Ripperology

Ripperology

Edited by Paul Begg

BARNES & NOBLE

NEW YORK

Contents

1. VICTIMS

Contents

2. SUSPECTS

3. POLICE

4. PEOPLE

Contents

5. AUTHORS AND COMMENTATORS

6. COMMENT

7. ANALYSIS

1. VICTIMS

The Ripper in America

Michael Conlon

EDWARD FITZGERALD did double duty as both bartender and night clerk at the East River Hotel in the heart of New York City's squalid Fourth Ward. By all accounts the hotel was a boisterous and forlorn dive. Huddled beneath a skyline ponderously overarched by the massive span of the Brooklyn Bridge and offering subdivided, cell-like rooms at 25 cents a night, it was typical of the many flophouses which lined the bustling docksides of lower Manhattan. Located on the corner of Water Street and Catherine Slip and facing the East River, it catered to a rough clientele comprised mainly of sailors, dockworkers and prostitutes.

Fitzgerald was a veteran of this establishment which the *Morning Journal* succinctly called a 'festering resort of vice and misery,' and by the spring of 1891 would certainly have settled into the interminable routine of brawls and debauchery, the nightly ebb and flow of wizened whores and rowdy, dissolute men. It must have been with benumbed resignation that, after another long night's work, he once more made his morning rounds of the seedy rooms, going mechanically from door to door, making certain that

1

all the previous night's lodgers had cleared out. It was not a place that expected or encouraged lengthy stays.

No doubt Fitzgerald was a man inured to casual brutality and unpleasant sights, but nothing could have prepared him for what lay behind the door of room No. 31 on the morning of 24 April 1891. We are informed that he '. . . went to the room and rapped on the door. There was no response and he forced the door. The dead body of the old woman was found lying on the bed. It was shockingly cut and mutilated. The body was completely naked. A deep gash extended from the lower part of the abdomen upward to the breast, which disembowelled it completely. The entrails had apparently been torn from the body and were scattered over the bed. There were also two deep cuts crossing each other on the back in the form of an exact cross. It is believed the murderer strangled his victim first and then proceeded to his horrible butchery.' The *New York Herald* ominously alluded to a missing organ, stating that what the killer '. . . had cut away had disappeared. He must have taken it with him. There was no sign of it in the room.'

News of the slaying quickly spread across the city, around the nation and over the seas. Homicide was not uncommon in the Fourth Ward but slaughter on this scale sold papers, not the least because of its uncanny resemblance to five notorious murders committed three years before. True, they occurred far across the Atlantic, but the entire world was now aware of the distinctive handicraft of the fiend called Jack the Ripper who had mysteriously disappeared without a trace . . . at least, so the papers had hinted, until now. There were few city news agencies which did not proclaim the likelihood that the Ripper had made Manhattan's teeming streets his new killing fields.

It was a sensational story for the press and so, perforce, a high priority for the police. Indeed, there was a certain irony involved in this case which was not lost on either the papers or the police. During the hunt for Jack the Ripper three years prior, the Chief Inspector of the New York Police Department had somewhat brashly volunteered, via the American press, some unsolicited advice to Scotland Yard on police methodology, gratuitously pointing out that should the Ripper ever relocate to New York's metropolis he would undoubtedly be apprehended within two or three days. Not surprisingly, Scotland Yard was less than grateful for this unbidden exercise in comparative constableship and it fostered something of a grudge between the two forces.

As it happened (much to the glee of the London police), the perpetrator of this fraternal faux pas yet presided over the detective force of the NYPD.

Chief Inspector Thomas Byrnes was no stranger to controversy. The New York press had made (and would continue to make) some unsavoury allegations about his associations with criminal gangs, bribe-taking and police brutality. Now he had left himself open to more criticism and the papers weren't missing their chance. Characteristic of a spate of journalistic jibes, the *Chicago Tribune* taunted that: 'The Scotland Yard officials are exultant over the fact that Inspector Byrnes, whose sometime criticism of the London police still rankles in the bosom of those functionaries, has now the opportunity to exercise his powers in a direction which has baffled Londoners.'

Byrnes found himself in a pressure-cooker of scrutiny and derision and, with much of the world watching, began what the press called the biggest manhunt in New York's history, continuously reminded by the papers that '. . . he had been known to sneer at the failure of the London police to catch the "Ripper".'

Some facts emerged quickly. It was initially learned that the murdered woman was a local prostitute who had entered the East River hotel at some time between 10.30 p.m. and 11.45 p.m. on the evening of 23 April with a man half her age. Edward Fitzgerald had his hands full that night tending the bar and so asked Mary Miniter, a local prostitute and habitué of the place, to assist the incongruent couple in procuring a room. Miniter brought the man a tin can of beer, a candle and the key and directed them up the rickety staircase to room No. 31 on the top floor. Miniter remembered the woman as drunk and giddy, the man as silent and grim.

Mary Miniter immediately became Byrne's prime witness. She felt that she had gotten a good look at the man and could probably recognize him again. She described him as being about five feet eight inches tall, about thirty years old, with brown hair, a brown

3

moustache, and sharp nose, and wearing a Derby hat and cutaway coat. From the few words he spoke, she thought he must be a foreigner. Byrnes soon sequestered Miniter and prevented the press any further access to her.

Reporters pressed Byrnes on whether he believed the Ripper was loose in New York, but 'The Inspector was much disinclined to be interviewed on the subject and was guarded in his talk. He said, referring to the Whitechapel murders, that he never criticized the work of the London police . . . he did not know under what difficulties they may have laboured to catch "Jack the Ripper." Byrnes may have exhibited a new-found reticence on the topic, but the newspapers were soon drawing their own conclusions: 'The points of similarity between this crime and those attributed to "Jack the Ripper" are numerous . . . The murdered woman belonged to the lowest class of fallen women from whom "Jack the Ripper" always selected his victims . . . The same horrible act of disembowelment and mutilation which distinguished the Whitechapel atrocities was performed upon this unfortunate hag . . . There was the same abstraction or attempted abstraction of certain organs. The instrument used – a big-bladed knife – is similar to the weapon used by the Whitechapel fiend . . . The district in which the murder was committed corresponds . . . to the Whitechapel district of London, especially in respect to the character of many of its inhabitants.'

It was the character and identity of one former inhabitant in particular which soon consumed the attention of the press and it was not long before they uncovered the sad vicissitudes of the murdered woman's tragic life. Carrie Brown was, ironically enough, born in England sixty years before. As a child she had come to America and eventually married a prosperous sea captain in Salem, Massachusetts. There she lived happily for a time, raising three children and keeping a conventional household far from the world of Whitechapel and New York's violent waterfront.

The details of the long, sordid decline which ended in a blood-spattered room off the East River are now lost to history, but family and friends hinted that alcoholism, boredom and dreams of becoming an actress in New York all conspired to form a fatal

4

prodigality. In New York she apparently led a bohemian life which seemed to have involved forms of entertainment more socially acceptable than those of her latter days. In the end however, she became familiar in the district as one more dissipated dreg, prostituting herself for the price of a drink and a room for the night. At sixty, she must have seemed an even sadder specimen than most of the broken women who haunted the wharves and bars of the quarter. Perhaps all that intimated a once more refined and sensitive existence was her penchant for quoting from the Bard's plays, earning her the sobriquet of 'Old Shakespeare'. In an epilogue worthy of the kind of music-hall melodramas in which she may once have performed, a married daughter materialized just in time to save her earthly remains from an anonymous pauper's grave, returning her body to a place of happier days, in Salem, Massachusetts, where she was laid to rest in a family plot beside the grave of her son.

True to his words of three years before, Byrnes announced to the press, on the third day after the murder, that the identity of the Ripper was now known: 'He is a cousin of one of the suspects who was arrested on [the night after the killing]. This suspect was known in Water Street as "Frenchy" . . . Possibly that is also the name of his cousin, the murderer.' The two were said to be '. . . the most vicious creatures in the quarter . . . They had a mania for vice in its lowest form.' Both men were reported to be Algerians. Several local prostitutes affirmed that the two 'cousins' (now dubbed "Frenchy No. 1" and Frenchy No. 2') were in the habit of 'prowling around Water Street' together, often abusing the street-walkers. 'When the Inspector heard the woman's' story he sent for . . . Minetur (sic) . . . she then recalled the fact that "Frenchy" was in the house that night, and said she recognized the man who came in with the murdered woman as "Frenchy's cousin".'

Everything seemed to be falling into place for Inspector Byrnes. It was now just a matter of time before 'Frenchy No. 2' was swept up in the dragnet. The police were now focusing on sailors and were searching ships. Mary Miniter was shown a parade of suspects but couldn't identify any of them as the wanted man. It was said that Byrnes was growing impatient with her.

Much to the surprise and bewilderment of the newspapers (and some of his officers) Byrnes announced to the press that . . . the police were no longer confining themselves to the description generally accepted . . . the people depended upon to give it were a drunken lot, without enough intelligence to remember how the man looked.' Further confusing matters, the next day the *Morning Journal* printed 'Byrnes' Extraordinary Denial' wherein the Inspector enigmatically stated: 'I wish to deny emphatically that we believe that Frenchy No. 2 . . . is suspected of the murder. I never thought so or said so.' The bemused reporter went on to write: 'The Inspector undoubtedly had some deep reason for making such strange denials, but what he meant by them even his oldest detectives cannot fathom . . . later in the day the Inspector when again questioned in regard to his denial, refused to either deny or confirm his original denials.' One paper could not resist reminding Byrnes that ' . . . the detectives of Europe are watching his movements with eager interest and perhaps restraining with difficulty a disposition to smile.'

A week after Brown's mangled corpse was found by Fitzgerald, Byrnes dropped a bombshell on the press. It seemed the real killer was the man they had had in custody as a material witness since the day after the murder – Frenchy No. 1. This man, whose real name was Ameer Ben Ali, was known from early on in the case to have been present in the East River hotel on the night Brown died.

Not unreasonably, the papers asked why a week-long manhunt, gathering up well over a hundred suspects, had been conducted if the police believed they had the killer all along. Byrnes replied that new evidence had been analyzed which pointed to Ali as the killer. Apparently, a blood trail leading from room No. 31 across the hall to room No. 33 (Ameer's alleged room) had changed the whole direction of the investigation.

A highly sceptical press asked: 'Why was it that intelligent reporters did not see those bloody tracks leading across the hall from Room No. 31, the woman's room, to Room No. 33, Frenchy's room, or, at least the marks of their erasure? And how was it that they failed to notice that No. 33 had the appearance of a slaughter-house, as Mr. Byrnes says it had?

In the opinion of the general public Inspector Byrnes must look

6

a good deal further before he finds the real Jack the Ripper. Sympathy is entirely with Frenchy, and there is a general belief in his innocence. Byrnes must soon admit himself as badly baffled and as much at sea as was Scotland Yard during and after the London butcheries.'

Another report scoffed: 'It was openly said in many quarters . . . that Byrnes does not really believe in the guilt of "Frenchy No. 1".'

The papers published an intriguing story about some behind-the-scenes 'politics' that were alleged to be involved in Ali's prosecution: 'There is in this city a very influential body of men who have no love for Inspector Byrnes . . . they control money and have an underhanded sort of political pull. These men . . . have an interest in the profits of gambling houses.' The story explained that 'these men' constituted a West Side gang which was in bitter rivalry with its East Side counterpart, an organization that seemed quite cosy with Inspector Byrnes. A spokesman for the West Side coalition said that they were contributing money to Ali's defence because, they claimed, '. . . unless Byrnes convicts the man he can never be made Superintendent of Police,' which was, they claimed, Byrnes's real aim and the East Side gang's fond desire. 'It is charged by the enemies of the Inspector that he is really prosecuting Frenchy to make good his word that a Jack the Ripper could not live here two days in safety.' They claimed that Byrnes had several times stated the '. . . belief privately that the prisoner Frenchy is not the murderer of Carrie Brown.'

Mary Miniter, who maintained that Frenchy No. 2 was the culprit, was now curtly dismissed by Byrnes who insisted that she was 'an opium fiend, and has associated with Chinamen.'

The Coroner's Inquest did little to allay the dubiety of the newsmen. Ali's lawyer, Frederick House, was able to establish that reporters were indeed on the murder scene in great numbers before either Brown's body or any evidence was removed. They had, in fact, examined all of the rooms on the floor, and none had seen any blood trail or blood evidence outside room No. 31. He also elicited contradictory statements from detectives as to when the blood evidence was discovered and removed. Ali's trial, witnesses and hotel records would support Ali's claim to have stayed in a

7

different room from the one in which the alleged evidence was found, and suggestions that evidence was planted and that testimony was 'corrupt and perjured' persisted throughout the trial. Prosecutors failed to establish that the blood evidence was human, let alone from Brown.

Despite press insistence that the case was weak, circumstantial and possibly contrived, Ali was found guilty in July of that year. Many papers expressed shock and gave ample space to the protestations of one of the jurors who claimed that the jury had been 'packed' and a miscarriage of justice done. Ameer Ben Ali was sentenced to life imprisonment.

After serving eleven long years, he was pardoned following a reinvestigation of the case which disclosed serious doubts about police conduct and Ali's guilt. He was said to have returned to Algeria, never to be heard from again.

And what of Frenchy No. 2, the man whom Mary Miniter positively identified as Brown's companion on the fatal night? It seems he was, in fact, located, but not before machinations against Ali had gone into high gear. Following press persistence in knowing what had become of this man who had after all been the object of a massive week-long quest, Byrnes admitted that: 'We arrested Frenchy No. 2 . . . we found that he spent the night of the murder four-and-a-half miles from the East River Hotel . . . The people he was living with satisfied us that he was not away for that period during the night and we simply turned Frenchy No. 2 loose.'

It seemed strange that the man formerly sought with such exigency should be so lightly exonerated on the mere testimony of some of his companions. This facile dismissal seemed all the stranger following the revelation of some remarkable and strangely suggestive facts concerning Frenchy No. 2. We are informed that his . . . arrest was made on information published in *The World*, which was received from one of its New Jersey readers. This statement is as follows: There is a man named 'Frenchy' who answers the description of Frenchy No. 2, and who was arrested in London about a year-and-a-half ago in connection with the Whitechapel murders . . . During the past two or three years this man has been crossing back and forth between this country and England on the freight steamers that carry cattle. He is noted for his strength and physical prowess . . . The sailors on the cattle ships tell horrible stories of his cruelty to the dumb brutes in his care. When one of these animals would break a leg or receive some injury that necessitated its slaughter, "Frenchy," they say, would take apparent delight in carving it up alive while the sailors looked on. No one dared oppose him, his temper was so bad. When he was arrested on suspicion that he was "Jack the Ripper" he knocked down the officer who tackled him and made things very lively for half a dozen men before they got him under control.'

Needless to say, Inspector Murphy, the Chief of the Jersey City police, was proud and eager to turn this prime suspect over to the New York authorities, certain that he had apprehended Brown's killer and quite possibly nabbed Jack the Ripper.

A detective sergeant was sent over to question the culprit. Much to the amazement of Murphy and the press, after a cursory interview, '. . . the detective concluded that the cattleman could not have roomed with "Shakespeare" on the fatal night, and he was released.'

Understandably, Murphy expressed some confusion and consternation at this unexpected turn of events, but was laconically informed that the New York police had changed their description of the wanted man and were no longer interested in Frenchy No. 2. But the press remained very interested in him, especially given the startling revelations of his Whitechapel connection.

Reporters tracked him down to a lodging house, pointing out his close resemblance to Miniter's original description. They pressed him for details: 'The night of the East River murder,' he claimed, 'I passed in this lodging house . . . my name is Arbie La Bruckman, but I am commonly called John Francis. I was born in Morocco twenty-nine years ago. I arrived here on the steamer Spain April 10 from London . . .' The reporter asked, 'Why were you arrested in London?' La Bruckman replied, 'About 11 o'clock one night a little after Christmas, 1889, I was walking along the street. I carried a small satchel. I was bound for Hull, England, where I was to take another ship. Before I reached the depot, I was arrested and taken to London Headquarters. I was locked up for a month, placed on trial and duly acquitted. After my discharge the Government gave me £100 and a suit of clothes for the inconvenience I had suffered.'

The *Daily Continent* learned that, 'For the past fourteen years (La Bruckman) has been employed by Meyer Goldsmith as a cattleman on the steamers of the National Line, plying between this port and London. La Bruckman felt so bad about his arrest that he wept when locked up in a cell to await instructions from the New York police. Detective Sergeant McCloskey went over to Jersey City in the afternoon, glanced at the prisoner, and said he was not wanted . . . Detective McCloskey said that the fellow was the man familiarly known as Frenchy No. 2, but he was not the murderer . . . (La Bruckman) freely acknowledged that he was arrested in London eighteen months ago on suspicion of being the Whitechapel murderer. He claims that his trial for killing one of Jack the Ripper's victims lasted two weeks, and when he was acquitted the Government gave him £100 and a new suit of clothes . . . He has signed to sail on the steamer Buffalo next Saturday.'

Two later reports stated that La Bruckman admitted to being arrested a year-and-a-half earlier . . . in London on suspicion of having killed nine women in the Whitechapel district, but after being in jail for a month was discharged.'

Obviously this scenario makes more sense, in that a Jack the Ripper trial would surely have been worldwide news. Certainly, the anonymous New Jersey tipster who first implicated La Bruckman to the press and police made no mention of any trial but merely of an arrest on suspicion. Given the great amount of detail he was able to provide about La Bruckman, a Ripper trial would certainly have been noted if it occurred. It is likely that La Bruckman may have confused his long interrogation with a trial and his discharge with an acquittal. His claim of monetary compensation is not implausible, especially given his lengthy detention and his American citizenship.

Further, though cryptic, confirmation of La Bruckinan's arrest on suspicion of being the Ripper emerged in the context of an intriguing story.

It seems that in the pre-dawn hours following Brown's murder, a man closely matching La Bruckman's description entered the

Glenmore Hotel not far from the murder site. He spoke with an accent and his hands, shirtfront and sleeves were covered in fresh blood. The suspicious clerk, not liking the man's appearance and agitated demeanour refused him both a room and his request to wash up in the lobby lavatory. It was subsequently learned that La Bruckman was a sometime lodger at the Glenmore. People who had previously encountered him there stated that '. . . he was regarded as a "bad man" should anyone provoke him . . . Shortly after he left the Glenmore the attachés learned that "Frenchy" had been arrested in London in connection with the Whitechapel murders.' This is interesting, because from the context of the story, the attachés appear to be police officials who independently seem to have confirmed this information, but how they discovered this is not stated. In the same story it is disclosed that La Bruckman possessed no fixed abode and, when not crossing the seas, worked in slaughterhouses near his ports of call.

La Bruckman, the former Whitechapel suspect, was headline news for a couple of days until Byrnes announced that Ali was the killer and the spotlight permanently shifted to the hapless Algerian. A month after Ali was convicted of Brown's murder, a new, gruesome killing caused the press to once again question whether the authorities had the right man. A story in the *Morning Journal* appeared under the headline, 'Is It Jack's work?', telling of the discovery in the East River, not far from Brown's murder site, of the badly mutilated body of a forty-five-year-old prostitute murdered in a manner said to be similar to the way in which 'Old Shakespeare' had been killed.

'The theory that a sailor had killed Shakespeare . . . [and] after the deed had gone to sea in a sailing vessel . . .' continued to appear in the press well after Ali's incarceration.

It is particularly interesting in regard to La Bruckman that similar stories of sailors and cattle steamers circulated in the London papers during the Whitechapel killings. It is well known that the London Customs clerk, Edward Larkins, pestered Scotland Yard with his theory that the Ripper was one or more Portuguese cattle boatmen. His theory was investigated and found untenable. What is of real interest, however, are stories involving Scotland

Yard's continued concern with cattle boats (especially American cattle boats) long after Larkin's theory had been dismissed. In September of 1889, following a renewed Ripper scare instigated by the discovery of a woman's mutilated torso in Pinchin Street, it was reported that 'the Thames Police . . . at once got their various craft on the river, and boarded all vessels at the mouth of the Thames dock. Attention was particularly directed to cattle boats from Spain and America.'

After another scare in February 1891, involving the murder of Frances Coles, we are told that 'a policeman who saw the unfortunate woman a short time before the murder said that she was talking to a man who looked like a sailor. The police searched all the cattle ships but found no reason to arrest anyone. Late in the evening, a man was arrested on the docks and locked up on suspicion.'

James Sadler, a sailor, was eventually arrested, though never convicted, for this murder, but he cannot have been the sailor mentioned in this story because he was arrested the day after this report, at a pub in the middle of the afternoon. Maybe the most interesting story in this regard appeared in January of 1890: 'During the past few days there has been an increase of vigilance on the part of the East London police owing to "information received".' A number of the police have been watching some cattle boats which have arrived at the docks from the United States, and a very sharp lookout is being kept at night in the neighbourhood where the recent tragedies were committed by Jack the Ripper. We are not told what this 'information received' consisted of or from whence it came, but it is highly provocative that this 'vigilance' coincides with the period in which La Bruckman was arrested in London on suspicion of being the Ripper.

One last bit of circumstantial evidence rounds out what I submit is a strong argument for at least considering Arbie La Bruckman as a valid new suspect in the Whitechapel murder case: a comparison of Lloyd's Ship Registry for La Bruckman's firm, the National Line, with the apposite arrivals and departures schedules published in the *New York Times* shipping records, disclosed that National

Line cattle boats were docked in London during each and every one of Jack the Ripper's murders!

At this point it is impossible to say how much we may ever know about Arbie La Bruckman and his precise role in the killing of Carrie Brown or the Ripper slayings. The fact that a Jack the Ripper suspect was also the object of a massive, New York manhunt in the Ripper-like slaughter of a prostitute eighteen months later suggests, to me, more than mere coincidence. Right now, however, we are left with an incomplete but tantalizing story – a story that just may follow a blood-soaked trail through the moribund warren of Whitechapel back-streets, down into the fetid holds of rusty cattle steamers, up the dark stairwells of decrepit, East River tenements and ending finally, wretchedly in some anonymous, raging and forsaken eclipse into history's perpetual reprobation.

This essay appeared in *Ripperologist* magazine No. 38, December 2001.

Eddowes's Apron

Paul Begg

A T 12.55 A.M. ON SUNDAY, 30 September 1888, Catherine Eddowes was released from Bishopsgate Police Station where she had slumbered for the last few hours after being arrested early the night before for drunkenness. She turned left out the doorway, which took her in the opposite direction to what would have been the fastest way back to Flower and Dean Street. Fifty minutes later, at 1.45 a.m. her body was found by PC Watkins in Mitre Square. It would have taken Eddowes between five and ten minutes to have reached Mitre Square, which leaves forty minutes unaccounted for. We have no idea what she was doing during that time.

At 1.35 a.m., however, three men in Duke Street saw a woman standing with a man at the corner of a passage leading into Mitre Square. The woman had her back to them and they paid her scant attention, but one of the men, Joseph Lawende, later identified her by her clothing as Catherine Eddowes. The police seem to have accepted that the woman was indeed Catherine Eddowes – Joseph Lawende being called upon years later to identify a possible suspect – and it is rarely if ever doubted by Ripperologists, but the divisional police surgeon, Dr Gordon Brown, told the inquest that the injuries done to Eddowes 'might be done in five minutes. It might take him longer; but that is the least time it could be done in,' and this makes the timings, if they are accurate, very tight, only ten minutes separating the sighting by Lawende and his companions from the discovery of Eddowes's body.

Before leaving the murderer sliced off a piece of Eddowes's apron and took it away with him. A City policeman, Detective Constable Halse, is credited with having said that, 'When I saw the dead woman at the mortuary I noticed that a piece of her apron was missing. About half of it. It had been cut with a clean cut.' (Jones & Lloyd, *The Ripper File* p. 126) Major Henry Smith also wrote that 'about one-half of the apron was missing. It had been severed by a clean cut.' (Sir Henry Smith, *From Constable to Commissioner*, p. 152). Aprons could be quite large, so we might be talking about a sizeable piece of material, possibly 3–4 square feet.

At 2.20 a.m. PC Alfred Long's beat took him through Goulston Street and he would later confidently assert that Catherine Eddowes's apron was not there at that time. When he came back though Goulston Street at 2.55 a.m., the apron was there.

Where was the apron?
Photographs of the Wentworth Model Dwellings show that its entrance opened into a short passage leading to stairs. The passage was little more than a porch, no more than three or four bricks deep. The walls were painted black from the floor to a height of about four feet and above that they were painted white. The apron was found on the floor and above it was some writing, the famed Goulston Street Graffito. According to PC Long's own testimony he found the piece of apron '*lying in a passage* leading to the staircases of 108 to 119 Model Dwelling House' (my italics). According to Detective Halse 'there were three lines of writing in a good schoolboy's round hand. The size of the capital letters would be about 3/4-inch and the other letters were in proportion. The writing was on the black bricks, which formed a kind of dado, the bricks above being white.' (the *Daily News*, 12 October). A dado is the lower part of an interior wall which has a different colour or decoration to the upper part. This conflicts with Sir Charles Warren, who said, 'The writing was on the jamb of the open archway or doorway visible to anybody in the street and could not be covered up without danger of the covering being torn off at once.'

A door jamb is the upright part of a door frame or the inside vertical face of an opening and Sir Charles Warren clearly meant the latter, which in the photograph is the brick or brick-and-a-half lip that's painted black. If Warren is right then the writing was at the entrance and little more than a brick in length. The apron was below the writing and would have been at the entrance to the passage, virtually on the pavement.

It's worth examining this a little more closely. A policeman or two could have been posted outside the entrance to prevent access or egress (except to residents) and thereby stopped or restricted the chance of any covering being removed, but this would not have been so easy if the writing was on the entrance bricks and it would explain why Warren chose to wash the writing away. The writing being on these entrance bricks also explains why some policemen thought the writing would have been rubbed out or become blurred by people entering and leaving the building and therefore concluded that it was fresh. On the other hand, placing policemen at the entrance may not have been in Sir Charles's mind or, indeed, been practicable, which may also explain why Sir Charles chose to erase it, and the writing would more likely have been blurred by people brushing against it as they went up and down the narrow stairs than it would have been at the fairly wide entrance. Sir Charles Warren's statement also conflicts with PC Lamb who said the apron was 'lying in a passage leading to the staircases' and with Detective Halse who said, 'The writing was in the passage of the building itself . . .' (*The Times*, 12 October). There is also a report by Donald Swanson which states that according to PC Long the apron 'was found in the bottom of a common stairs' (HO 144/221/A49301C, ff184-94, Report by Chief Inspector Donald S Swanson dated 6 November 1888). We must also take into account PC Long's statement that he saw the writing after he had seen the apron, but could he fairly have missed the writing if it had been painted on the black facia of the jamb? So, it seems unclear whether the writing was on the entrance jamb or on the wall inside the passage. The writing was not at man's height – whoever wrote it was not standing up – but on the black facia of the bricks, which were only painted black to a height of about four feet. The writing was low down and the writer was probably on his haunches when he wrote it.

We might be able to deduce one or two other things from the scanty facts we possess. Detective Halse said that the writing was in a 'good schoolboy's round hand,' by which he meant that the handwriting had been taught. The writer had therefore received a basic education, which probably rules out an immigrant foreigner. It may also rule out an adult because compulsory schooling didn't exist until the 1880s. A correspondent to the *Daily News* (13 October), who signed himself 'A Writer with Chalk,' observed that 'There are very few people who can write easily and freely upon a black board until they have had considerable practice, and writing upon a less regular surface is more difficult still.' This correspondent was suggesting that the chalked handwriting on the wall probably wouldn't have reflected the author's normal handwriting, but the observation makes one wonder if the 'good schoolboy round hand' with its ¾-inch capitals and proportionate lower case letters means that the writer was someone like a school teacher who was used to writing with chalk. This suggestion will no doubt please those who support the candidacy of Montague Druitt as the Ripper, but the strange sentence construction and the spelling of the word Jews suggests that the writer was not well educated. Perhaps Halse was unknowingly closer to the truth when he said the writing was in a 'schoolboy's round hand' – a child would have had less opportunity for his good round hand to become sloppy, and if he came from a poor family he was probably educated at a charity school that kept costs to a minimum and where children practiced their writing with chalk on slates. That the writing was chalked less than four feet from the ground might also support the idea that the writer was a child.

And not Jack the Ripper!

We don't know for certain where the apron was, except that it was below the writing, and we're not sure whether the writing was on the jamb, as Sir Charles Warren said, or inside the passage as PC Long and Detective Halse maintained, possibly at the bottom of the stairs. We also don't possess another piece of crucial information that would help determine how visible the apron was, and that is the direction PC Long walked down Goulston Street. If PC Long merely flashed his light into the passage as he approached, it's possible that the apron may have remained unobserved in the shadows in that part of the passage behind him, particularly if it was obscured behind the jamb. Equally, if PC Long had directed his lamp up the stairs, the apron may have remained obscured in the shadows at the bottom of the stairs. There is no reason to suppose that PC Long lied when he said the apron wasn't there at 2.20 a.m., but we can't be sure that he wasn't mistaken. That Detective Halse provided independent support of PC Long's story, as some commentators have claimed, isn't true. Detective Halse said, 'At twenty minutes past two o'clock I passed over the spot where the piece of apron was found, but did not notice anything then. I should not necessarily have seen the piece of apron.' (*Daily Telegraph*, 12 October 1888)

We'll never know whether the apron was there or not, but the apron itself might provide us with a few clues. We have inadequate descriptions of the piece of apron, but at the inquest PC Long said that one corner of it was 'wet with blood' (inquest papers and newspaper reports; see *Daily Telegraph*, 12 October, *The Times*, 12 October). Otherwise Long said, 'there were blood stains on it, and one portion of it was wet' (*Daily News*, 12 October). According to the testimony of Dr Frederick Gordon Brown at the inquest, it was stained with 'some blood and apparently faecal matter' (Inquest papers). The *Daily Telegraph* (5 October) reported Dr Brown as saying 'I fitted that portion which was spotted with blood . . .' and *The Times* (5 October) reported him as saying that 'there were smears of blood on one side as if a hand or a knife had been wiped on it.' Therefore, as far as we can tell, although one corner was wet with blood, the apron was not otherwise heavily stained with blood and in fact only one side of the apron was marked, so the blood and faecal matter was insufficient to penetrate into the material. We can therefore almost certainly rule out any idea that the apron was used to carry the kidney and uterus because these would have deposited a greater quantity of blood on the material and left distinctive marks. No such marks were visible to Dr Brown, who believed the apron had been used by someone to wipe his hand or his knife, or both.

If the apron was simply used by the murderer to wipe blood and faeces from his hand, it is unlikely that he'd have held on to it for any length of time. He would have discarded it as soon as he was finished with it. We must also consider that it was incriminating evidence, that it had a corner wet with blood that could have got onto his hands and stained his clothing and that, because of the faecal matter, it was something the murderer would not have wanted to carry around with him for any length of time. If the apron was something the murderer discarded soon after use, it follows that he did not hang around the murder scene or take a long and circuitous route to get to Goulston Street. It is also highly improbable that he would have reached home, then ventured out to the vicinity of the murder scene to dispose of an incriminating piece of evidence that he could have burned on the fire.

Thus, the condition of the apron suggests that the murderer went from Mitre Square and dropped the apron as he passed through Goulston Street. The apron was there when PC Long passed through at 2.20 a.m., but he didn't see it.

This essay appeared in *Ripperologist* magazine No. 57, January 2005.

The Carrie Brown Murder Case: New Revelations

Michael Conlon

N ATURE, WE ARE TOLD, abhors a vacuum, and so also, it would seem, does the average armchair detective. How else can one explain the enduring interest in the mystery of Jack the Ripper and the 115-year endeavour to fill its void with answers?

Perhaps part of the reason resides in the multifarious nature of the enigma, there being very little that even the experts seem able to agree on as indubitable fact concerning the case. There is, of course, the central and perennial puzzle of the killer's identity, from which extend the equally vexing questions of his motive and method. But even beyond these perplexities, it is hard to find any substantial footing upon which to confidently begin the search.

Take, for example, the question of the Ripper's death toll. A number somewhere between three and over a dozen is often cited, with five victims commonly being deemed 'canonical.' It remains one of the more confounding aspects of the case, premised as it is on implicit criteria for assessing similarity in the killings. Such criteria usually involves a whole host of variables including motive, location, method, 'victimology' and, in the parlance of modern forensics, 'signature.'

At best, these components constitute rough indicators for gauging the probability that two or more murders separated by time and location are attributable to the same killer. Thus, the linkage any investigator ascribes to a series of murders reflects the relative weight he may give to any or all of these interpretable factors. Someone stressing the importance of victimology might presumably be less inclined to accept inclusion of a victim who was not associated with prostitution or from the lower classes despite the presence of other suggestive similarities such as wounds or methodology. Someone giving priority to locality or a 'comfort zone' might be disinclined to include a similar homicide committed outside of Whitechapel.

Finding a single hermeneutic key to unlock a proper assessment of all these forensic indices is only further complicated when evidence is scant – a deficiency all too typical of the Ripper case. Many investigators specializing in the field of serial killers would undoubtedly point to the element of 'signature' as the most significant feature in determining which murders are assignable to the same killer, 'signature' constituting the invariable motive elements which all the killings share. Succinctly put, it is the evidential link between the motive and what the killer deems to be its satisfactory accomplishment and is manifested in specific, consistent patterns or clues left behind at the crime scene.

It is interpretive in the sense that motive is deduced from physical fact – from evidence that forms a consistent pattern which may be deemed characteristic of the slayings. In this sense, such patterns become heuristic, pointing toward established typologies as regard both criminal psychology and predictable characteristics of the murders reflective of that psychology. This is commonly related to the idiosyncrasies manifested in ritual-like behaviour superfluous to the actual act of killing and what this suggests about the psychopathology of the killer. It is a deduction buttressed by empirical evidence amassed from in-depth analysis of past serial cases but, involving as it does prognostic skill, it is not an exact science, although its tenets appear to be regularly borne out in case studies.

For those who feel that such analytic tools are of some probative value in the Jack the Ripper case, there appears to be a consensus that 'signature' in these killings is characterized by mutilation targeted specifically at the female genitalia, and the handling and/or extraction of viscera and organs. The motivation this pattern

21

suggests is clearly psychosexual in nature, this again being based on the accumulated analyses of similar serial murders. Given the paucity of hard evidence in the Ripper case, it is inevitable that questions concerning motivation resort to promising systems such as the one employed by the FBI to profile serial killers as outlined above. Method (which may well suggest motive) is perhaps one area in the Ripper case where existing evidence is more helpful.

Detailed coroners' reports and some post-mortem photos survive for many of the supposed Ripper victims. It does not seem unreasonable that consistent, recurrent features in these killings are significant enough to serve as templates for assessing the probability that non-canonical killings may or may not fall within the ambit of the Ripper's horrible handiwork.

The 23 April 1891 murder in New York City of an aged prostitute named Carrie Brown has been speculatively linked with the Jack the Ripper series since the time of its occurrence. Until quite recently, our ability to accurately assess this association has been severely limited, and restricted almost exclusively to analyzing contemporaneous press coverage to glean forensic information. Now, new information has come to light which permits a fuller and more accurate comparison of this New York murder with those of Whitechapel. Despite this, it may still remain an open question whether this new information will be of any more help in resolving the issue of Brown's possible status as a Ripper victim.

While researching original documents concerning the murder of Carrie Brown, I was surprised to uncover the court case file which included two post-mortem photos of the victim, in addition to a small tintype of her from life. This case file also contained the original indictments, outlining the wounds and causes of death. A wealth of news reports also exists which contain on-the-spot descriptions of the murder scene as well as descriptions of the wounds by the coroners involved in the case. The disclosure of Brown's autopsy report in a recent and excellent article by Wolf Vanderlinden supplies important supplemental information on the killing and allows for a more detailed and definitive comparison of this case with the Ripper series. By examining these in combination with what we know about genuine Ripper murders, we are in a far better position to assess whether certain 'signature' elements are present in Brown's murder, leaving her status as a possible Ripper victim open to possible inclusion.

First, a brief word about the clarity of the photos is called for. It is unfortunate that the most important photo for our purposes is also the most degraded. The frontal view of Brown's mutilated body is, sadly, rather faded and grainy. It is, I believe, sufficiently clear however for the purposes at hand. These disturbing post-mortem photos appear to give grim corroboration to the accuracy of the recently discovered autopsy report, disclosing the three-inch deep 'ripping' wounds to the abdominal cavity, cuts to the genital area, and clearly showing the curious 'X' incised on the victim's left buttock. What the photos do not disclose is the important revelation found in the autopsy report concerning the extraction of organs. It had been widely and sensationally reported in the press that Brown's intestines had been torn out, and this is indeed proven by the report, which states that parts of the intestines had, in addition to being pulled out, been cut off and found on the bed. Many stories also claimed that 'certain organs' had been cut out. The autopsy report now conclusively proves that this was also true, as Brown's left ovary had been found in the blood-soaked bed linen, disclosing an interestingly consistent pattern with Ripper murders in its concentration on and removal of organs of reproduction.

It remains a matter of speculation, however, whether death resulted from strangulation or from the knife wounds. The indictment record I discovered in the original case file cites three counts, each sufficient in itself to have caused death. In the first count, it states that Brown was: '. . . willfully, feloniously and of malice aforethought, choked, suffocated and strangled by both hands [of the assailant] about her neck of which cause . . . she then and there died.'

The second count details: '. . . a certain piece of cloth which [the assailant] did fix, bind, tie and fasten about Caroline Brown's neck and upon her head and face and did choke, smother, suffocate and strangle her so that she died then and there.'

The third count covers the knife wounds, starkly stating that the assailant: '. . . did strike, thrust, cut, stab and wound, giving unto her the said Caroline Brown, then and there . . . in and upon the breast, belly, abdomen, back and sides . . . divers mortal wounds of which said mortal wounds she . . . then and there died.'

During the Coroner's Inquest to indict Ameer Ben Ali (the suspect accused, convicted, and ultimately pardoned of this crime), Deputy Coroner Jenkins, the man who conducted the autopsy, was asked whether Brown had died from asphyxiation or from knife wounds: 'He said he found the woman's face livid and some fluid blood in the left auricle of the heart. This, he said, was sure evidence of strangulation. There was a semi-circular mark on the left side of her neck, as if made by a thumbnail, and her tongue protruded, more evidence of strangulation. He explained various wounds and their location, and said that while the evidences of asphyxiation by strangulation were apparent, he found it a difficult matter to determine whether or not life was wholly extinct when incisions were made.'[1]

While this new forensic evidence, coupled with what was previously known of the case, has inclined Mr Vanderlinden to a position of some diffidence, if not disinclination, concerning the Ripper-like nature of this killing, it has persuaded me that there is nothing, prima facie, militating against its inclusion in the series, at least insofar as it can be said to manifest a strong parallelism in terms of what modern forensic science would focus on as salient and indicative. Applying the criteria of 'signature' permits for a recognized method of sorting out which features in a series of killings are merely coincidental, variable, functional and inconsequential and which elements are motive-specific and essential. This differentiation may be broadly classified into what is termed 'method' (or 'modus operandi') and what is specified as 'signature.'

Thus construed, those elements which appear problematic or anomalous – the absence of throat cutting being, perhaps, the most notable – are features which, when viewed in context, apply to method, which may or may not remain uniform in a series depending on contingencies of expedience and utility. The act of throat cutting is a feature of method and not signature. It is functional in intent – a commodious step towards achieving the fulfillment of the motive by dispatching the victim so that mutilation, the primary aim, may be enacted.

It has also been sensibly suggested by researchers that, in addition to swiftly causing incapacitation and death, the massive and quick blood-letting accomplished by cutting the throat is a convenient and intentionally combined means by which the Ripper could both dispatch his victim and avoid becoming imbrued during the mutilation process, a consequence which would otherwise render him highly conspicuous on the streets. Throat cutting would be a logical method when the killer was fully clothed and outside in a public place, but would be a necessity obviated by being indoors and undressed, as Brown's killer almost surely was. It is also clear that the killer was able to clean up in a bloodstained washbowl found in the room. Seen in this context, throat cutting is an adventitious and variable element of method. It should also be pointed out in passing that the clothing, which was so tightly tied around Brown's throat that it had to be cut off, would have prevented the killer from cutting her throat had he wished to do so subsequent to strangulation, as occurred in the Chapman murder.

The fact that there is apparently some variance in the type of knife used on Brown when compared to those supposed to be used in the Ripper series is, again, shown by studies to be inconsequential in terms of these types of murders, as the key element is the fact that the genitalia were mutilated with a knife and organs and viscera were targeted and 'handled.' It is, quite simply, unrealistic to expect a sexual serial killer to always kill and mutilate his victims in precisely the same manner with precisely the same weapon every time, especially over a space of years. Studies of such killers show that this is simply not the case. They do, however, show that features, such as (in the Ripper case) the targeted mutilation of the genital region, the 'ripping' of the abdomen, and extraction of viscera and organs associated with reproduction will be largely consistent and similar in all connected cases. Other interesting but ancillary similarities exist between Brown and the traditional Ripper victims, such as 'extraneous' and glyphic cuttings or markings as represented by the inverted 'V's or triangles on Eddowes cheeks and the inscribed 'X' on Brown's buttock, as well as facial bruising indicative of a 'blitz-type' attack, as in the cases of Nichols, Chapman and Eddowes.

The objection that no organ was taken away by Brown's killer disregards the evidence of other, similar cases in which 'trophies' were sometimes taken and sometimes not. It should also be remembered that not all of the 'canonical' victims had organs taken away. Again, what is very significant is the extraction of viscera and an organ of reproduction from Brown's body – a feature highly specific to the Ripper murders.

While the evidence clearly suggests to me that Brown's murder cannot be excluded from the Ripper series, it is not impossible that a copycat killer or sexual killer with an almost identical 'signature' was at work in New York three years after the ostensible cessation of the London killings. Given what we now know, it is simply impossible to say. There is, however, one intriguing link which might strongly connect Brown's murder with the Ripper's, and thus exponentially increase the likelihood that we are dealing with more than a copycat.

My discovery of an individual who was both the initial prime suspect in the Brown murder and had, rather remarkably, also been arrested in London on suspicion of being Jack the Ripper may just constitute such a link (see 'The Ripper in America', *Ripperologist*, December 2001). I will not recapitulate my findings here, but I would like to briefly address some recent objections made against this intriguing suspect, Arbie La Bruckman, and his candidacy as Brown's slayer. The only real objection to this suspect is that Mary Miniter (the sole eyewitness) gave at least two somewhat dissimilar descriptions of the man who accompanied Brown on the fatal night. Although one description seems to match La Bruckman[2], another, more widely published description, varies from La Bruckman in terms of mustache and/or hair colour and physique.

As regards physique, it has been pointed out that La Bruckman was described in one article as a 'Hercules' leading some to perhaps think La Bruckman was brawny, as opposed to the more slender man described by Miniter. In actuality, this is an inaccurate assumption, for although he is described as muscular, it is also stated elsewhere that '. . . there is not an ounce of spare flesh on his wiry frame.'[3] 'Wiry frame' would certainly not suggest brawniness, but rather, slenderness. Newspaper descriptions of La Bruckman state that he had dark hair and a brown moustache, while Miniter's more widely circulated description speaks of a man with light hair and a light moustache who spoke with an accent that may have been German. The accent was a feature common to both descriptions given out by Miniter, and significantly it was stated that La Bruckman spoke with an accent, although we don't know what it sounded like.

Upon La Bruckman's arrest, the reporter for the *World* stated:

> He is a villainous-looking man of about twenty-nine years and of remarkably strong physique. He is about 5 feet 7 inches in height and weighs about 180 pounds . . . He is very far, however, from answering the description of the murderer given out by the New York police. The alarm sent to the police all over the country by Inspector Byrnes . . . was as follows:
>
> General Alarm: Arrest a man 5 feet 9 inches high, about thirty-one years old, light hair and mustache, speaks broken English. Wanted for murder. The prisoner, on the contrary, has black hair and a dark brown mustache, and is only 5 feet 7½ inches in height.'[4]

It will be noted, first of all, that, with the exception of the hair colour, the description is, in fact, not very different from La Bruckman (the only disparities being constituted by a difference of two years in the estimated age, and 1½ inches in height!). Later, in the same article, however, the reporter sarcastically alludes to the confused description being given out of the killer:

> So far the undisputed admissions of Inspector Byrnes and his aides seem to be that old 'Shakespeare' was murdered at the East River Hotel on Thursday night or early Friday morning last, that she was horribly mutilated in true 'Jack the Ripper' style; that she was an outcast; that she is dead beyond doubt; that the murderer was the Greek, Italian, German or Swede with a long nose and light or dark mustache who accompanied the old woman up to room 31 at 11 o'clock last Thursday night . . .'

But more importantly regarding La Bruckman as a suspect, we learn in this same article that the New Jersey police, who made the arrest of La Bruckman, confirm that he is, indeed, the man sought as the prime suspect: 'Chief Murphy declared that there was no doubt of the identity of his prisoner with "Frenchy No. 2 . . . We have made a most important arrest at the request of the New York police authorities. We have been impressed by them with the idea that it is the most important arrest that could be made in the case of the Jack the Ripper butchery of Carrie Brown".'

Several other press reports also noted that the police positively confirmed La Bruckman as Ali's 'cousin', 'Frenchy No. 2.' Interestingly, it was also discovered that the two men shared at least one alias.[5]

Two facts emerge from the news and police reports: there was inconsistency in the descriptions, and there was, despite this, great and persistent interest in La Bruckman as a suspect. It is worth noting that the informant who first brought the attention of the press and police to the startling fact that La Bruckman had been arrested in London on suspicion of being Jack the Ripper, specifically stated that La Bruckman, '. . . answers the description' of Miniter's suspect.[6] Regarding the 'standard' description circulated concerning a light-haired man, two points need to be made. The first is that Miniter saw the suspect at night in the darkened hallway of a hotel, where he was said to be acting in a furtive manner, keeping in the background as if anxious to avoid being seen. The second and more important point actually makes the preceding point moot. It is well attested in the contemporary papers and by the police that Miniter came to be highly problematic as a witness. It is a fact that she provided at least two descriptions of the suspect. It is also a fact that coupled with the one description she gave which generally matched La Bruckman, Miniter recalled that the suspect was the man known as Ali's cousin, 'Frenchy No. 2,' something which the authorities clearly took to be of more importance and reliability than her other description of a light-haired man[7]. It is also well attested that the police came to believe that Miniter's description of the suspect with the light hair and blonde moustache was, in their words, 'wholly unreliable.'

This was stated, by the police, on several occasions. On 29 April, for instance, just five days after the murder, the papers were already reporting:

The confidence in Mary Miniter's ability and willingness to identify the man to whom she let the room that fatal night is not so strong now. The police fear she has not given a correct description of him. The alarm sent out is therefore far from accurate in its description of the man who accompanied poor old Shakespeare. Proprietor Jennings has expressed a disbelief of the woman's statements . . . If the woman's veracity is impeached so soon she will be of little use in identifying anyone whom the police may happen to arrest and who answers the description she has given . . .[8]

The *Daily Continent* summed up the consensus of both the press and the police when it stated, 'Mary Miniter's fame as a professional identifier is rapidly waning . . .'[9]

The police, whose distrust of Miniter began growing from the moment they learned she was an alcoholic prostitute and opium addict, came to believe that Miniter was intentionally giving a false description of the suspect and would probably not identify him even if confronted with him. The *New York Herald* lamented:

The police were nearly paralyzed last night to discover that the most important witness in the case, Mary Miniter, housekeeper at the East River Hotel, would be wholly unreliable when called upon to make an identification of the suspected murderer. It was somehow learned that she has not given a correct description of the man who was last seen with the woman who was murdered. It is hinted that she may be actuated by motives to shield the fellow, who was an acquaintance of hers.[10]

As previously noted, Miniter later recalled that the man she had seen accompanying Brown was Ali's companion, 'Frenchy No. 2,' from which it logically follows that he was an 'acquaintance,' at least by sight. Given the man's stated reputation as an abuser of women in the district, Miniter's reluctance to identify such a person would be understandable.

In this same article, it mentions that Ali's 'cousin,' 'Frenchy No. 2,' remained the focus of the police manhunt: 'This man . . . the cousin, is the fellow for whom Inspector Byrnes and the entire force of 3,500 police have been looking in vain for the week past.' It is clear that the thing which the police took to be of the most importance in the investigation was not Miniter's description of the suspect, but Miniter's identification of the suspect as Ali's friend or 'cousin,' who was later positively determined to be La Bruckman. Should anyone suggest that Miniter's description was being negated so as to 'fit up' Ali for eventual prosecution, I would simply point out that there is no evidence whatsoever, beyond mere speculation, that this was the case. Additionally, as the article shows, 'Frenchy No. 2' remained the focus of the investigation.

Further evidence of Miniter's highly questionable veracity was demonstrated when, in the course of the trial against Ali, she was forced to admit to lying to the police that the man who accompanied Brown had claimed to be named 'Kniclo.' It was brought out at trial, that no such person really existed, and that no names were given by Brown or the suspect on the night of the murder. Miniter confessed at trial that:

Shakespeare paid me with a silver dollar that she got from the man, and asked him to get some beer. I got some mixed ale for her. I did not put the names in the hotel register that night, and next morning Tommy Thompson [the bartender] told me to say that C. Kniclo and wife had occupied room No. 31 the night before. I did not put it down in the register.

Miniter admitted that the name was invented and put in the register by the bartender the following day to 'make it appear right': 'As a matter of fact,' said lawyer House, 'does anyone ever register at the house?'

'No sir,' was the reply.

'Then you lied to the police when you told them the man had registered as Kniclo?'

'I did,' was the frank admission. [11]

Having now placed Miniter's suspect description and reliability in their proper context, and having assessed the forensic findings, including autopsy, news reports and morgue photos in comparison with Ripper killings and what is known about the 'signature' of serial lust-killers, it seems justifiable, especially in light of the La Bruckman 'link,' to suggest that the murder of Carrie Brown remains, at this point, a possible Jack the Ripper killing. Future research and revelations may eventually confirm or rebut this assessment, but nothing we know thus far comes close to dismissing it as a viable supposition. In conclusion, I would merely suggest that it might be instructive to ask: had this murder occurred two or three years earlier in London rather than in New York, would anyone doubt that Brown's murder would quickly have been classed by the authorities as the probable work of the infamous Whitechapel fiend? I would cautiously suggest that the rather amazing linkage between the London and New York killings supplied by the ocean-going slaughterman, Arbie La Bruckman, keeps this possibility open and intriguing.

Footnotes

1. The *New York Recorder*, 13 May 1891.
2. The *New York Herald*, 25 and 26 April 1891.
3. The *World*, 30 April, 1891.
4. The *Evening World*, 30 April 1891.
5. Ameer Ben Ali was known as 'George Francis' (The *New York Times*, 26 April 1891) and La Bruckman was known as 'John Francis' (The *World*, 30 April 1891).
6. The *World*, 30 April 1891.
7. The *New York Herald*, 21 April 1891.
8. The *New York Recorder*, 29 April 1891.
9. The *Daily Continent*, 30 April 1891.
10. The *New York Herald*, April 1891.
11. The *Morning Journal*, July 1891.

All of the above citations can be found in roll #11 of the *New York District Attorney's Scrapbooks*, vols. #83–90, housed in the New York City Municipal Archives. Citations where only the month and year are given reflect that arrangements of newspaper clippings compiled in the NYDA's scrapbooks. They are arranged chronologically, but the clippings do not always include exact dates.

Select sources

Begg, Paul, Fido, Martin and Skinner, Keith, *The Jack the Ripper A-Z*
Douglas, John and Olshaker, Mark, *Mindhunter – Inside the FBI's Elite Serial Crimes Unit*

Victims

Douglas, John, with Burgess, Ann W., Burgess, Allen G. and Ressler, Robert K., *Crime Classification Manual*

The New York City Municipal Archives, *The Court of General Sessions, District Attorney Indictment Record Inventory*

The New York City Municipal Archives, *The New York District Attorney's Scrapbooks*

Vanderlinden, Wolf, 'The New York Affair, Part One' in *Ripper Notes* 16, April–June 2003: 33–45

This essay appeared in *Ripperologist* magazine No. 46, May 2003.

Was Annie Chapman Drunk
When She Left Her Lodgings?

Paul Begg

IN *JACK THE RIPPER: The Facts* I said that Annie Chapman was drunk when she left her lodgings at 35 Dorset Street in search of money for a bed for the night. Several readers have challenged this claim, pointing out that Dr George Bagster Phillips said that Chapman's body didn't contain any alcohol.

In fact, although this is what many newspapers reported, at the inquest Dr Phillips actually said that that he was convinced she had not recently taken 'strong alcohol' and on page 80 of the book I point out that this was a term usually applied to spirits and I say she was probably drunk on beer and that it had either passed through her system or was not looked for or mentioned by Dr Phillips. I said Annie Chapman was drunk when she left her lodgings because we're told she had been drinking beer, because we're told it didn't take much to get her intoxicated, and because we're told by two sources that she was drunk when she left to find her lodging money.

According to the inquest testimony – see the *Daily Telegraph*, 12 September 1888, for a good account – the night watchman, John Evans, saw Chapman come into the lodging house soon after 12.00 midnight. Soon afterwards she sent one of the lodgers for a pint of beer. This was possibly William Stevens (whose name was erroneously given as Frederick Stevens in the *Star*) who said he drank a pint of beer with her at about 12.30 a.m. (see the *Star*,

8 September 1888). Chapman then went out again and returned shortly before a quarter to two. Timothy Donovan was sitting in his office which faced the front door and he saw Chapman go past and down to the kitchen. John Evans's wife was in the office with him and he asked her to find her husband and send him downstairs to ask Chapman for the money for her bed. Chapman, who was eating potatoes, came up to the office followed by Evans and said, 'I have not sufficient money for my bed. Don't let it. I shan't be long before I am in.' She left the house. Asked if she was drunk, Donovan said, 'She had had enough; of that I am certain. She walked straight. Generally on Saturdays she was the worse for drink. She was very sociable in the kitchen. I said to her, "You can find money for your beer, and you can't find money for your bed." She said she had been only to the top of the street – where there is a public house.' John Evans testified that she 'was the worse for drink, but not badly so' and said that 'before he spoke to her about her lodging money she had been out for a pint of beer.' (see *The Times*, 11 September 1888, for Evans's statement that she had been for a beer.)

We know that it didn't take much for Chapman to get drunk because we have the testimony of her friend Amelia Palmer or Farmer, who told the inquest that Chapman 'could not take much drink without getting intoxicated' (the *Star*, 10 September 1888). Against this we have the testimony of Dr Phillips, who was asked at the inquest if there was any appearance of Chapman having taken 'much alcohol' and replied, 'No. There were probably signs of great privation. I am convinced she had not taken any strong alcohol for some hours' (the *Daily Telegraph*, 14 September 1888). Dr Phillips's testimony is at variance with the testimony of at least three witnesses that Chapman had been drinking beer. An explanation is therefore necessary and I suggest that while there was no evidence of Chapman having taken 'much alcohol' – and it didn't take much to get her tipsy – Dr Phillips was looking for 'strong alcohol,' namely spirits, not beer. Beer was still considered nutritious and part of a healthy diet in 1888 and a licence wasn't even needed to sell it, as was the case with spirits, and unlike licensed pubs, beer houses like the Britannia weren't shown on *Ordnance*

Survey maps. My conclusion was also reached by the *Daily Telegraph* (27 September 1888), or perhaps the news agency from which the newspaper took the story, which reported, 'it was probably only malt liquor that she had taken, and its effects would pass off quicker than if she had taken spirits.' I should add that 'malt liquor' meant beer, not a spirit like malt whisky. Pie and mash shops still refer to the parsley sauce as liquor.

I conclude that Annie Chapman had been drinking, that it didn't take a lot to make her drunk, that she was tipsy when she left the lodging house and that by the time of her death she had sobered up and the beer had passed through her system or wasn't looked for by Dr Phillips.

(I might observe that although some evidence suggests that Elisabeth Stride had spent most of the evening drinking, Dr Phillips was asked by a juror specifically 'Was there any trace of malt liquor in the stomach?' to which Dr Phillips answered, 'There was no trace.' Whether we take this to mean that Stride hadn't been drinking or that she had and it had passed through her system is for those with the appropriate knowledge to determine.)

This essay appeared in *Ripperologist* magazine No. 57, January 2005.

Martha Tabram: The Forgotten Ripper Victim

Jon Ogan

O F ALL THE WOMEN murdered in that Autumn of 1888, the least known is Martha Tabram, otherwise known as Turner. She was a woman typified in the subsequent murders. But perhaps more interest would have been shown in her case if it were not wrongly assumed that she had been killed with a bayonet. But first to the background, and events leading up to the murder.

In 1888, August bank holiday Monday fell on the sixth. Throughout the night the celebrations went on in typical bank holiday spirit. More particularly, in Whitechapel where two women were helping two soldiers celebrate the event. One of the women – Pearly Poll Connally – had set herself up with a corporal; her friend had been paired off with a private. From at least 10.00 p.m. the foursome had been drinking around the inns and taverns of Whitechapel. But for the women, their work may have begun much earlier. At 11.00 p.m. they were seen drinking together in the White Swan Public House on Whitechapel Road by her friend's sister-in-law, Anne Morris. Forty-five minutes later the two women separated each with her prospective client. Connolly left with the corporal to go down an alley for what was coyly referred to as 'immoral purposes.' Her friend left with the private, entering George Yard Buildings for a similar purpose. Connolly never met up with her friend again.

For some, the night's celebrations were slowly winding down

36

and the revellers were leaving the taverns to find refuge in their beds. For others not even the holiday would break the monotonous drudgery of life. One such person was the unemployed John Saunders Reeves, resident of 25, George Yard Buildings. At 4.50 a.m., Reeves descended the communal stairway looking for work. On the first floor landing, he came across the body of a woman 'lying in a lake of blood.' Her clothing had also been disarranged.

The local bobby, PC 226 H. Barrett, found that the woman had been ferociously stabbed. He at once searched the stairway, but found no trace of weapon, or of blood leading up or down from the spot. Evidently she had been murdered where she lay.

Dr Timothy Keleene, the local physician, was astonished to find no fewer than thirty-nine stab wounds on the neck, body and private parts. One account has them separated into nine in the throat; seventeen in the breasts; and thirteen in the stomach. But Keleene's official disclosures at the inquest are even more accurate: 'The left lung was penetrated in five places, and the right lung was penetrated in two places. The heart, which was rather fatty, was penetrated in one place and would be sufficient to cause death. The liver was healthy but was penetrated in five places. The spleen was penetrated in two places and the stomach, which was perfectly healthy, was penetrated in six places.' Keleene added ominously, 'Whoever it was knew how and where to cut.' He believed that two weapons had been used, perhaps simultaneously. One was a narrow-bladed, dagger-like instrument. But the other posed more problems. It must have been strong enough to have broken the sternum. The reasoning went that it must have been a bayonet.

PC Barrett remembered a soldier he had seen in Wentworth Street at 2.00 a.m. He was a Grenadier, twenty-two to twenty-six years of age, 5 feet 9 or 10 inches tall, fair-complexioned with a small brown moustache turned up at the ends. He had no medals, but wore one good conduct badge on his tunic. When challenged by the constable the soldier said he was waiting for a 'chum who had gone off with a girl.' One report stated that he was seen in the building itself. However, a married couple called Mahoney had been down the steps and out of the building at the time, but had seen neither body nor soldier.

Another potential witness was licensed cab driver Albert Crow. At 3.30 a.m. he had finished his night's work and was heading up the stairway to his room. On the first-floor landing, Crow encountered 'something.' Concluding it was a tramp, sleeping rough, he decided to let him lie and went on to his own bed in room thirty-seven. But Chief Inspector Donald Swanson believed that although it was common for tramps to sleep out on stairways, he felt sure that the 'something' Crow saw was indeed the murdered woman.

But as yet, she still remained unidentified. Well, at least not formally. The description released ('Age: 27; Length: 5 feet 3 inches; Complexion and Hair: Dark; Dress: Green skirt, brown petticoat, long black jacket, brown stockings and side-sprung boots, black bonnet') turned up three possible victims. The most likely was a woman named Withers, but fortunately she was found alive and well the following day.

In the meantime, the officer handling the case, Inspector Edmund Reid, arranged for an identity parade to be held at the Tower including all the men out on leave over the bank holiday. His aim was for Barrett to pick out the man he saw loitering around George Yard Buildings.

In addition to the constable two other witnesses were located. A mother and daughter from Aidgate called Guildhawk, said they saw a man from the Guards and a woman, together on the day before the murder. They failed to pick out anyone from the row. Barrett on the other hand picked out two. After the constable was warned by his superior that a great deal depended upon his actions he was directed along the rank. The first chosen he admitted was a mistake on account of his medals. The man he saw had none, so the Guardsman was released without further questioning. The second, Private John Leary, was asked to account for his movements on the Monday night. His alibi involved another soldier called Law. Leary said they headed for Brixton on the bank holiday. They remained in the area until the taverns closed. Just before they left the last inn, Leary went outside to the rear. When he returned Law had gone. He looked around trying to find him, but couldn't see him, so headed off towards Battersea, alone, by way of Charing Cross and the Strand. At 4.00 a.m. he caught up with Law on the Strand, walked towards Billingsgate, had a last drink and returned to Barracks at 6.00 a.m. Law, who was questioned separately, was able to substantiate his friend's statement and both men were allowed to leave the orderly room.

One soldier who did not appear in Reid's line-up was the absent-without-leave Private Benjamin who had been missing since the Sunday night. Benjamin reappeared on the Tuesday, directly after the identification parade. At once, Reid took possession of his clothing, bayonet and a statement. According to Benjamin he spent the weekend's impromptu leave at his father's hotel at Kingston-on-Thames. Enquiry was made at the Canbury Hotel and Mr Benjamin verified his son's statement.

On Thursday the ninth, Pearly Poll finally came forward to tell the Police what she knew of the events and the victim's name: Martha Turner. The following day another parade was arranged at the Tower's Barracks. Connolly agreed to attend, but when Sergeant Caunter of the CID went to her address at Crosingham's Lodging House on Dorset Street she could not be found. When she was located a second parade was fixed for 11.00 a.m. on the thirteenth. This time Connolly did appear, but failed to pick out anyone. Instead she boldly asserted: 'They are not here, they had white bands around their caps.' This meant the two men Connolly saw were from the Coldstream Guards, a totally different regiment from the Tower-based Guards.

Yet another parade was arranged for the fifteenth, this time at the Wellington Barracks, and it appeared to have had some success.

Connolly picked out two men. One, whom she believed to be the corporal was in fact a private called George, and had two good conduct badges to his name. The second man she identified as the victim's companion was another private named Skipper. But Reid's optimism was short lived. George was able to prove that he had been at home, on the Hammersmith Road from 8.00 p.m. of the Monday and only left at 6.00 a.m. the following morning. There was another such failure in the 'suspects' case. Skipper was found to have returned to Barracks at 11.00 p.m. and did not leave the compound. The books kept in the Guardhouse confirmed this and Skipper was eliminated from Reid's inquiries.

Several days later – sometime between the inquest's adjournment on the tenth to its resumption on the twenty-third – a Danish sailor and husband to the deceased, Henry Tabram, came forward. Now resident at 7 River Terrace, East Greenwich, he confirmed the identification as Martha Tabram (which should remain as her 'official' name because the couple were married). They had been separated for thirteen years so her husband could add little more.

A more recent acquaintance was Martha Tabram's landlady. The police report, written in longhand, gives her name as something like Sunhurst. But Tom Cullen writing in his book *Autumn of Terror* renders it as Bousfield. Both sources agreed on her address as 4 Star Place, a narrow street running off the southern side of Commercial Street. Tabram lived there for some four months, along with her fellow resident Henry Turner whose name she then took, leaving six weeks before her murder. The Turners knocked Bousfield for the rent and disappeared.

Subsequent police enquiries turned up another address and a new name. After her hasty departure from Star Place, she lived at number 19 George Street under the name of Emma, thus avoiding any further contact from her former landlady. It was an astonishing coincidence that the name Emma and an address on George Street, admittedly not number 19, were both the name and address used by one of the other alleged Ripper victims, Emma Smith. Her murder was to be attributed to different hands – 'hands' being the operative word.

After so many false starts, Reid was forced to abandon the idea of identity parades. Reid's report to his superiors admitted that since both witnesses had picked out wrong men, that even if another positive identification could be made their evidence would be 'worthless,' and his investigation ground to a halt. The two soldiers were never found, nor did they come forward.

A perfect circumstantial case could be built up against Connolly's soldier, one which had stood for over one hundred years.

1. Tabram had been seen in the company of two soldiers by a number of eyewitnesses.

2. She had gone off alone with one of the men.

3. Tabram had been killed with something thought to have been a bayonet.

Almost unshakable, but if we look at numbers one and two first, a different picture begins to emerge. The length of time between the soldier last being seen with the victim, and the discovery of her body was four-and-three-quarter hours, which gave Tabram ample time to have entertained her companion and to have found another. Mary Kelly had done this. At 11.45 p.m. on the night of her murder, she was seen with Widow Cox's blotchy-faced individual. At 2.00 a.m. she was seen with Hutchinson's stereotypical music-hall villain. Two totally different men.

Careful analysis of Stride's movements on the night of the 'double event' similarly point to her having more than one client over her last few hours and it is certain that these were not the only women.

Swanson, too, believed that it was possible. Even though police enquiries were unable to find anyone who had seen the deceased with anyone other than the soldier, he said: 'From the lapse of time, it is possible that she might have been.'

The chief protagonist in the 'soldier theory' is Sir Melville Macnaghten, although he was not drafted in to head the CID until 1889, a year after the murders. His 1894 memo has still been the final word on the subject, particularly regarding the number of murders and those now infamous three suspects. In the paragraph on Tabram's murder he reviews the old ground, the soldier, the victim's friend Connolly. But then his account deviates from the facts. He states that the two soldiers had been arrested. But Connolly 'failed or refused to identify, and the two soldiers were eventually discharged.' This seemed to indicate that Reid had found the two men. Clearly, he had not. Both Connolly and PC Barrett had failed to recognize anybody in the line-ups; there was never enough evidence to arrest any soldier. Macnaghten had also tactfully drawn a veil over the constable's shortcomings.

With respect to part three of the circumstantial case, the bayonet, Macnaghten too had his say. He described that 'the body had been repeatedly pierced' – a curious expression to use – '*probably* by a bayonet'. That assumption was wrong. Although no post mortem report remains, a short note appended to a Home Office document gives the revised official view that 'some of the wounds are so narrow that a bayonet *was first* suspected as the weapon. *But* bayonet wounds are quite *unmistakable*' [my emphasis]. Indeed Keleene hinted as much, that the murder weapon may have been some sort of surgical instrument.

All of which makes sense, if a soldier had killed Tabram in a fit of rage, then only one weapon – his bayonet – would have been used. But of course, Tabram had been killed with two separate knives which fact alone suggests premeditation. The murder would hardly seem to be the work of someone who killed in a drunken rage. If then, Macnaghten's notes have been shown to be 'faulty,' and they remain the only source attributing Tabram's murder to a different culprit, there is now every reason to include her name in the list of victims killed by Jack the Ripper. Indeed, the circumstantial evidence can be taken one step further. The date fits in with one particular suspect, a surgeon, in fact, called Puckeridge. He was released from a Lunatic Asylum on 4 August, three days before Tabram's murder. The suspect appears in the Home Office file in a letter written by Sir Charles Warren to the Home Secretary's assistant, Mr Ruggles-Brice. Sir Charles added, 'We are still looking for him.' But that is a different story.

Postscript

At the initial stage of the police investigation the murder was seen to be included in the Whitechapel murderer's tally. However, it should be added that the (unlikely) case of Emma Elizabeth Smith was similarly linked to this crime series. It was only with the publication of Macnaghten's memoranda that her case lost favour in the eyes of more recent investigators.

There are several points that would appear to suggest a link with the 'bona fide' Whitechapel Murders.

1. A bayonet was not the murder weapon, as indicated in the Home Office annotation: 'Some of the wounds are so narrow that a bayonet *was first* suspected as the murder weapon. *But* bayonet wounds are *quite unmistakable*' (my emphasis).

2. Neither Connolly nor the constable was able satisfactorily to identify the man.

3. The dates of the murder fit into a 'rostered' pattern of crimes as with subsequent murders.

The only drawback has been the apparent lack of extensive abdominal mutilations characteristic of the Nichols (et al) murders. PC Barrett described the victims' clothing as being 'turned up as far as the centre of the body, leaving the lower part of the body exposed.' Barrett believed that sexual intercourse had taken place. However Doctor Keleene revealed that 'from appearances sexual intercourse had not taken place.'

More importantly, Dr Keleene noticed the presence of a wound three inches long and an inch deep, in the 'lower portion of the body.'

Therefore, the clothes were disarranged solely to carry out the mutilations. The offences featured are highly indicative that Tabram/Turner was the Whitechapel Murderer's first victim.

Select sources
Home Office Files A 49301 Series
Mepol Files 3/140 (Victim's File)
The Times, 10 August 1888
Cullen, Tom, *Autumn of Terror*

This essay appeared in *Ripperologist* magazine No. 5, March 1996.

Elisabeth's Story

Daniel Olsson

E LISABETH'S STORY started early in the nineteenth century. There was great excitement at farmer Carl Larsson's home as his wife was about to give birth. It was 4 July 1810 when a healthy baby girl first saw the light at Stora Tumlehed, a small village by the sea in Torslanda parish, Hising Island, not far from Gothenburg. They baptized her on 12 July at the Torslanda church. The name they gave her was Beata Carlsdotter.

During her teenage years, Beata worked as a domestic servant to help support her family. In the mid-1830s, she met Gustaf Ericsson, born on 5 September 1811 in Alingsås parish, 60 km north-east of Gothenburg. He had recently arrived in rural Gothenburg, where he worked as a farmhand. Beata and Gustaf soon fell in love. On 27 October 1839, they became husband and wife at the Torslanda church.

The newlyweds' first priority was to find a place of their own. It wouldn't have suited them, financially or practically, to work for somebody else. They bought a small piece of land on the outskirts of Stora Tumlehed, where they could grow potatoes, carrots, oats and wheat. In the winter of 1840, they began to build their own farmhouse.[1]

Three months after their wedding, Beata became pregnant. That was fine with them, as they had a home and a steady income. A baby was more than welcome!

Nine months later, on 15 October 1840, Anna Christina

Gustafsdotter duly arrived. She was followed three years later, on Monday, 27 November 1843, by the Ericssons' second child: another girl. At her baptism, on 5 December 1843, they named her Elisabeth Gustafsdotter. Gustaf and Beata would have two more children: Carl-Bernhard Gustafsson, born on 4 January 1848, and Svante Gustafsson, born on 22 July 1851.

You may wonder why the boys and girls have different surnames. In Sweden, in those days, children were often given their father's first name as a surname. The girls born to Gustaf and Beata accordingly had the surname Gustafsdotter, which means daughter of Gustaf, and the boys the surname Gustafsson, which means son of Gustaf.

During my research I have ascertained that the family lived in a very safe environment. I consider Stora Tumlehed, in the nineteenth century and still today, as an ideal place to raise children: clean air, verdant farm landscapes as far as the eye can see, and, just beyond them, the rolling grey waves of the North Sea.

All four children worked hard alongside their father on the farm. This meant early mornings and late nights, and undoubtedly gave the children good moral values and strong physiques.

Elisabeth's older sister, Anna Christina, left the farm in 1857 to move to the city of Gothenburg. She married Bernhard Olsson, a shoemaker born in 1828. They had five children: Johan Edward, born 1867; Sven Hugo, born 1873; Gustaf Teodor, born 1876; David Emanuel, born 1879; and Hulda Maria, born 1883.

I was able to track down two of Anna Christina's relatives, both elderly ladies still living in the Gothenburg area. Unfortunately, they had no information to contribute to my research. They also asked to remain anonymous, a wish I am bound to respect.

The only records concerning Elisabeth during the first sixteen years of her life are parish biblical instruction logs. Religion played a major role in Swedish society in the nineteenth century and the Lutheran Church exerted strict control over the faithful. Priests regularly visited the villages in their parish to test the villagers thoroughly on their biblical knowledge. Failure in the tests brought shame upon the persons examined and their families.

Elisabeth's name can be found in the parish logs for the years

1845, 1848, 1851 and 1854. Nothing much is said about her, however, except that her biblical knowledge was good. After the logs, the first entry concerning her relates to her confirmation, held on 14 August 1859 at the Torslanda church where her parents had been married twenty years before. The confirmation record tells us that her knowledge of the bible was very good.

As Elisabeth approached her seventeenth birthday, she grew restless and bored with farm life. Only 20 km away, Gothenburg beckoned. With a population of more than 100,000, it must have looked to her like a teeming metropolis. She decided to seek her fortune in the city. Her application for a certificate of altered residence was approved on 25 October 1860. The certificate indicated that her behaviour was 'good' and her religious knowledge 'extensive.'

No information exists concerning her whereabouts between 25 October 1860 and February 1861. I have not so far found her in any records of that period. In February 1861, she found work as a domestic servant. Her employer was Lars-Fredrik Olofsson, born on 9 August 1825. He resided in Carl Johans parish, Majorna district.

Before we move on, I'd like to clarify something. I had always believed that Lars-Fredrik was a widower when Elisabeth came to work for him. I was therefore amazed to find that his wife was alive and well at the time. Her name was Johanna Carlsdotter Nilsson, born in Hönö on 21 April 1828. She lived for another eleven years and died on 9 August 1872, at forty-four years of age, of Bright's disease, an inflammation of the kidneys.

Lars-Fredrik and Johanna had a total of six children: Johanna Elisabeth, born 1853 (died at only 7 years old, in 1860, from pneumonia); Carl-Otto, born 1856; Johan Fredrik, born 1857; Anders Gustaf, born 1863; Augusta Theresa, born 1865; Hjalmar, born 1867. Lars-Fredrik worked as what in Sweden we call a *Månadskarl*. This means that he sold his labour to various employers one month at a time. Apparently he drew a good wage.

What strikes me is how well the Olofssons managed to make both ends meet. Their household was large, as it consisted of the couple, three children (who would later be joined by two more) and two servants: Elisabeth and Lena Carlsson, who was born in 1826. I find their accomplishment very impressive.

Once again, no information has come to light about the three years Elisabeth spent with the Olofsson family. We can safely assume that she had to work hard. Since she had grown up on a farm, however, she was no doubt used to it.

Yet she left her job in February 1864, apparently a bit hastily. The reason why, we can only speculate. Had her responsibilities become too much for her? After all, Lars-Fredrik and Johanna already had three children at this time and a fourth one would be born the following year. Did Elisabeth neglect her duties and was fired? Perhaps the job didn't stimulate her enough. We will probably never know.[2]

What we do know is that sometime during 1864 Elisabeth drifted into prostitution. Yet we don't know what drove her to the streets or even where she lived at the time, since she is not mentioned in any records.

During the summer of 1864, Elisabeth's life began to fall apart. On 25 August her mother died, at the age of fifty-four, in Stora Tumlehed. The cause of death was given as 'chest disease,' which most likely was pneumonia or tuberculosis. In September, Elisabeth became pregnant, perhaps by one of her clients.

That must have been a real disaster for her. The number of prostitutes in the streets of Gothenburg was quite high and with so much competition about a pregnant woman would not have much of a chance.

What would she do for money? How would she survive? She must have asked herself those questions, over and over again. But she had no other option but to keep the child. An abortion is never pleasant, but 140 years ago it must have been a truly frightening prospect.

To top it all, on 4 April 1865, Elisabeth found herself in Kurhuset, Gothenburg's hospital for the treatment of venereal diseases.[3]

Kurhuset was founded in 1728. It was originally located in Ekelundsgatan Street, far from the city centre.[4] In 1804, the building was completely destroyed by fire. For a number of

47

years, patients were treated in temporary premises. Late in 1815, Kurhuset moved to Örgryte parish – today a very upscale area of Gothenburg – where it remained for twenty years. In 1835, it was relocated to a building at Lilla Bommen, near Gothenburg harbour and the red-light district. This is where Elisabeth was treated on three occasions in 1865.

Kurhuset would remain at this location until 1894, when it moved to Landala parish. At this time it changed its name from Kurhuset to Holtermanska Sjukhuset, after philanthropist J. P. Holterman, who donated a large sum of money to the newly built hospital.

When she first visited Kurhuset, Elisabeth was infected with genital condyloma, or venereal warts. She was also pregnant. Something went horribly wrong during her stay in hospital.

On 21 April, Elisabeth went into labour after only seven months of pregnancy. She gave birth to a stillborn girl. There are two records of her birth: one, in the Kurhuset log book, and one in the register of baptisms in the local church.

The baptism record shows that Elisabeth gave birth to a stillborn girl: in Swedish, *dödfödd* means stillborn, *flicka* means girl and *oäkta* denotes an illegitimate child. The girl was not christened.

The record also gives Elisabeth's surname as Gustafsson instead of Gustafsdotter and her occupation as domestic servant. It looks like nobody was yet aware that for the past fourteen months she had not made her living as a servant but as a prostitute.

On 13 May, Elisabeth was pronounced healthy. She immediately went on the streets again. To earn a living, to pay for food and lodgings, she had no choice but to continue working as a prostitute.

On 30 August, she was back in Kurhuset. This time she suffered from a chancre, a venereal ulcer, which is the primary stage of syphilis. Her treatment took about three weeks after which she was discharged as cured on 23 September.

Only a few weeks later, on 17 October, Elisabeth appeared for the first time on police records. According to entry number 97 in the official ledger, Elisabeth '. . . worked in the countryside and later began to work here in the city until March 1865 when she was

48

registered.' It is not clear, however, whether she was registered as a prostitute. At any rate, she does not appear on the police records for March 1865 or any other date until 17 October.

The ledger gives her physical description and personal data as follows: 'Blue eyes, brown hair, straight nose, oval face and slight build. Born 27 November 1843 in the parish of Torslanda. Daughter of farmers now dead.'

The last entry is not wholly accurate, since Elisabeth's mother had died earlier in 1864, but her father lived until 1879. Apparently Elisabeth also told the police that she had been confirmed at the age of seventeen, when in fact she was only fifteen at the time. Oddly enough, her occupation is not recorded.

It is also worth noting that she said that she lived in Pilgatan Street, in Haga parish. This is the only mention of Pilgatan Street in connection with her. But, did she really live there? According to the census for Östra Haga (the Eastern part of the parish), no one named Elisabeth lived in Pilgatan Street in 1865. In fact, the only person born in 1843 – the year of her birth – who lived in Pilgatan Street in 1865 was a man. It is, of course, possible that Elisabeth's landlord forgot to mention her to the census takers.

Bearing this in mind, I spent over fifteen hours searching for Elisabeth in the 1865 and 1866 censuses, not only in Pilgatan Street but in the whole of Östra Haga. But I could find no trace of her.

Did she lie to the police about living in Pilgatan Street? We might never find out. It is not likely, however, that her landlord forgot her two years in a row. The staff at the public records office where I did my research assured me that censuses are highly reliable sources of information.

Were there any reasons for Elisabeth to lie about her address? Perhaps. If the police found out that she was homeless, for instance, they would most probably have sent her to prison, though not for a very long time. It would nevertheless mean a loss of income for her.

If Elisabeth gave a false address, why did she choose Pilgatan Street? In the 1860s, many prostitutes lived in Pilgatan Street, though it was not the main 'Prostitutes' Walk' in Gothenburg. The red-light district was located in Sillgatan Street, now called

Postgatan Street, which was near the harbour. It was a logical place for the prostitutes to frequent, since most of their clients were sailors. Besides, Sillgatan Street was full of convenient small hotels renting rooms by the hour.

Since Elisabeth was registered as a prostitute, it was unlikely that the police would check whether she really lived in Pilgatan Street. This is, of course, pure speculation. The fact remains that she is nowhere to be found during this period.

It is worth noting that prostitution was not illegal in Sweden in 1865. The only reason why the police would intervene was to prevent the spread of venereal diseases.[5]

At any rate, on 17 October the police sent her to Kurhuset, for what would be the third and last time, to be treated for a chancre. She remained in hospital until 1 November, when she received a clean bill of health.

During the next two weeks she had to report regularly to the police. She was confirmed as healthy in police records for 3, 7, 10 and 14 November. On this day, the police struck her off the prostitutes' register.

Now, to be struck off the register was quite hard for someone entered as a prostitute. The old saying, once a tart always a tart, was correct in most cases. There were only two ways to get off the register: to get married or to get a job. But neither husbands nor employers were easy to find for women who made their living out of selling themselves. Moreover, prostitutes were often arrested for such offences as drunkenness, theft, assault or disorderly conduct. Their police records, particularly if they spent some time in gaol, would also conspire against their finding a way out of their profession through marriage or alternative employment.

But Elisabeth was fortunate this time. She secured a position as a domestic servant and, four days later, was struck off the prostitutes' register. By 10 November 1865, she was at work in her new job.

Some sources have named Elisabeth's new employer as one Maria Wejsner, residing at 42 Husargatan Street, Haga. There has been some speculation as to the exact nature of the job she offered Elisabeth. It has been hinted that Mrs Wejsner had too many domestic servants for a small household and it has even been suggested that she may have run a brothel where Elisabeth pursued her trade.

My research, however, has shown that all these speculations were quite groundless. Elisabeth's new employer was not called Maria Wejsner and did not live at 42 Husargatan Street. She was born Inga Maria Hansdotter on 23 May 1845 (which made her two years younger than Elisabeth). She took the surname Wenzel from her husband, Carl Wenzel Wiesners, and was therefore known as Inga Maria Wenzel. In the census for 1865, where I first located them, there is an annotation next to his name to indicate that he was not of Swedish origin. He belonged to the Christine German parish. Carl was also much older than Maria, as he was born on 27 April 1826. Their home was at 27–29 Husargatan Street.

From 1865 to 1866, Carl was employed as a musician at the newly-built Grand Theatre in Gothenburg. Later he joined the West Goetha Regiment.

To ascertain how many domestic servants lived in their household, I checked all census records from 1865 to 1870. During that period they had only two maids. Elisabeth was the first one. The second maid joined them in 1869.

While Elisabeth worked for them, the couple had no children. Inga Maria, however, was pregnant. Their first child was a boy, born in July 1866. They later had four more children.

Who was Mrs Wenzel? Why did she offer Elisabeth a job? She was obviously not the evil, calculating brothel-keeper some have made her out to be. Was she a kind soul, saving a young girl from a life of infamy? Was she a philanthropist who gave a prostitute who genuinely wished to change her way of life a chance at rehabilitation? Well, I couldn't say for sure. This is a question which requires further research.

In December 1865 or January 1866, Elisabeth received an inheritance of 65 Swedish crowns from her mother. That was a substantial sum of money in those days. It was probably at that time that she decided to go to London, now that she had enough money to pay for her journey and even to acquire a new wardrobe.

Elisabeth must have felt that she would finally leave her gloomy days behind and start a new life in London, the largest, most exciting city in the world. She applied for a certificate of altered residence from her current parish, stated to be Domkyrko (Cathedral) parish, to the Swedish parish in London. Her request was approved on 2 February. Her occupation was given as 'domestic servant.'

On Wednesday, 7 February 1866, Elisabeth left Sweden. She probably knew that she wouldn't see her family again. As her ship headed for the open waters of the North Sea, Gothenburg, which had brought her so much unhappiness, disappeared slowly in the distance. Possibly she couldn't hold back a smile any longer, for her new life started on that day. If she had only known that it was instead the beginning of the end. Poor Elisabeth.

Footnotes

1. Some authors have said that the farm itself was called Stora Tumlehed, not the village. There is, however, no evidence to this effect. There was Lilla and Stora Tumlehed (Lilla means 'Small', Stora means 'Big'). But it is doubtful that the Ericssons' farm was called Stora Tumlehed because it was, by comparison with other farms in the area, pretty small.
2. There has been some confusion among authors as to when Elisabeth left the Olofssons' service. Donald Rumbelow's *Jack the Ripper: The Complete Casebook* (Chicago: Contemporary Books, 1988) contains information on Elisabeth derived from Klas Lithner. On page 75, Rumbelow says that Elisabeth worked with the Olofssons 'until 1864.' He nevertheless adds, 'She moved again and on 2 February 1862 took out a new certificate [of altered residence] to the Cathedral parish in Gothenburg . . .' One suspects that here lies the origin of the error. The correct date is 2 February 1864.
3. In Swedish, the word 'Kurhuset' means 'hospital' or, more literally, 'house of healing.' 'Sjukhuset' means 'Infirmary.'
4. It should be noted that 'gatan' means 'street' in Swedish. Though they are therefore tautological, Ekelundsgatan Street, Pilgatan Street and other similar street names are used in this article for the sake of clarity.
5. The situation has since changed. Under the terms of a Swedish law introduced in 1999, men who seek the services of prostitutes are liable to fines and prison sentences. The law does not target the prostitutes, who are considered as victims of social injustice and inequality.

Acknowledgments

I wish to express my sincere gratitude to Eduardo Zinna, for his help with this essay.

This essay appeared in *Ripperologist* magazine No. 52, March 2004.

Kit, Kitty, Kitten

Andy Aliffe

'YOUNG WOMAN AGED approx. 24 years of age found mutilated in Millers Court. Seen earlier accompanying a man into house. Man described as foreign-looking about 5 ft 7 ins in height with a moustache: Another man seen earlier lurking by a lamppost opposite. Man who discovers body runs into McCarthy's shop. Established that young woman had been, at one time, in domestic service. Coroner's inquest reports she had eaten a meal of fish and potatoes shortly before she was murdered.'

This all sounds terribly familiar doesn't it? The date of the crime described above? 2 July 1909.

Let's return now to Millers Court and examine another date – February 1892.

It was at this time that Canadian journalist Kathleen Blake Watkins, known to her many readers as 'Kit' of the *Toronto Mail* visited some of the murder sites as part of a series of articles she was writing on London life.

Kit had joined the staff of the *Mail* in the autumn of 1890 aged thirty-six years, to write and edit a weekly column called 'The Woman's Kingdom.' She quickly broke with the tradition of recipes, fashion and gossip to write on social issues and what she called 'woman's rights and wrongs.'

Kit had originally arrived in London at the end of 1891 to write about the disappearing London of Charles Dickens, but 'after she had finished the trail of David Copperfield, Pip, Mr Pickwick, and Scrooge through London, she went in search of the Ripper of Whitechapel.' It was the victims and homeless she was to write about.

A chance encounter in Covent Garden led her eventually to the East End. Kit had been exploring the environs of the market and had seen huddled together a young boy and girl. 'The worst sight of all was to see two children lying on a heap of refuse near an archway. The boy had his two arms round the sleeping girl and he sat patiently there, his big brown eyes heavy with sleep and solemn with thoughts that did not befit his years, for he was only seven.' She took them for coffee, bread and butter and hot pudding and eventually learnt of their plight. 'Our mother? – dead – murdered down Spitalfields way; father a rag and bone picker who turned us out.'

She first visisted the Bucks Row crime scene after which she made her way to 29 Hanbury Street. 'It was a foul stinking neighbourhood, where the children are stunted little creatures with vicious faces, old features and where a woman's face would frighten one . . . here we go through a cats' meat shop into a narrow yard, in one corner of which another wretched victim was found murdered.'

From there Kit walked to Dorset Street and number 13 Miller's Court, which was 'reached by a narrow passage under an arch reeking with fifth and crowded with women and children.'

Still residing there was Elizabeth Prater, who lived above Mary Kelly on the night of her murder, but was now living opposite. She told Kit how she had been woken by her kitten 'Diddles' at about 4 a.m. and had heard a faint cry of 'oh murder' from somewhere near by.

Elizabeth then took Kit across the court to meet the current occupant of Mary Kelly's still blood-stained room of number 13, a lady who went by the name of 'Lottie.'

'I was her friend,' said Lottie, speaking with difficulty because of a broken and battered nose given to her by a kick from her husband's heavy boot. 'I was living further up the court then. She [Mary Kelly] says "I'm afraid to go out alone at night because of a dream I had that a man was murdering me. Maybe I'll be next. They say Jack's been busy in this quarter." She said it with such a laugh ma'am that it just made me creep. And been sure enough ma'am she was the next to go. I heard her through the night singin' – she had a nice voice – "The violets grow on your mothers grave" – but that's all we 'urd.' Lottie seemed to have no repugnance in sleeping in the room with its now blood-blackened walls.

Kit continues: 'Other women began to gather presently and grew voluble over the hideous details, like birds of prey. They had hard faces with an evil look on them – the demands for money, for beer, the curses, the profane language, jests about the awful fiend who did his deadly work here, the miserable shrewd-faced children listening eagerly: it was horrible beyond expression.'

Kit Watkins would write about this encounter again in eighteen years time so let us now journey that length of time into the future and to the events of 2 July 1909. 'Ghastly Murder in Spitalfields: A bright young girl cruelly done to death' cries the *Illustrated Police News*. 'Whitechapel Murder: Jack the Ripper crimes recalled' heads the *East End News*.

'A sensational discovery was made on Friday at a house off Duval Street, Commercial Street, Stepney. Shortly after two o'clock in the morning it was discovered that a young woman, locally known as "little Kitty" who was employed as an ironer at a lodging house in the locality, had been murdered, her throat having been cut from ear to ear apparently while she was sleeping, whilst her mouth was stuffed with a pocket handkerchief. The victim had been living, it is said, with a man who knew her as Kitty Ronan, at 12 Miller's Court.'

They had actually been living in the room formerly occupied by Elizabeth Prater.

Kitty Ronan's male friend was Henry Benstead, a news vendor who had been living with Kitty for about four weeks. It was reported that 'He left home on the morning of the tragedy about 9 o'clock, and left the deceased in bed. Witnesses described his subsequent movements until 1.30 the next morning when he parted from a man whom he knew at Spitalfields Church, and then went home. On reaching Miller's Court he found the street door open, and made his way upstairs. He found the bedroom door open, he lit a lamp and saw Kitty lying on the bed fully dressed. He said "Hello, Kitty," and then noticed blood on her neck and on the bed. She did not answer him, he rushed out crying, "Someone has cut Kitty's throat!" and into McCarthy's shop, then went on to Commercial Street police station.'

Detective Inspector Fredrick Porter Wensley took up the case.

The body was subsequently identified by both her mother, Mrs E. Dresch of Hoxton, and her father, Andrew Ronan, of Fulham, who said that she had been in domestic service when he had last seen her several years before.

The *Illustrated Police News* was quick off the mark to satisfy its reader's thirst for the morbid and graphic details of this atrocious killing.

Dated 10 July 1909 it reads: 'Several neighbours ran upstairs and found the girl lying in bed with a terrible gash in her throat. The room of the tragedy was the top apartment of a two-roomed house. There was about half a dozen white-walled houses in the court and the opposite houses are only a few feet apart. Two doors away on the right hand side near the entrance, is the house in which one of the last "Jack the Ripper" murders was committed. Andrew Stevens a seventeen-year-old market porter, who went into the house when the discovery was made told the following story. "I was standing out in the street opposite the court about five minutes to twelve last night and I saw Kitty come down the street with a strange man, pass up the court and enter her house. About 12.20 I saw him come down the court again. He looked round sharply once or twice and the walked briskly up to Commercial Street. From what I remember of him he struck me as being a man of military appearance or perhaps a sailor; but he was well set up . . . he had a moustache and was wearing a dark suit and a dark cloth cap. When I went upstairs I saw Kitty was lying in bed fully clothed. There was blood on the bedclothes. The room did not appear to have been disturbed in any way and there were no signs as if there has been a struggle. It looked to me as if she had been strangled first, and then her throat cut afterwards. On the floor I saw an ugly-looking knife with blood on it. It was a pocket knife but the blade was a thin one. I should think it was about three-and-a-half inches long. The point of the knife was about half an inch in length. At the time of the crime the court was quite deserted. You can hear everything in the ordinary way, but nobody heard a sound or a scream.

The only sound was the footfalls of the man coming out of the court. One of the neighbours I believe heard the sound of footsteps coming down the stairs, but nothing else."'

John Callaghan, a stableman who was living at Mary Kelly's old address, number 13, was also called as a witness, having taken charge of the murder weapon at the time.

At the inquest Dr John Clarke said he saw the body of the deceased on the bed. 'The woman was lying on her back with her head to the left side. There was an incised wound on the right side of the neck about one-and-a-half inches below the jaw; the wound divided the windpipe and all large vessels on the right side of the neck. There was a large quantity of blood on the right side of the neck but there was no sign of a struggle. In his opinion the injuries were not self-inflicted and must have caused instantaneous death.'

Police evidence was also given, including a statement from Detective Inspector Wensley who said that every inquiry had been made, and every clue followed, but without success.

The coroner in summing up, alluded to the mode of life led by the deceased (possibly part-time prostitution) and those associated with her. The jury returned a verdict of 'wilful murder against some person or persons unknown' and expressed the opinion that the police had done all they possibly could under the circumstances.

Had the 'Ripper' returned once more only to disappear so inexplicably again?

And so it was finally with this murderous event that Kit Watkins reported the news for the *Toronto Mail* recalling her first visit to the same mean street in the 1890s and the horrors which in time seem to have repeated themselves.

Select sources
Toronto Mail, 1892
Toronto Globe and Mail, 1988
East End News, July 1909
Illustrated Police News, July 1909
Begg, Fido, Skinner, *The Jack the Ripper A–Z* (1996)

This essay appeared in *Ripperologist* magazine No. 21, February 1999.

2. SUSPECTS

Díosy and D'Onston:
Black Magic and Jack the Ripper

Christopher T. George

I N AN ANONYMOUS ARTICLE, 'The Whitechapel Demon's Nationality: And Why He Committed the Murders (By One Who Thinks He Knows),' which appeared in the *Pall Mall Gazette* on 1 December 1888, the writer, usually thought to have been Ripper suspect Roslyn D'Onston Stephenson, put forth a theory that the Ripper murders were committed by a French practitioner of black magic.

The author theorized that the uterus, removed during the mutilation of several victims, was used by the killer in black magic ceremonies. One good reason to think that D'Onston wrote the article is that the suspect wrote to the City of London police on 16 October 1888 from Currie Wards, London Hospital, stating, 'I can tell you, from a French book, a use made of the organ in question, *"d'une femme prostituée,"* which has not yet been suggested . . .'

Arthur Díosy's claim
On 3 December, two days after the appearance of the article in the *Pall Mall Gazette*, the periodical, seemingly somewhat tongue in

cheek, reported that a man of the name of Arthur Díosy was 'aggrieved' by the claim made in the article and had made the assertion that he had been the first to come up with the black magic theory back in October. Indeed, Díosy said he told the police about such a 'necromantic motive' on 14 October, that is, two days before D'Onston wrote to the authorities.

Loyally, the *Gazette* stood by their unnamed writer, whom they referred to as an 'ingenious contributor' for having identified the nationality of the murderer and attributing the motive of necromancy for the murders. If Díosy had made the claim first, they stated pointedly, how was it no one had heard of it before? They then mentioned that Arthur Díosy 'darkly hints that the dates of the crimes have some occult relation to magical astrology.'

The *Gazette* challenged the upstart: 'It would be more to the point if Mr Díosy would tell us where the next murder ought to occur according to the dates of magical astrology.' Presumably, Díosy did not respond to the challenge, or, if he did, there appears to be no record of whether he made such a prediction of when the next murder would take place.

Who was Arthur Díosy?
Arthur Díosy was born in London on 6 June 1856, at Talbot House, Westbourne Terrace North, Paddington. His father, Martin Díosy, was a Hungarian exile, wine merchant, and commission agent. In that year, Martin had a business at 81, Bishopsgate Within, 'Martin Díosy & Co., mer[chants] & leather factors,' and he also acted as agent for the firm of Chollet, manufacturers of patent compressed vegetables, at that same address. Arthur Díosy's mother was the former Léonie Muller, daughter of an Alsatian officer and a Spanish lady. The elder Díosy was active both in commercial circles and in promoting Hungarian interests in England. During Arthur's boyhood years, the Díosys hosted the great Hungarian patriot Louis Kossuth, and, much later, in 1886, Franz Liszt, during the composer's stay in London in the last months of his life.[1]

Given his cosmopolitan background, it is not surprising that young Díosy became interested in affairs beyond the horizon of England. He attended the London International College beginning in

May 1868 and became interested in Japanese culture and language, teaching himself to speak the language from a book. He went on to attend the Realschule in Lippstadt, Westphalia, at the time of the Franco-Prussian War, and then the Realschule in Düsseldorf, in 1872. On his return to England in 1874, he enlisted in the Royal Naval Artillery Volunteers and began work as a provision merchant like his father. In 1877, he founded the Junior Cosmopolitan Club, comprising over seventy members, mainly Japanese, Hungarian, and English. On 6 June 1882, Díosy married Miss Emma Florence Assheton Hill, only surviving daughter of the late Mr G. W. Hill of Carnarvon, Wales, at Christ Church, Lancaster Gate. Díosy's major claim to fame would follow him within the next ten years with the foundation of the Japan Society. This organization, formed in 1891–1892, was, according to *The Times* of 5 January 1892, 'for the encouragement of the study of Japanese art, science, and industries; of the commerce and finance, the social life, the literature, the language, history and folk-lore of the Japanese.'[2]

Although the British populace and even the government of the day underestimated the Japanese society and how fast the Japanese were modernizing, Díosy was no dewy-eyed romantic. The common attitude toward the Japanese might be illustrated, humorously, by the fact that during a visit of the Crown Prince of Japan to Buckingham Palace in 1921, the Coldstream Guards chose to play a selection from Chu Chin Chow. By contrast, Díosy, with his understanding of gunnery and naval matters, was able to paint quite a different picture of Japan, as he lectured on the growing military menace of the Japanese from the 1890s onward.[3]

Arthur Díosy and the Whitechapel murders

In his memoirs, retired coroner S. Ingleby Oddie described a tour of the murder sites conducted by Dr Frederick Gordon Brown, the City of London Police surgeon, on 19 April 1905, that included Sir Arthur Conan Doyle, and other members of the Crimes Club (also called 'Our Society').

It is not clear whether Arthur Díosy was on this tour of April 1905, but we do know from several sources that he was a member of this same organization. Oddie wrote about Díosy's interest in the case:

Amongst the theories put forward was one by Arthur Díosy, a member of "Our Society." He thought the murders were the work of some practitioner of "Black Magic." According to him, amongst the quests of these people in the East is the elixir vitae, one of the ingredients of which must come from a recently killed woman. Díosy got quite excited when he heard of the bright farthings and burnt matches which he said might have formed the "flaming points" of a magical figure called a "pentacle" at each angle of which such points were found, and according to ritual certain "flaming" articles had to be thus disposed. Díosy said later that he had paid a visit to Scotland Yard to place his theories before the authorities, but had been received without enthusiasm, as one can well understand.[4]

Melvin Harris is dismissive of Díosy as a theorist on the murders, however, Harris was promoting his own theorist and suspect, Roslyn D'Onston, so it is not surprising that he puts Díosy in a subsidiary role. Harris quotes Bernard O'Donnell who interviewed Sir Max Pemberton years after the murders. Pemberton recalled that Díosy had pointed out to the police the existence at one murder scene of "a pentagon [that] had been formed of the stumps of five matches" that would have rendered the murderer invisible, and also that the theorist had persuaded the police to watch a certain bookshop frequented by people who bought books on the occult.[5]

Who came up first with the occult theory concerning the murders, Arthur Díosy or Roslyn D'Onston Stephenson? Did Díosy and D'Onston arrive at their black magic theories quite independently? Or else, did they know each other and they perhaps discussed the case some time in early October, then, during the middle of the month, two days apart, they separately contacted the police?

The note in the *Pall Mall Gazette* of 3 December 1888, following the anonymous article in the *Gazette* of 1 December 1888, might indicate that Díosy did not know who the author of the article was. Thus, we might imply that the two men came up with their ideas separately.

Nor is there any suggestion that Díosy might have suspected D'Onston of being the Ripper, as Melvin Harris suggested in the 1980s and Ivor Edwards has theorized more recently. A search of the letters of Arthur Díosy (1856–1923) might better clarify the relationship, if any, between the two men, as well as reveal further details of Díosy's interest in the case and his theory.

Was Díosy on the side of light, not of darkness?
The Irish-American writer Lafcadio Hearn (1850–1904), similarly to Díosy, developed a love for Japanese culture. After a career as an American newspaperman and a writer of horror stories characterized as 'Irish-Victorian Gothic,' Hearn settled in Japan in 1890, married a Japanese woman, and even adopted a Japanese name. He was made a member of the Japan Society by Díosy, but from a letter he sent to Díosy from Tokyo on 28 April 1903, in his last year of life, it appears he may never have met the Englishman. Nonetheless, there is an interesting aside in this letter that may have a bearing on Díosy's interest in black magic and the Ripper.

Hearn wrote to Arthur Díosy, in what might be an ominous aside, that '...I have reason to know that you are upon the side of Light, not of Darkness...'[6]

What is the significance of this statement for our story?
Patrick Lafcadio Hearn, despite being blind in one eye, became a prolific writer and world traveller. He was born to a Maltese mother and an Anglo-Irish British Army surgeon on the Greek island of Santa Maura. His writings prove that he had a lifelong interest in the grotesque and strange, as well as in superstitions and folk-lore, following in the footsteps of a writer such as Edgar Allan Poe (1809–1849). In 1884, Hearn wrote to his friend, William D O'Connor: 'I have pledged me to the worship of the Odd, the Queer, the Strange, the Exotic, the Monstrous.'[7]

Thus, was Lafcadio Hearn's remark a reference to Díosy's interest in black magic? It is true that Hearn's letter to Díosy appears to have been partly an attempt to get Díosy to exert influence to get Western interests in Japan to treat the writer more kindly. The letter indicates that Hearn believed he was the victim of persecution, as he put it, 'of a small clique of English officials' as well as Jesuits. The overall tone of the letter might suggest that the author was only interested in such practical matters as improving his own position (or alleviating his paranoia perhaps!) since Hearn writes near the end, I know myself on the right side in the order of eternal progress.' And yet Díosy at a dinner party in 1912 told Mrs Belloc Lowndes that he possessed 'a great number of letters from Hearn' but that they were 'too intimate for publication' – which might hint at deeper matters.[8]

If the letter did betray some knowledge of Díosy's dabbling in or at least interest in black magic, does it imply that Hearn had somehow learned that Díosy, while he had an evident interest in the black arts, used his knowledge for good, while someone like D'Onston, whether Jack the Ripper or not, was on the side of Darkness?

Footnotes

1. Adlard, John, *A Biography of Arthur Díosy*, pp. 2, 4 and 5.
2. Ibid., pp. 12, 18–19, 21–23, 43 and 51. *The Times*, 5 January 1892. In the 1890s, Arthur Díosy was also one of the founders, along with Sir Francis Vane, of the English Order of Christ. See Vane, Sir Francis Fletcher, Bart., KCOC, *Agin the Governments*, (London: Sampson Low, 1929) pp. 81–83. Vane credited Díosy as one of the men who helped him 'most in this adventure of reviving Chivalry as a practical scheme' and he singled out the merchant for his dynamic energy.
3. Adlard, John, *A Biography of Arthur Díosy*, pp. 43, 116–19 and 168.
4. Oddie, S. Ingleby, Inquest, p. 55.
5. Harris, Melvin, *The True Face of Jack the Ripper*, pp. 159–60.
6. Lafcadio Hearn to Arthur Díosy, 28 April 1903, quoted in Adlard, p. 136.
7. Lafcadio Hearn to William Douglas O'Connor, 29 June 1884, in Bisland, Elizabeth, *The Life and Letters of Lafcadio Hearn, Vol. 1* (Boston: Houghton Mifflin Co.) p. 328.
8. Lafcadio Hearn to Arthur Díosy, 28 April 1903, quoted in Adlard, p. 137. Susan Lowndes (ed.), *Diaries and Letters of Marie Belloc Lowndes, 1911–1947* (London: Chatto and Windus, 1971) pp. 38–39. Hearn has the distinction of having been the first writer to use the word 'tsunami' in English. In a work published in 1897, he wrote of a devastating tsunami of 17 June 1896, when 'a wave nearly two hundred miles long struck the north-eastern provinces of Miyagi, Iwaté and Aomori, wrecking scores of towns and villages, ruining whole districts, and destroying nearly thirty thousand human lives.' Hearn, Lafcadio, *Gleanings in Buddha-Fields: Studies of Hand and Soul in the Far East* (London: Kegan Paul, Trench, Trubner & Co., 1897) p. 16.

Select sources

Anonymous (usually attributed to D'Onston, Roslyn),'The Whitechapel Demon's Nationality: And Why He Committed the Murders. (By One Who Thinks He Knows),' *Pall Mall Gazette*, 1 December 1888.

Pall Mall Gazette, 3 December 1888, (Note beginning 'Mr Arthur Díosy is aggrieved . . .')

Adlard, John, *A Biography of Arthur Díosy: Founder of the Japan Society, Home to Japan, in Japanese Studies Volume 2* (Lewiston, Queensland, and Lampeter: The Edward Mellen Press, 1990).

Begg, Paul, Fido, Martin and Skinner, Keith, *The Jack the Ripper A–Z* (London: Headline, 1995).

Costello, Peter, *The Real World of Sherlock Holmes: The True Crimes Investigated by Arthur Conan Doyle* (New York: Carroll & Graf, 1991) pp. 57–69.

Harris, Melvin, *The True Face of Jack the Ripper* (London: Michael O'Mara Books, 1995).

Oddie, S. Ingleby, Inquest (London: Hutchinson & Co., 1941).

Robert D'Onston Stephenson' in Jakubowski, Maxim, and Braund, Nathan (eds.), *The Mammoth Book of Jack the Ripper* (London: Robinson Publishing Co., 1999), pp. 445–50.

Stephenson, Roslyn D'Onston, letter to the City of London Police (Corporation of London Records Office, Police Box 3.23, no. 390).

Acknowledgments

My thanks to Stephen P. Ryder, Chris Scott and Jeffrey Bloomfield for help with this article.

This essay appeared in *Ripperologist* magazine No. 57, January 2005.

The American Connection: Sandford Conover aka Charles A. Dunham and Dr Francis Tumblety

Carman Cumming

OR SOME YEARS NOW, the bizarre personality of Dr Francis Tumblety, a prime suspect in the Whitechapel murders, has been defined partly by the colourful description from Charles A. Dunham, a 'well-known' and, therefore, presumably, respectable New Jersey lawyer, who knew and had met Tumblety in Brooklyn and Washington. In a 2 December 1888 interview with the *New York World*, at a time when it seemed evident that the Irish-American quack doctor was suspected of being involved in the Whitechapel murders of that autumn, Dunham helpfully painted the 'Indian herb doctor' in lurid terms: as a psychotic, an exhibitionist, a misogynist, and a charlatan healer who kept in his office an evil collection of female body parts. Several writers have quoted this account as being true, but it is now clear that Dunham himself was also a most remarkable liar and scoundrel, possibly the least reliable witness who ever faked a newspaper column. Therefore, his account of Dr Tumblety must be treated with great caution.

A man of many identities and many frauds, Dunham was a Civil War spy, 'reptile journalist' and agent provocateur whose career as a con artist in both North and South began well before the war and extended beyond it, peaking when he testified (as Sandford Conover) that the Confederate government had ordered Abraham Lincoln's assassination. Dozens of his stories, written for various papers under various names, have now been exposed as ingenious frauds. Presumably many more have still to be spotted.

So, is his description of Dr Tumblety a total fabrication?

Not necessarily. Dunham often used a base of reality for his best inventions, and in the Tumblety case there are indeed elements of truth. For instance, Dunham claimed he was a very young army colonel when Tumblety entertained him at his 'tasteful' quarters in Washington and showed off his cases of female body parts. The fact is that Dunham was indeed in Washington at the time he mentioned, shortly after the 1861 First Battle of Bull Run, as self-proclaimed 'colonel' of a New York regiment. Dunham's 'Cameron Legion' eventually collapsed and was probably a fraud from the start. His claims of recruiting success did not stand up, and his officers were a shady lot of Brooklyn cronies. The most impressive officer listed was a Major Sandford Dockstader, a regular army officer trained at West Point – but that name fails to show up in West Point or US Army records.

Dunham's description of Dr Tumblety in the 2 December 1888 *New York World* colourfully paints the doctor as one of the most prominent characters in wartime Washington, DC. As such, the account is typically detailed, vivid, and unprovable. Much of it could have been taken from newspaper accounts, but the basic facts are consistent with other descriptions of the herb doctor, and they also give a striking view of the wartime capital. When he arrived in July 1861, Dunham recalled, the first-class hotels were like beehives, packed with strangers, mainly in uniform:

Among them were many fine-looking and many peculiar-looking men, but of the thousands there was not one that attracted half as much attention as Tumblety. A Titan in stature, with a very red face and long, flowing mustache, he would have been a noticeable personage in any place and in any garb. But, decked in a richly embroidered coat or jacket, with a medal held by a gay ribbon on each breast, a semi-military cap with a high peak, cavalry-trousers with the brightest of yellow stripes, riding boots and spurs fit for a show window, a dignified and rather stagy gait and manner, he was as unique a figure as could be found anywhere in real life. When followed, as he generally was, by a valet and two great dogs, he was no doubt the envy of many hearts.

Dunham's description of Tumblety's role in Washington is also based on accounts that say Tumblety was a ubiquitous presence:

> Go where you would, to any of the hotels, to the War Department or the Navy Yard, you were sure to find the 'doctor.' He had no business in either place, but he went there to impress the officers whom he would meet. He professed to have had an extensive experience in European hospitals and armies, and claimed to have diplomas from the foremost medical colleges of the Old World and the New. He had, he declared, after much persuasion, accepted the commission of brigade surgeon at a great sacrifice pecuniarily; but, with great complacency, he always added that, fortunately for his private patients, his official duties would not, for a considerable time, take him away from the city.

The crucial (and apparently uncorroborated) part of Dunham's account, however, comes with claims of an intimate association with the doctor and especially with revelations made by him at a dinner attended by 'my lieutenant-colonel and myself.' We should note here that Dunham's 'lieutenant-colonel' was in fact a Brooklyn colleague in crime named Charley Bishop who had helped Dunham in pre-war 'missing heirs' swindles. As Dunham told it:

> One day my Lieutenant-Colonel and myself accepted the 'doctor's' invitation to a late dinner – symposium, he called it – at his rooms. He had very cosy and tastefully arranged quarters in, I believe, H street . . . His menu, with colored waiters and the et ceteras, was furnished by one of the best caterers in the city. After dinner there were brought out two tables for play – for poker or whist. In the course of the evening some of the party, warmed by the wine, proposed to play for heavy stakes, but Tumblety frowned down the proposition at once and in such a way as to show he was no gambler. Someone asked why he had not invited some women to his dinner. His face instantly became as black as a thunder cloud. He had a pack of cards in his hand, but he laid them down and said, almost savagely: 'No, Colonel, I don't know any such cattle, and if

I did I would, as your friend, sooner give you a dose of quick poison than take you into such danger.' He then broke into a homily on the sin and folly of dissipation, fiercely denounced all woman and especially fallen women. Then he invited us into his office where he illustrated his lecture, so to speak. One side of this room was entirely occupied with cases, outwardly resembling wardrobes.

When the doors were opened quite a museum was revealed – tiers of shelves with glass jars and cases, some round and others square, filled with all sorts of anatomical specimens. The 'doctor' placed on a table a dozen or more jars containing, as he said, the matrices of every class of women. Nearly a half of one of these cases was occupied exclusively with these specimens.

Not long after this the 'doctor' was in my room when my Lieutenant-Colonel came in and commenced expatiating on the charms of a certain woman. In a moment, almost, the doctor was lecturing him and denouncing women. When he was asked why he hated women, he said that when quite a young man he fell desperately in love with a pretty girl, rather his senior, who promised to reciprocate his affection. After a brief courtship he married her. The honeymoon was not over when he noticed a disposition on the part of his wife to flirt with other men. He remonstrated, she kissed him, called him a dear, jealous fool – and he believed her. Happening one day to pass in a cab through the worst part of the town he saw his wife and a man enter a gloomy-looking house. Then he learned that before her marriage his wife had been an inmate of that and many similar houses. Then he gave up all womankind.

Shortly after telling this story the 'doctor's' real character became known and he slipped away to St Louis where he was arrested for wearing the uniform of an army surgeon . . .

This account is so richly detailed that it beggars belief, especially since it adds much to the profile of an enigmatic figure. This kind of authenticity, however, was a hallmark of Dunham's technique. He was a master of the art of choosing convincing detail – the small touches that gave 'presence' to his stories. In Tumblety's case it is not even certain the subject was in Washington at the time of Dunham's July visit. However, Dunham apparently visited the capital several times in 1861 and may well have been present for a contretemps he described in which Tumblety, as a publicity stunt, burlesqued himself at the Canterbury Music Hall and then pretended fury at the hall for lampooning him. An ad for the hall in the Washington Star of 4 December 1861 lists 'Tumblety Undone' as one of its attractions.

In this as in other cases, Dunham may have drawn the dramatic detail from other accounts – or simply from his rich imagination. His testimony was, for instance, a highlight of the 1865 military commission trial of Lincoln assassins. He told of being present in the Montreal office of rebel officer Jacob Thompson when fateful orders arrived from Richmond approving Lincoln's killing. Thompson, he said, tapped the paper with his finger, and said: 'This makes the thing all right.' As with much of Dunham's work, this story is discredited mainly on the grounds that almost any statement of Dunham's that can be checked, from the pre-war estate swindles to post-war political scams, is a lie.

Dunham's faked characters included, for instance, the formidable Southern spy Colonel George W. Margrave (or Rhett, or Haynes), an aristocratic villain who had developed an elaborate plan for capturing or killing Lincoln. As Sandford Conover of the *New York Tribune*, Dunham told of defecting from the Confederate war department and bringing with him documents that included a Margrave report on plots in the North to promote fake peace plans: 'He is one of the most cool and reckless villains in the Confederacy – one who can smile, and murder while he smiles. For a villainous and desperate enterprise, no better leader could be found. He is now in the Canadas, and I verily believe for the purpose of heading a gang of desperadoes to commit some depredation on our frontier.'

In fact, no historical trace of Rhett/Margrave has ever been found, and Dunham himself is now known to have passed as Margrave. For instance, Margrave's 'report' told how in spring 1863 he had obtained a pass in Baltimore in the name of Isaac E. Haynes. When Dunham was captured in the South around that time he was carrying Union passes from Baltimore and Harper's Ferry in the name of Haynes. Again, when he was freed and sent north a few months later, Dunham posed as Margrave at least once to sell a fake document (later exposed, of course) to the disloyal *New York News*.

Again, in 1864, when Dunham went to Canada as James Watson

Wallace, he carried a Confederate commission authorizing 'Colonel Margrave' to recruit men for border raids. Ironically and significantly, Dunham himself had in 1863 proposed to Lincoln a plan to capture Jefferson Davis that was similar to 'Margrave's' plan for the capture of Lincoln.

Another Southern spy who cropped up in Dunham's Northern journalism poses even more interesting problems of credibility. This was the woman known to history as Alice Williams or Loreta Janeta Velazquez (among other names), who was supposed to have fought in the Confederate army as Lieutenant Harry Buford. Velazquez produced controversial post-war memoirs telling how as a Confederate agent she had duped the formidable (but by now conveniently dead) Colonel Lafayette Baker, chief detective in the Union war department. Since an 'Alice Williams' did indeed appear on Baker's payroll in fall 1863, this account has been given some credence. Recent research, however, shows a curious twist: Williams showed up on Baker's list shortly after Dunham, as Harvey Birch of the *New York Herald* 'exposed' her as a Southern 'she-wolf' working as a spy in Washington. Because Dunham was known to have been in touch with Baker at least once in this period, and since Baker's bureau would hardly have missed the prominent *Herald* warning, it is likely the 'Williams' Baker hired was a fake of some kind, possibly one of the women he used to spy on suspected traitors. Dunham (as Birch) claimed he had met the 'she-wolf' in Richmond's Castle Thunder prison, and this is almost certainly true, since both are known to have been held there in spring 1863. But the spy story may be a fiction since Dunham later exploited the she-wolf's story at least one more time. This was in the fall of 1865 after Secretary of War Edwin Stanton personally hired him to seek evidence of rebel complicity in Lincoln's death. Working in the South as W. E. Harrison, Dunham reported discovery of another plot for Lincoln's murder, approved by Confederate President Jefferson Davis, which was 'quite as diabolical as the one which resulted in his death' and was to be carried out by Alice Williams/Harry Buford. Dunham said Williams wanted to emulate Charlotte Corday, the aristocratic French woman who was guillotined for slaying Jean-Paul Marat in his bath, 'except that she proposed to employ poison instead of a dagger.' This incident, too, has been cited by some writers as support for the Velazquez memoirs.

Further tangling the 'she-wolf' story is the fact that 'Velazquez' gave considerable credit for her post-war memoirs to an editor/collaborator identified only as C. J. Worthington, 'late of the US Navy'– another name that does not show up in military records. Since Velazquez's adventures often paralleled Dunham's, especially on Southern spying and raid threats from Canada, it seems possible he could have been this elusive collaborator, exploiting her story for a third time. While that invention seems fantastic, it is topped by Dunham's most remarkable confirmed wartime ploy, in which, after becoming 'Conover,' he transformed his original 'Dunham' identity into yet another vicious Confederate agent. He used this villainous Colonel Dunham in several ways, including a cunning ploy to discredit Democratic candidate General George McClellan during the run-up to the 1864 election.

After the war, too, Dunham created a full stable of fake witnesses (including his wife and sister-in-law) who swore to the guilt of Confederate officers in Lincoln's assassination. When this scam was eventually uncovered (to the horror of the War Department), Dunham was sentenced to ten years' hard labor. He then continued a series of plots in prison, first devising evidence that President Andrew Johnson had associated with John Wilkes Booth, then disclosing the fake evidence to the president in an eventually successful bid for a pardon.

After his release, Dunham's life becomes almost as shadowy as Tumblety's. He did indeed do legal work in New Jersey before his death there in 1900, but again, his status is uncertain and his work seemed focused on efforts to tap into large estates. His account of Tumblety in the *New York World* – which reads more like a written article than an interview – must, therefore, remain in the highly doubtful category. One odd little sidelight on the article is that Dunham recalled an incident in which Tumblety, at the time of the assassination, was briefly confused with Luke Blackburn, the Kentucky doctor (later governor of the state) who had mounted a wartime effort from Canada to spread yellow fever infection in the

Union. Dunham remarked as an aside that Blackburn had been 'falsely accused' of the yellow fever plot. The irony is that Dunham knew the Blackburn plot, admitted even by Thompson's own secretary, was real. He knew as well the falsity of an additional charge: that Blackburn and others had plotted to cut off New York City's water supply by blowing the great dam at Croton, New York (Dunham's hometown) and then poisoning the remaining water in conduits and reservoirs. He would have known all about this because he himself had devised the Croton plan, pressed it on reluctant Confederate officers, and then exposed it in his Washington testimony.

So while the truth of his Tumblety story remains clouded, there can be no doubt whatever of the complexity of Dunham's lies. Each part of his Tumblety story will therefore have to be tested, piece by piece, against other available evidence.

This essay appeared in *Ripperologist* magazine No. 63, January 2006.

Pedachenko Revisited: The British Secret Service and the Assassination of Rasputin

Stepan Poberowski

T HESE DAYS, WHEN Ripperology flourishes and new Ripper suspects pop up as regularly as clockwork, it is difficult to imagine the times when the police files on the Whitechapel murders were closed, the memoirists had not yet named any suspects and the Mcnaghten memorandum, the Swanson marginalia and the Littlechild letter were still unknown. Only journalists speculated then on the Ripper's identity: Carl Muusmann named Hungarian murderer Alois Szemeredy; Leonard Matters, Harley Street physician Dr Stanley; and William Le Queux, Russian homicidal maniac Dr Alexander Pedachenko. Their tales all appear to have combined in various degrees truth and fantasy. Of them, perhaps none has fallen into more discredit than the story told by reporter, popular novelist and amateur spy William Le Queux. The question remains, however, did Le Queux make it all up? Or was there any truth to his stories? The British Embassy in St Petersburg started employing writers and journalists in its propaganda and intelligence operations early in the twentieth century. During the decade leading to the First World War, when Sir George Buchanan was Ambassador to the Court of the Romanovs, many British literary figures came to St Petersburg. Their names read like a best-sellers' list: Maurice Baring, Harold Begbie, Arnold Bennett, G. K. Chesterton, John Galsworthy, Compton Mackenzie, Sir Hugh Walpole and H. G. Wells, followed

74

later by T. E. Lawrence (Lawrence of Arabia) and W. Somerset Maugham. When the war broke out, both Robert Wilton, the correspondent for the *Times*, and Harold Williams, the correspondent for the *Manchester Guardian*, who was married to Russian journalist Ariadna Tyrkova, lived in St Petersburg. Another journalist, Major Stanley Washburn of the Special British Diplomatic Mission to Russia, was war correspondent for *The Times*. At the outset of the war, Russia sent the largest army in the world against her German and Austro-Hungarian enemies and scored significant victories. One year later, she had exhausted her military potential, debilitated by huge battle casualties, widespread inefficiency and corruption, the rapacity of quartermasters and the inability of Russian industry to supply her armies with guns and munitions. As Russia tottered on the brink of collapse, her British and French allies tried to prop her up with financial and military aid while the Germans attempted to woo Tsar Nicholas II with the offer of a separate peace – which would free up as many as 350,000 German troops for the Western Front. The Tsar spurned the German advances, dismissed his commander in chief and assumed the command of the armed forces. While he was at the front, his wife, the Tsarina Alexandra, ruled the Empire. But the Tsarina was German-born, and as the war continued disastrously for Russia, she became an object of increasing hatred. Even more universally disliked was her confidant and adviser, the Siberian peasant Grigory Yefimovich Rasputin, whose wild-eyed, swarthy and bearded countenance can be seen in contemporary photographs and newsreels. Rasputin was an unordained, wandering holy man, a *staretz*.[1] He had gained great influence over the Tsar and the Tsarina through his uncanny ability to heal Tsarevitch Alexei, who suffered from the royal disease, hæmophilia.[2] Malicious rumours circulated about Rasputin's relationships with the ladies of the court and the Tsarina herself. Some claimed that he was secretly working against Russia together with the Tsarina. In December 1916, a group of conspirators assassinated him, ostensibly to save the Tsar from his pernicious influence. It was to no avail. Only two months later, a popular uprising led to the abdication of the Tsar and the establishment of a provisional government committed to continuing the war. At the end of 1915, the British Foreign Office instructed Robert Wilton and Major Washburn to set up a British Propaganda Office in Russia to counter pro-German sympathies and anti-war sentiment. They placed Hugh Walpole and Harold Williams at the head of the Petrograd[3] office and Bruce Lockhart at the head of the Moscow office. Despite their labours, the failure of the Gallipoli campaign against Turkey in 1915–1916 and the Irish Easter Uprising in 1916 undermined Russian confidence in Britain and reinforced the impact of both German and Russian anti-war propaganda. By June 1917, Walpole and Williams could report that the Germans had succeeded in instilling in the Russian people some suspicions regarding British and French war aims.[4] William Le Queux and W. Somerset Maugham arrived in Petrograd in 1917 to bolster the British Propaganda Office's efforts to shore up the Provisional Government headed by Alexander Kerensky and combat anti-war feelings and the growing strength of Bolshevism. Le Queux already had over ten years' experience in the performance of various secret government missions in Europe. It is hard to assess his intelligence work in the Russian capital, however, inasmuch as neither the Bolshevik revolution in October 1917 nor the subsequent withdrawal of Russia from the war could be prevented. Le Queux did not remain long in Russia. Back in Britain, he wrote a series of articles about Rasputin which ran in the *Illustrated Sunday Herald* during June-August 1917. Later in the year, he segued with Rasputin, the Rascal Monk, where he claimed to reveal the *staretz*'s pro-German machinations on the basis of documents given to him by the Provisional Government.[5] The success of *Rascal Monk* led him to write *The Minister of Evil: The Secret History of Rasputin's Betrayal of Russia*, which was published in August 1918. This time the provisional government had given him the papers of Fedor Rajevski, Rasputin's private secretary. According to Le Queux, Rajevski was in fact a secret agent whose superior, General Kuropatkin, had introduced him to Rasputin and secured a place for him as the *staretz*'s secretary. Kuropatkin was also said to have engineered the first meeting of the Tsar and the Tsarina with Rasputin at Sarov in July 1903. Le Queux asserted that during the war the Tsarina and Rasputin had worked together to contrive Russia's defeat. To that end, Rasputin had travelled secretly to Berlin, accompanied by the ubiquitous Rajevsky, to meet the Kaiser. In 1919, Le Queux returned to the subject with Rasputin in London, a novel claiming to be an exposé of an erotic religious movement created by Rasputin. Finally, in October 1923, Le Queux published a book of memoirs, *Things I Know about Kings, Celebrities and Crooks*, where he averred that the Provisional Government had also given to him a manuscript dictated in French by Rasputin which had been found in a safe in the cellar of his house. This manuscript, entitled *Great Russian Criminals*, revealed the identity of Jack the Ripper. He was Dr Alexander Pedachenko, a homicidal Russian maniac. Pedachenko was an obstetrician in the staff of the maternity hospital at Tver, the capital of Tverskaya Province, north of Moscow, where he lived in the first floor of a house in Millionnaya Street. The Okhrana, the Russian secret police, sent him to London in order to embarrass Scotland Yard. Pedachenko's accomplices in the murders were a man called Levitski and a tailoress called Winberg. Old Russian revolutionary and Anarchist Nicholas Zverieff, a member of the Jubilee Street Club, an anarchist centre in the East End of London, told the story to a Russian agent named Johann Nideroest who was also a member of the Club. Le Queux's tale is well known – as are the further elaborations of Donald McCormick, who expanded upon it in *The Identity of Jack the Ripper*, as well as in *The History of the British Secret Service* (1969) and *The History of the Russian Secret Service* (1972), both published under his pseudonym, Richard Deacon. On the face of it, Le Queux's claim to have received the manuscript of *Great Russian Criminals* from Kerensky's Provisional Government appears nonsensical. Why would the Provisional Government give such a manuscript to a British journalist? At the time of Le Queux's sojourn in Russia, an extraordinary court of inquiry established by the provisional government was investigating Rasputin's role as an intermediary between the Tsar and interest groups seeking the appointment of ministers, department presidents and other senior officials of the Empire. Had the Provisional Government found any documents in Rasputin's house, it would have been under an obligation to hand them to the extraordinary court. On the other hand, Le Queux had close connections with the British Secret Service, which was anxious to neutralize Rasputin, who openly opposed the war. How far the Secret Service was willing to go to achieve this end has been revealed only recently. Rasputin's assassins were Prince Felix Yussupov, a wealthy aristocrat who was married to the Tsar's niece; Grand Duke Dmitri Pavlovich Romanov, the Tsar's cousin; Vladimir Purishkevich, a right-wing member of the Duma, the Russian Parliament; Dr Stanislaus Lazavert, Purishkevich's physician; and Lieutenant Sukhotin, a young officer of the crack Preobrazhensky Regiment. On the night of 29 December 1916 – 16 December according to the Julian calendar that was still used in Russia at the time – Yussupov invited Rasputin to his palace on the Moika Canal. What happened next is known to us largely from the memoirs left by the conspirators. Yussupov gave his memoirs the title *Rasputin, His Malignant Influence and His Assassination*; Purishkevich, more tersely and dramatically, called his *How I Killed Rasputin*; and Dr Lazavert was content with an untitled report. They all recounted how Yussupov led Rasputin to a dining room in the basement where he plied him with Madeira wine and chocolate cake laced with potassium cyanide. But the poison seemed to have no effect. Yussupov got a revolver from the study where his co-conspirators waited and shot Rasputin in the back. An hour later, he returned to the murder scene to discover with horror that the *staretz* was still alive. As Yussupov leaned over him, Rasputin leapt to his feet, pushed Yussupov aside and fled into the courtyard. Purishkevich ran after him, firing his gun wildly. Rasputin, hit twice, collapsed. Yussupov then beat him savagely about the head with a rubber club. The conspirators bound Rasputin's hands and legs, bundled him up in a sheet and carried him to the river Neva, where they dropped him through a hole in the ice. The river police found the body. Rasputin had still been alive when they threw him in the river. He had not died from either poison or his wounds, but had drowned in the freezing waters, still struggling to free himself. Akulina Laptinskaya, a peasant woman whom Rasputin had known since 1907, stripped and washed his body at the house of Anna Vyrubova, the tsarina's lady-in-waiting and intimate friend. The tsarina prayed over the corpse, covering it with icons and flowers. Two days later, they buried him on the Imperial park at Tsarskoe Selo.[6] Newly uncovered evidence, however, points in a different direction. During the weeks leading to Rasputin's assassination, there were many contacts between the conspirators and British officials. Two weeks prior to the assassination, Purishkevich met Samuel Hoare, who was the chief of station at the British mission in Petrograd from 1916 to 1921 and would serve as Britain's Foreign Secretary in the 1930s.[7] The Ambassador, Sir George Buchanan, learnt about the plans for the assassination a week before they were carried out. Major Washburn discussed the assassination in a telephone conversation with General Handbury-Williams, the head of the British Mission to the Stavka – the Russian High Command – long before the news became known to the Russian police and public. On 30 December, the Tsar told Sir George Buchanan that he suspected a British subject 'who had been a college friend of Prince Felix Yussupov' of having participated in Rasputin's murder. Who was the Tsar's suspect? In his book *Ubit' Rasputina* (*To Kill Rasputin*), Russian historian and journalist Oleg Shishkin fingers Hoare, who had been at Oxford with Yussupov. Shishkin asserts that the British Secret Service played a central role in the conspiracy to assassinate Rasputin because of his anti-war stance. Hoare was at Yussupov's palace on the night of Rasputin's assassination. He did not plan to intervene, thinking that Yussupov could manage on his own. Yet, when Yussupov failed to finish off the *staretz*, Hoare intercepted him as he tried to escape and shot him dead. Shishkin avers that the report on the post-mortem examination of Rasputin's body carried out by Professor Dmitry Petrovich Kosorotov on 21 December 1916 proves that Yussupov and his accomplices lied about his death and concealed the name of the real killer. Kosorotov was a member of the Medical Council of the Ministry of the Interior who performed the post-mortem at the chapel of the Chesmenskaya Hospice at the behest of the Petrograd District Court Chief Investigator, Victor Nikolaevich Sereda. Kosorotov stated that Rasputin had sustained multiple wounds, many of which were inflicted after his death. He had not died by drowning in the freezing waters of the Neva, but from 'an abundant loss of blood from a gunshot wound to the stomach . . . at almost point-blank range.' The gunshot wound and type of bullet used were not consistent with a shot fired by Yussupov and pointed to the existence of another gunman. Only Kosorotov and Chief Investigator Sereda were present at the post-mortem. A representative of the gendarme corps at the joint staff had visited Hoare, whose home was on the Moyka Canal near Yussupov's Palace, to invite him to be present at the post-mortem as a foreign observer. But Hoare declined the invitation for fear of provocation by Russian counter-espionage agents. In a later report he described the post-mortem in detail, but it is likely that he obtained the relevant information from his contacts. In *Who Killed Rasputin?*, a BBC Timewatch documentary aired on 1 October 2004, intelligence historian Andrew Cook and former Metropolitan Police Commander Richard Cullen relied on the same information to formulate a different theory which, however, still points to the involvement of the British Secret Service in Rasputin's assassination. Examining Kosorotov's post-mortem report, Cullen also found that existing accounts of the *staretz*'s death did not tally with the forensic evidence. Yussupov and Purishkevich both stated that they alone had shot Rasputin. Yet the three bullet holes in his body were of different sizes. This means that the bullets were fired from three different guns, which points to the existence of a third gunman. In particular, a gunshot wound was found in the forehead whose precise positioning suggests that it was fired by a trained killer at close range; yet Purishkevich shot Rasputin from behind and at a distance. Photographs taken at the palace after the discovery of Rasputin's body show a long, straight line of blood across the courtyard ending in a pool of blood near a gate where a car was waiting. In all probability, after both Yussupov and Purishkevich shot Rasputin, the conspirators carried him across the courtyard to the car they would use in disposing of his body. Before they reached the car, Rasputin showed faint signs of life. The third gunman promptly dispatched him with a bullet to the head. Both his superiors and the Russian conspirators, who were eager to gain the glory for themselves, kept his involvement secret.

Who was the third gunman? Cullen names Oswald Rayner, a British Secret Intelligence Service agent who, like Hoare, had been with Yussupov at Oxford before the war. Rayner was working alongside Captain John Scale, a senior SIS officer. Scale's daughter Muriel clearly recalls that her father 'was involved in the planning of Rasputin's death,' a memory also shared by relatives of other British officers said to have participated. In his official documentation, Scale refers to Rasputin by the codename 'Dark Forces' and describes him as a real threat to Britain. He openly discusses a 'sinister' force clogging the Russian war machine: 'Rasputin the drunken debauchee who is influencing Russian policy.' Through his close contacts with members of the Duma, Scale learnt of secret plans to make a separate peace with Germany. Shortly afterwards, Scale and his fellow British intelligence officers Rayner and Stephen Alley were holding regular meetings with Yussupov and Grand Duke Dmitry Pavlovich, undoubtedly to discuss Rasputin's assassination. In a further book of memoirs published in 1952, *Lost Splendour*, Yussupov mentions Rayner in his account of the day following Rasputin's assassination: 'As I went down to dinner, I met my friend Oswald Rayner, a British officer whom I had known at Oxford. He knew of our conspiracy and had come in search of news. I hastened to set his mind at case.'[8] After the *staretz*'s death, Stephen Alley addressed to Scale a memorandum which read: 'Although matters have not proceeded entirely to plan, our objective has clearly been achieved. Reaction to the demise of Dark Forces has been well received by all, although a few awkward questions have already been asked about wider involvement. Rayner is attending to loose ends and will no doubt brief you on your return.' If Rayner was indeed the killer, he never spoke about what he had done. He left Russia before the end of the war, burnt all his papers and took all his secrets to the grave in 1961. Cook has since uncovered more evidence about other covert operations involving the same intelligence officers in the two years following Rasputin's murder, including further assassination plans and efforts to help the Tsar and his family escape from captivity. This new evidence also reveals efforts by intelligence officers to entice Lenin's Bolshevik

Government to re-enter the war even after it had signed the treaty of Brest-Litovsk with Germany.[9] It is therefore not so improbable, after all, that Kerensky's Provisional Government could have given Rasputin's documents not to the extraordinary court of inquiry but to Le Queux. Most members of the provisional government, including Kerensky himself, had close contacts with British diplomats and intelligence officers. Le Queux was a well known anti-German propagandist who could be relied on to use any information received to advance the cause of the warlike provisional government in Britain and castigate the timorous Tsar, the traitorous Tsarina and their sinister adviser Rasputin for their ill-conceived rapprochement to the German foe. Some serious difficulties nevertheless remain regarding the documents Le Queux claimed to have in his possession. He averred that in his books on Rasputin he had relied on the papers of the *staretz*'s private secretary, Rajevski. But no one called Rajevski was ever a member of Rasputin's inner circle. His friends and advisers were well known. Many among them described themselves as his secretaries, though they were in fact adventurers and intriguers with an unsavoury past. They included Ivan Manasevich-Manuylov, a former Okhrana agent; Aaron Simanovich, a Moscow jeweller who represented certain Jewish interests; Michael Otsup, a contributor to the newspaper *Vechernee Vremya* (*Evening Times*) who was also Rasputin's personal photographer; Prince Michael Andronnikov; and Ivan Dobrovolsky, a collegiate counsellor[10] and inspector of the board schools who was one of Rasputin's most devoted admirers. They served as a buffer between Rasputin and the suppliants who brought petitions addressed to the *staretz* together with money to press them forward – two thirds of which stuck to the so-called secretaries' hands. Only Akulina Laptinskaya could be considered as Rasputin's secretary in the true sense of the word. Shortly before his death, he dictated to her his memoirs, the manuscript of which is nowadays kept in the State Archive of the Russian Federation. Not only Fedor Rajevski was not a member of Rasputin's circle, but no one by that name lived in Petrograd at the time. According to the *All Petrograd Directory*, the only person bearing that surname who was registered in Petrograd in 1916 was

Andrei Fedorovich Rajevsky. He was a collegiate secretary[11] and manager of Savings Bank No. 162 who lived in a house, no longer extant, which was then at No. 6, Babigonskaya Street in Peterhof – some 100 metres from the home of the author of this essay. Another Rajevsky, Lieutenant-Colonel Michael Fedorovich Rajevsky, had served in the Moscow Military District and from the beginning of the War had been a senior aide-de-camp in the intelligence branch of the army. He most likely did not know Rasputin at all. The brother of Rasputin's above-mentioned 'secretary' and photographer, Michael Otsup, was the poet Georgiy Otsup, who used the pen name G. Rajevsky. But there is no evidence that he was acquainted with Rasputin. Besides, Rajevsky is an aristocratic surname, well known in Russia because of several distinguished members of the family who lived in the first half of the nineteenth century. In all probability, Fedor Rajevsky never existed. Le Queux gave his name to a character in his book in the same way that a Hollywood producer could have named a character in a film General Pushkin or Dostoevsky. Little in the so-called Rajevski manuscript makes sense. Le Queux asserted that General Kuropatkin had schemed to ensure that Tsar Nicholas II and the Tsarina met Rasputin at Sarov in July 1903. But, contrary to Le Queux's claims, General Kuropatkin never headed the secret service. He was in fact the Minister of War. In July 1903, moreover, he was in the Far East. As for Rasputin, he was still in Pokrovskoe, his native village in Siberia. He first met the Tsar and Tsarina on 1 November 1905, at Grand Duchess Militsa's home. During the First World War, Rasputin never left Russia and, in particular, never met the Kaiser, as Le Queux maintained. According to Le Queux, *Great Russian Criminals* was dictated in French by Rasputin, who knew the language slightly. The truth is that Rasputin knew no French whatsoever and was barely able to read and write Russian. Le Queux also said that the manuscript had been found in the cellar of Rasputin's house. But Rasputin did not live in a house but in apartment No. 20 on the second floor of a building at 64, Gorokhovaya Street, St Petersburg. The cellars of such houses usually contained woodsheds and laundries for the tenants.The manuscript itself, though full of absurdities, contains a

Suspects

modicum of truth about Tver, where Pedachenko allegedly lived. In the early nineteenth century, Millionnaya Street was indeed one of Tver's main streets, lined by two-storied private residences. Furthermore, Tver really had a maternity hopital. Unfortunately, no detailed directories for Tver were issued in 1870–1880, and it would be impossible to find a list of members of the maternity hospital's staff without carrying out extensive research in local archives. But then the manuscript becomes increasingly nonsensical. It purports to be a history of Russian criminals, but Rasputin – as his daughter Maria told Colin Wilson – had no interest whatsoever in this subject. Besides, little or nothing was known in Russia about criminals at the time. The first Russian serial killer – Nikolay Radkevich, also known as Vadim Krovjanik, or Bloody Vadim – became known only in 1909. Le Queux's stories about alleged Russian agent Nideroest and his associates were already being ridiculed upon the publication of his book. Old Russian revolutionary and Anarchist Nicholas Zverieff is nowhere to be found, not even in the *Dictionary of Characters of the Russian Revolutionary Movement*, an extremely detailed multi-volume publication that lists even people who attended a revolutionary meeting or two only to drop out after a first encounter with the police. Yet there is a possible source for at least part of Le Queux's story. The surnames of most characters allegedly mentioned in *Great Russian Criminals* can be found in a directory called the *Address-Calendar of the Russian Empire for 1888*. They are all within one or two pages from the entry on Peter Ivanovich Rachkowsky, whose name is identical to that of the head of the Foreign Agency of the Okhrana in Paris from 1884 to 1902. As we know, Le Queux claimed that Pedachenko committed the Ripper murders at the behest of the Okhrana. Could Le Queux have learned of Rachkowski's existence during his sojourn in Russia? It is possible, since the Extraordinary Court of Inquiry was at the time investigating the Foreign Agency's operations. Furthermore, some related documents were already public knowledge. Alternatively, Le Queux could have learnt about Rachkowski from an interview with Princess Ekaterina Radzivill which appeared in issue No. 15 of *American Hebrew*, published in 1921, where she described

Rachkowski's role in the fabrication of the notorious *Protocols of the Elders of Zion*. The Rachkowski in the *Address-Calendar*, however, was a totally different person. He was the founder and head of the first maternity in Krasnoyarsk, the capital of Yenisei Province, in Siberia, and the chief obstetrician for the province. Could this be the origin of Dr Pedachenko, who was also described as an obstetrician and member of the staff of a maternity hospital? If my assumptions are correct, Le Queux tore off several pages from the *Address-Calendar* and kept them on hand during the writing of his book as a reference source for Russian names. This would explain why so many characters in the so-called manuscript bear names found in these few pages. For example, the governor of Yenisei Province, Lieutenant General Ivan Pedachenko, may have lent his surname to Dr Pedachenko, the alleged Whitechapel murderer; the postmaster of Karginsky post office, Pavel Levitsky, to the Ripper's accomplice Levitski; either the head of the Cheremkhovsky post office, Nikolay Zverev, or the district doctor in Verholensk, Nikolay Zverev, to 'old revolutionary' Nicholas Zverieff. In the shelves of a library somewhere in Britain there is perhaps a copy of the *Address-Calendar of the Russian Empire for 1888* bearing Le Queux's *ex libris* and missing the pages where columns 313 to 316, containing the names Rachkowski, Pedachenko, Levitski and Zveriev, appear.One final question might be asked. Did Le Queux, whose contacts in the intelligence services have been well documented, know that the British Secret Service had been involved in Rasputin's assassination? If he did, he could well have thought that ascribing the Jack the Ripper murders to an agent of the Okhrana, the Russian secret police, would be no more and no less than poetic justice. If he didn't, we would be faced with a remarkable coincidence.

Footnotes

1. It is widely believed that Rasputin belonged to a sect known as the 'Flagellants', the *Khlysty* – probably a corruption of *Khristy*, meaning 'Christs' – who believed that Christ could enter into living individuals – usually peasants who were seized by some mysterious spirit and wandered round the villages attracting followers. (See Figes, Orlando, *Natasha's Dance*.)

2. It has been theorized that the Tsarevich took aspirin, which was then considered a wonder drug, but which, in fact intensified the bleeding. Rasputin advised discontinuing the use of aspirin, which caused the bleeding to stop.

3. When the First World War broke out, the Russians – in whose language Peter is rendered as Pyotr – thought that the name Sankt Peterburg (St Petersburg) was too Germanic. On the initiative of the Tsar, the city was renamed Petrograd on 31 August (18 August, Julian calendar) 1914.

4. After the war, Wilton joined Victor Marsden, a correspondent for the *Morning Post* who had also lived in Tsarist Russia, in promoting the idea of a Jewish conspiracy in Britain. Marsden translated into English the *Protocols of the Elders of Zion*, now widely believed to be an Okhrana forgery.

5. The full title of the book was *Rasputin the Rascal Monk, Disclosing the Secret Scandal of the Betrayal of Russia by the Mock-Monk Grichka, and the Consequent Ruin of the Romanoffs*.

6. There have been persistent rumours that a relic of the *staretz* still exists. It was said that a very aged, very frail lady of Russian origin living in Paris kept for many years Rasputin's legendary 12-inch (30-cm) penis in a velvet-lined box of polished wood. In April 2004, Dr Igor Vladimirovich Kniazkin, head physician at the St Petersburg Prostate Research Centre, announced that he had paid $8,000 for a box containing Rasputin's penis together with a letter from Akulina Laptinskaya to Rasputin's daughter Matrena which read: 'I have a part of your father's body. Here is a relic of the Holy *Staretz*.' Following Rasputin's death, Laptinskaya remained for twenty-four hours alone with his body. During that period she could well have removed his penis. The relic is at present an exhibit in a newly established museum of erotica in St Petersburg.

7. Samuel John Gurney Hoare, Lord Templewood, 1880–1959. After the war, he served as secretary of state first for air and then for India. He was appointed foreign secretary in 1935 as the Italians prepared to invade Ethiopia. Hoare and Pierre Laval of France secretly agreed on a compromise plan by which a large portion of Ethiopia would have been surrendered to the Italians. The plan was leaked to the press and Hoare resigned. He re-entered the cabinet in 1936, served as special ambassador to Spain from 1940 to 1944 and was raised to the peerage in 1944.

8. Rayner later translated Yussupov's memoirs, *Rasputin*, into English and named his son Felix after him.

9. The full story of the plot to kill Rasputin and the operations which followed has been covered in Andrew Cook's book, *Who Killed Rasputin?* (Tempus, 2005).

10. Collegiate counsellor was a rank in the civil service determined in accordance with the table of ranks for the civil and military hierarchies introduced by Tsar Peter the Great in 1712. It was the equivalent of a colonel in the army or a captain first grade in the navy.

11. Civil rank equivalent to a staff captain of infantry or cavalry.

Select sources

Alexeev, Michael, *Voennaya Kontrrazvedka Rossii. Pervaya Mirivaya Voyna (Military Counter-espionage in Russia. First World War)*, Vol. 2 (Moscow: 2001)
Begg, Paul, Fido Martin and Skinner, Keith, *The Jack the Ripper A–Z* (Headline, 1994)

Figes, Orlando, *Natasha's Dance: A Cultural History of Russia* (London: 2002)
Harris, Melvin, *Jack the Ripper: The Bloody Truth* (London: 1987)
Le Queux, William, *Things I Know about Kings, Celebrities and Crooks* (London: 1923)
McCormick, Donald, *The Identity of Jack the Ripper* (1971)
Oakley, Jane, *Raspoutine* (Paris: 1990)
Platonov, Oleg, *Zhizn' za Tsarya (A Life for the Tsar: The Truth about Grigory Rasputin)*
    (St Petersburg: 1996)
Shishkin, Oleg, *Ubit' Rasputina (To Kill Rasputin)* (Moscow: 2000)
Wilson, Colin, *Rasputin and the Fall of the Romanovs* (Secaucus, 1971)
Zinna, Eduardo, 'The Ripper People: William Le Queux', in *Ripperologist*, Issue 46, May
    2003
Address-Calendar of the Russian Empire for 1888
Daily Telegraph, 19 September 2004
Dictionary of Characters of the Russian Revolutionary Movement, 1870–1904 (1933)
Nezavisimaya Gazeta, 28 April 2004

Acknowledgments
My thanks to Eduardo Zinna and Artemy Vladimirov for their help in the preparation of this essay.

This essay appeared in *Ripperologist* magazine No. 58, March 2005.

Nikolay Vasiliev: The Ripper from Russia

Stepan Poberowski

B ETWEEN NOVEMBER and December 1888 several British and
international newspapers identified a new Ripper suspect:
Nikolay Vasiliev, also called Nicolas Vassili or Wassily.
Not only that, but two books brought out in America during the
same period, *The History of the Whitechapel Murders: A Full and
Authentic Narrative of the Above Murders* (Richard K. Fox,
Publisher and Printer, New York) and *Leather Apron; Or, the
Horrors of Whitechapel, London* (Philadelphia), no doubt inspired
by press reports, fingered Vasiliev as the most likely suspect.[1]

From the press reports one can sketch a biography of this new
suspect. Vasiliev was born to well-off parents in 1847 in Tiraspol,
Kherson Province (called Cherson Province in contemporary
newspapers), Russia. He was educated in Tiraspol and at Odessa
University. At twenty-five years of age, he was one of the heads of
the *Skoptsy*, a sect of Castrati or eunuchs, who were referred to in
English-language newspapers as 'The Shorn.' In 1872 Vasiliev
exiled himself to France to escape the persecution of the Russian
government. He carried letters of introduction for members of the
local Russian community who helped him to settle down in Paris.

For a couple of months he rented lodgings in the Rue
Mouffetarde.[2] In the daytime he worked away amid piles of books
and when night came went out into the streets to wander about until
dawn, calling on streetwalkers to repent and join the *Skoptsy*. Soon
he became known as the 'Saviour of Lost Souls'. But he gradually

88

changed his methods: from entreaty to curses, from generosity to compulsion. And then the unexpected happened.

Among the women he tried to reform was a young girl called Madeleine whom he met in the Rue Richelieu.[3] Vasiliev fell in love with her and, hoping to redeem her and rescue her soul, secured lodgings for her with a respectable tradeswoman, Mme Guidard, in the Rue Serrurier.[4] He also found her a place in a lace-making establishment. But after a few weeks his beloved ran away and Vasiliev left his lodgings to search for her.

Two months later he caught up with her in the same place where he had seen her for the first time – the Rue Richelieu – and stabbed her in the back. Two days after Madeleine's death, he murdered another prostitute in a quiet street of the Faubourg St Germain. Three days later another was found, wallowing in blood, with the same wounds, in the Quartier Mouffetarde. Within the space of two weeks, five more victims were found butchered in the *arrondissement* of the Pantheon, between the Boulevard St Michel and the Boulevard de l'Hôpital. Their money, purses, jewels, etc. were intact in all cases. Vasiliev was caught red-handed when a streetwalker he attempted to kill in the Rue de Lyon cried out for help.[5]

During his trial his lawyer, Maître Jules Glaunier, claimed that his client was insane and Vasiliev was confined in a private asylum at Bayonne. According to some reports, he was later sent to Russia where he spent sixteen years in an asylum at Tiraspol; according to other sources, he remained in the asylum in France.

The newspapers described him as tall, lean, with a brawny form, a pale, waxy complexion (which may have been a side-effect of castration) and burning black eyes. He was released from the asylum on 1 January 1888, when he was forty years of age.

Unfortunately, the press reports on Vasiliev do not contain enough data that could be checked against other sources. The town where he was born, Tiraspol, is today the capital of the breakaway Transdnistria Region, west of the Dniester River, while Chisinau, 73 km away, remains the capital of Moldava. Tiraspol was founded in 1792, at the same time as the Sredinnaya Fortress, on the left bank of the Dniester in the Ochakovskaya area annexed by Russia pursuant to the Iasi Treaty which cemented its victory in the Russo-Turkish War (1787–1791).

In 1806 Tiraspol became a district town of Kherson Province, most of which lies today in the Ukraine. By the mid-nineteenth century, its population was about 10,000.

The railway reached Tiraspol in 1867 and Chisinau in 1873, bringing about the rapid development of the town, which did a brisk trade in grain and wine. Tiraspol's main street was Pokrovskaja Ulitsa, which was lined with government buildings, luxury shops and the houses of the wealthy – in one of which Vasiliev was probably born. Interestingly, Tiraspol was granted its coat-of-arms in 1847, the year of Vasiliev's birth.

In the mid-1860s there were two educational institutions in town preparing students to enter university: the Tiraspol Secondary School and the Tiraspol Orthodox Spiritual School. Unfortunately, no documents about these educational institutions are available. Although some documents are probably kept in the Tiraspol archives, the disintegration of the Soviet Union, the proclamation of the Transdnistrian Republic and the ensuing tensions within Moldova render access to these archives very difficult.

Vasiliev was well educated at Tiraspol and at the University of Odessa. The Imperial Novorossiysk University of Odessa was founded in 1865 and originally consisted of the School of History and Philology and the School of Physics and Mathematics. To have time to complete his studies, become a leader among the *Skoptsy* and emigrate to France in 1872, Vasiliev must have been among the university's very first students. But there is no Vasiliev among either students or non-credit students at the university during its first years of existence, though some students came from Tiraspol. No Vasiliev can be found either among the graduates from the University until at least 1890.

We have seen that Vasiliev became a *Skoptsy* leader. The fact that he was from Tiraspol points quite accurately to the *Skoptsy* group to which he belonged. The *Skoptsy* cult was a heresy that emerged in the second half of the eighteenth century and blossomed in St Petersburg and Moscow under the leadership of Kondratiy Selivanov. In the mid-nineteenth century, during the reign of Tsar Nicholas I, the Russian government persecuted the *Skoptsy*. It was considered as the most dangerous of all sects and membership in it was declared illegal. Many members of the *Skoptsy* fled to Romania and Turkey, where they settled mainly in such towns as Iasi, Bucharest, Galati, Ismail and Nikolaevka, which were near to the border between Russia and Romania as well as to Tiraspol.

The *Neo-Skoptsy* movement was founded in Galati in 1871. Its objectives were to elaborate theoretically the *Skoptsy* teachings, especially conversations about the angels, the soul and the Holy Spirit, and to ameliorate the religious and moral conditions caused by the decline of religion. The *Neo-Skoptsy* cult spread to the Danubian towns near the border. A peasant, Kuzma Fedoseyev Lisin, and his associate Kupreyanov became its leaders and invested the movement with a messianic character. Lisin declared himself to be the second messiah and the reincarnation of Tsar Peter III and Kondratiy Selivanov. As a god, he ranked higher than Jesus Christ, and as a man, higher than the sovereign. The sect was headed by the Svyatoe Izbranie, or Holy Elite, composed of forty persons. Vasiliev may have been one of them.

When Lisin joined the *Skoptsy* he was castrated with 'the great or Tsar seal,' which involved the removal of his penis as well as his testicles. Yet the *Neo-Skoptsy* preached spiritual castration and held that there was no need to submit to physical castration upon joining the sect; castration could be performed at any time, even in the face of death.

At *Neo-Skoptsy radenies*, prayer meetings, future preachers were revealed to Lisin by divine intervention. The chosen ones divested themselves of all their possessions, abandoned their homes and went forth to spread the sect's message across Russia. In 1875 Lisin and some of his associates were arrested, tried and banished to Siberia. They concealed the identity of other adherents of the sect from the prosecution. It is therefore possible that Vasiliev, who was not on trial, was among those who were not named.

But most newspaper reports about Vasiliev contain a significant detail which indicates either that he was not in fact a member of the

Skoptsy or that journalists who were not familiar with the sect thought up this part of the story. In effect, the newspapers said that Vasiliev pored over religious books all day and when night came went out to preach or, later, to carry out his self-imposed mission of revenge. But the *Skoptsy* had no books. They rejected the authority of the Bible, believing in the revelations of the Holy Spirit which were set forth in their *raspevetses*, spiritual verses, which were sung at their prayer meetings. The *raspevetses* contained basic ideas of the *Skoptsy* worldview, some events of the history of the sect, and moral norms and principles. Therefore this clue does not confirm the existence of Vasiliev.

A police officer investigating a counterfeiting case in St Petersburg in 1818 came across two adjacent houses belonging to two merchants: Vasiliev and Solodovnikov. Members of the *Skoptsy* were found at both houses. The main adherent of the sect, Kondraty Selivanov, lived at Solodovnikov's home, and a 'virgin of rare beauty,' named Bogoroditsa or the Blessed Virgin, whom the *Skoptsy* revered as a divinity, lived secretly at Vasiliev's home. The St Petersburg authorities did not follow up the case but instead hushed it up. There is, however, no evidence connecting the merchant Vasiliev with Nikolay Vasiliev.

On 17 November 1888, the London *Star*, in an article entitled 'A Fictional French "Ripper"' recounted briefly Vasiliev's story and concluded: 'It is doubtful, however, whether such a man as Wassili [sic] ever existed. M. Macé, a former Chef de la Sûreté, who is thoroughly posted in the criminal history of France, has said to an interviewer that no such person committed murders in Paris in 1872. The only Parisian case in any way resembling the London assassinations was one which occurred about 1875. A certain individual terrified the women in the Rochechouart quarter by repeated assaults. He was captured after five or six of these outrages, and was pronounced insane. He was a foreigner, but not a Russian, and in any case he killed none of his victims.'

Despite this apparently final verdict on Vasiliev, his newspaper trajectory was not yet finished. On the same day, 17 November (5 November according to the Julian calendar), the St Petersburg newspaper *Novosti* published a brief article reporting the murder of

Mary Kelly and speculating on the possible identity of the murderer: its readers' fellow Russian, Nikolay Vasiliev.

On 28 November 1888, both the *Pall Mall Gazette* and the *Daily Telegraph* published articles which began as follows: 'The *Novosti*, a Russian paper, is responsible for the following startling revelation regarding the Whitechapel murderer: "He was born in Tiraspol in South Russia in 1847, and graduated at the Odessa University. After 1870 he became a fanatical Anarchist, and emigrated to Paris, where he went out of his mind".' The articles concluded: 'He went to London, and there lodged with different compatriot refugees until the first woman was assassinated in Whitechapel, since which time his friends have not seen him'.

An article worded somewhat differently was published on the same day, 28 November, in the *Star*, which two weeks before had denied Vasiliev's existence. None of the articles said anything about Vasiliev's membership of the *Skoptsy*, but affirmed instead that he was an anarchist. In this connection it is worth noting that revolutionaries such as the *narodovoltsy*, the members of the *Narodnaya Volya*, the People's Will, who assassinated Tsar Alexander II in 1881, considered the *Skoptsy* as potential allies. However, the original Russian article published in the *Novosti* on 17 November was actually a reprint of foreign, most likely French, press reports which said nothing about anarchists but repeated the version known to us about the *Skoptsy*.

The rumours about Vasiliev were picked up by the newspapers soon after the double murder on 30 September 1888. On 12 October, the British newspaper *Weekly Herald* ran an article entitled 'A French Whitechapel Murderer,' which managed to tell the entire story without ever mentioning Vasiliev's surname or his nationality. On 2 November, the Russian journalist (and rumoured Tsarist agent) Olga Novikoff, a friend of Gladstone, Madame Blavatsky, Henry M. Stanley and William T. Stead, who named her the 'MP for Russia' because of her tireless work on behalf of her country, asked her Parisian correspondent for information on Vasiliev. Press reports published in mid-November gave Belgium and Switzerland as the sources of the initial information about Vasiliev. Later France was also included in this list.

At that time, the Foreign Bureau of the Tsarist Secret Service, the *Okhrana*, had its headquarters at the Russian consulate in Paris and maintained a network of agents in Switzerland. The Foreign Bureau used provocation primarily to persuade the French to take action against Russian radicals and cooperate with the *Okhrana*. The most notorious provocation occurred in Paris in 1890, when an *Okhrana* operative, Arkadiy Harting, organized a team of bomb-throwers whom he later betrayed to the Sûreté. Their heavily publicized arrests helped convince the French public of the dangers posed by Russian radicals in France.

The head of the Foreign Bureau, Pyotr Rachkowski, was a specialist in provocation who refined the art of what is known today as active measures or perception management techniques. Rachkowski paid subsidies to journalists to write articles favorable to Russian interests and acquired or subsidized such periodicals as *Le Courier Franco-Russe* and *Revue Russe*. He also founded the *Ligue pour le Salut de la Patrie Russe* to promote positive views towards Russia among French citizens.

The articles published in the *Pall Mall Gazette*, the *Daily Telegraph* and the *Star* resemble other articles planted in newspapers by the *Okhrana* as part of its provocation campaigns and may have been based on the assumption that Mary Kelly's murder would be followed by more murders in November or December. Giving 1870 instead of 1872 as the year when Vasiliev emigrated to Paris would have served to link his name more closely with the radical *Commune of Paris* and with the slaughter of hostages by the *Communards*.

In addition, Vasiliev could be safely described as an anarchist because this definition was applied to practically all foreign radicals, since the British public were not familiar with all revolutionary trends. Members of the International Working Men's Educational Club, the Socialist club in Berner Street, for instance, were frequently described as anarchists.

The press reports stating that Vasiliev lodged with compatriot refugees may have been aimed at inducing the Metropolitan Police to interrogate Russian immigrants, thus gathering valuable information about Russians in London which the *Okhrana* could collect through its agents in Scotland Yard. Contemporary *Okhrana* documents mention the names of two agents, John and Murphy, both of whom probably served in the Special Branch.

By 1888 the *Okhrana* Foreign Bureau had completely infiltrated and demoralized Russian immigrant communities in the Continent, but it could not reach the revolutionaries living in Britain. The *Okhrana's* interest in the British capital is shown by Rachkowski's journey to London in June 1888, as well as by a veiled mention of a trip to Britain by secret agent Gurin, who was known for his active participation in the destruction of the *Narodnaya Volya* printing press in Geneva in 1886.

But the provocation – if that was indeed what it was – did not go any further and left no trace except for one newspaper report. When the Ripper vanished, the possibility for the *Okhrana* to use his name for its own purposes vanished with him. By the New Year, 1889, Vasiliev had disappeared from the pages of the newspapers. He remains an elusive legend, which probably had some basis in reality, but was mostly embellished by the journalists who wrote it up.

Footnotes

1. *The History of the Whitechapel Murders* gave as its source for the Vasiliev story the journalist John Paul Bocock, of the *New York World*.
2. The places Vasiliev allegedly frequented while in Paris are real and, what is more, still exist. The Rue Mouffetard – not Mouffetarde – is on the Left Bank, south of the Seine. It is one of the oldest streets in Paris, going back to Roman and medieval times. Until recently, it was also one of the most disreputable. Its name was derived from *moufette* (skunk) because of the stink caused by the activities of the tanners and tripe butchers who once plied their trade along the banks of the Brève river, which now runs underground.
3. The Rue Richelieu runs from Montmartre to the Palais Royal and the Louvre.
4. The Boulevard Serrurier is in the 19th *arrondissement*, north of the Seine, which in Vasiliev's time was a semi-rural area .
5. The Faubourg St Germain, in the 7th *arrondissement*, is where many ministries, embassies and homes of the very rich are located.
6. The *arrondissement* of the Pantheon is in fact the 5th *arrondissement*. The Pantheon is a former church which, during the French Revolution, between 1831 and 1852 and today, has served as a final resting place for great men and women. Among those who lie there are Mirabeu, Voltaire, Rousseau, Victor Hugo, Braille and Zola.
7. The Rue de Lyon is in the Bastille quarter, north of the Seine.

Suspects

8. Interestingly, there was one Nikolay Vasiliev among the accused at a political trial in St Petersburg in 1861, but his biographical data do not tally with Vasiliev's data as published in the newspapers.
9. For more information on the Narodnaya Volya see Zinna, Eduardo, 'A Passion for Justice: Jacob Rombro and the Berner Street Club', *Ripperologist*, 39 (2002).
10. According to one source, Rachkowski was also involved in the production of *The Protocols of the Elders of Zion*, arguably the most notorious political forgery of the twentieth century.

Select sources

Begg, Paul, *Jack the Ripper: The Uncensored Facts* (Parkwest Pubs, 1990)
Begg, Paul, Fido, Martin and Skinner, Keith, The *A–Z Jack the Ripper: A to Z* (Headline, 1994)
Belkin, A. I., *Tretiy pol: Sud'by pasynkov prirody* (*The Third Sex: Destinies of Nature's Stepsons*) (Moscow, 2000)
Burtsev, V. L., *Za sto let, 1800–1896, Vol. 2* (*During a Hundred Years, 1800–1896*) (London, 1898)
Dilevskiy, G. Y., *Kishinev, Bendery, Tiraspol* (Kishineu, 1982)
Engelstein, Laura, *Skoptsy i Tsarstvo Nebesnoe* (*Castration and the Heavenly Kingdom*) (England, 1999; Moscow, 2000)
Markevich, A. I., *Dvadzatipyatiletie Imperatorskogo Novorossiyskog Universiteta* (*The Twenty-Fifth Anniversary of the Imperial Novorossisk University*) (Odessa, 1890)
Nevskiy, V., *Istoria Departamenta Politsii* (*History of the Police Department*) (Manuscript in the possession of the author's widow, 1930)
Panchenko, A. A., *Christovszhina i skopchestvo: folklor i traditsionnaya cultura russkikh mischeskikh sect* (*Christovszhyism and Skoptsyism: folklore and traditional culture of Russian mystical sects*) (Moscow, 2002)
Spisok studentov i postoronnih slushateley Novorossiyskogo universiteta za 1865/66; 1866/67, 1867/68, 1868/69 akademicheskiy god (*List of students and non-graduate students at Novorossiysk University for the academic year*) (Odessa, 1866, 1867, 1868 and 1869)
Stepanov, S. A., Rudd, Charles A., *Fontanka, 16: politicheskiy sysk pri tsaryakh* (*Fontanka 16: The Tsar's Secret Police*) (Moscow, 1993; McGill-Queens University Press, 1999)
Russian State Historical Archive, files of the 796 fond (the Holy Synod)
Casebook: Jack the Ripper (www.casebook.org)
Daily Telegraph (London), 28 November 1888
The *East London Observer* (London), 1 December 1888
The *Evening Star* (Washington, DC), 14 November 1888
The *Manchester Guardian*, 15 November 1888
The *Montreal Daily Star* (Canada), 14 November 1888
Novosti (St Petersburg), 5 (17) November 1888
The *Ottawa Citizen* (Canada), 16 November 1888
The *Pall Mall Gazette* (London), 28 November 1888
The *Star* (London), 17 and 28 November 1888

Nikolay Vasiliev

Sudebny Vestnik (Judicial Bulletin) (St Petersburg, 1874–1876)
The *Toronto Globe* (Canada), 15 November 1888
The *Weekly Herald* (UK), 12 October 1888

Acknowledgments
My thanks to Eduardo Zinna, Artemy Vladimirov and Alexander Chisholm for their help in the preparation of this essay.

This essay appeared in *Ripperologist* magazine No. 50, November 2003.

3. POLICE

Anderson's Quirkiness

Martin Fido

ON THE INTERNET 'Casebook: Jack the Ripper' site, I was asked by contributor David Radka if I thought 'Anderson's acceptance of his suspect as the murderer may have been based on his quirkiness.'

I think Anderson's quirkiness would probably only have affected his insistence that the Ripper's identity was known insofar as it was of a kind to leave him very confident and assertive when holding a minority opinion. Let me elaborate.

Anderson was a milleniarist: he believed the second coming of Christ, with attendant Last Judgement etc. was imminent. This was and is a minority opinion (held most notoriously today by Jehovah's Witnesses). Most people disagree with it strongly enough to call the belief 'barmy,' but equally recognize that individual Jehovah's Witnesses (or similarly milleniarist Plymouth Brethren or Seventh Day Adventists) are perfectly sane and may prove to be be quite admirable people when one knows them well.

In Anderson's day the belief was minority enough to be cranky, but was shared by such notable figures fringing the Ripper case as his chief, James Monro, and the East End evangelizing philanthropist Dr Barnardo. (Tho' Barnardo, who became quite an energetic social climber, gave it up and became an Anglican when this helped his public recognition and acceptance.)

Much more seriously quirky was Anderson's belief that Satan is the Lord of this World – like Billy Graham, he supported this and other curious views on the grounds that 'the Bible said so', and anything the Bible said was indisputably true. This led him to deduce, uniquely, as far as I know, that all wordly institutions were under the control of Satan. And since all the churches held land and money, they too, had fallen under Satan's control. Anderson believed that everybody could see how obviously true this was of the Church of Rome! But he was unusual in thinking that all Protestant churches were heading fast to the same damnation. Therefore the true Christian had to prepare for the Last Judgement by *not* joining any church, and going to ad hoc tent meetings and revival crusades rather than endorsing a particular sect.

Anderson preached for Barnardo, but did not join him in the Plymouth Brethren. Instead he joined lay Protestant associations, like the revolting Protestant Truth Association which within my certain memory was still publishing the pornographic and fraudulent 'Maria Monk' as an attack on the Catholic Church – (about as reputable as touting *The Protocols of the Elders of Zion*).

Now, what Anderson did to himself by deciding against any sort of formal church membership was something Dr Johnson had observed about Milton. He invited dangerous crankiness, lacking the observation and concern of others to keep him within generally agreed bounds.

This is obviously important where a personal philosophy rests on faith – by definition something which is not a matter of pure reason based on demonstrable fact. (It doesn't protect against mass hysteria, which probably seems a greater danger to us today, but which was less significant when a large majority of thinking people were committed to one or other of a number of competing faiths, whose competition for the endorsement of sensible men normally kept them within the bounds of common sense.)

Since he was quite accustomed, then, to working out his own theology and sticking to it no matter whether the rest of the world disagreed, Anderson's cast of mind inclined him to accept his own judgement and push aside challenges. His thinking could be strikingly original: for example, he believed that it would be sensible to impose life imprisonment on all habitual criminals, no matter how trivial their offences (down to the theft of sixpences) rather than using a sliding scale of penalties relating to the seriousness of the crimes. But he also thought that prisons should then be made as comfortable as possible, with pleasant prospects and all possible facilities for legitimate entertainment and occupation, as society's justified self-protection did not warrant turning incarceration into a punishing imposition of severe circumstances.

He explicitly believed that being a detective necessitated an undesirable (unchristian) attitude of suspicion, however. But he did not feel that he had a Christian duty to give this up. As far as can be seen, his approach to detection was perfectly rational, and except insofar as he was hair-splittingly concerned about how far equivocation and deliberately misleading questioning might be employed, quite unaffected by his quirky Christian and penological beliefs.

He would, however, be intensely unwilling to abandon a conclusion he had finally reached. Littlechild's dismissive 'Anderson only thought he knew . . .' was a fair characterization of the man's capacity to insist on his personal opinions as a matter of truth, even though, as far as it goes, the same thing is equally true of you, me and everyone else who has a definite opinion about either the identity of the Ripper or the impossibility of forming one in the present state of knowledge. We all 'only think we know' everything that isn't a matter of our own definite experience, but Anderson was 'more equal than others' in this respect.

I don't think his crankiness would have affected him in the slightest in deciding whether the Ripper was or was not Jewish or Gentile, local or extra-East End, poor or rich. It would have led him to resist counter-arguments once he had made up his own mind on perfectly sensible grounds.

This essay appeared in *Ripperologist* magazine No. 34, April 2001.

Anderson's Solutions:
The Lighter Side of Historical Reality

Jeffrey Bloomfield

I T CANNOT BE DENIED that measured by the standards of government service, Robert Anderson had a successful career. He proved his worth in his work in Ireland undoing plots by the Fenians and successor groups against the British government. He was brought to London to confront the dynamiters of the 1880s, and rose to be Assistant Commissioner of Scotland Yard. Finally he was knighted – a rewarding career with only one blemish: he took his 1888 vacation plans too seriously and robbed the regime of Sir Charles Warren of his expertise in searching for the most notorious criminal of the nineteenth century.

Whether or not Sir Robert would have helped catch the Ripper I leave unanswered. His reappearance came too late to have any marked effect on Scotland Yard's efforts. I am inclined to wish him the benefit of the doubt and leave it at that. That said, I would add that he would have been wiser (from the point of view of posterity) if he had resisted the temptation of commenting on Whitechapel in his memoirs. He would be respected as a successful spy master, and that would have been enough. Instead, he is seen as something of a self-important windbag, who claimed to know more than he may have had access. To be fair, however, the temptation was probably too great for him to ignore. Despite his experience and ability, he probably got a lot of teasing over his vacation plans in 1888 (i.e. 'So, did you find any clues among the yodelling in the

Alps, Sir Robert?', or 'Is it true that on the Matterhorn you found somebody wrote in the snow, "The Juwes are not the persons who go skiing for nothing?"'). It was not the stuff to try to build a legend on . . . at least not a creditable legend.

Because of the Ripper chapter in his memoirs, *The Lighter Side of My Official Life* is rarely looked at for anything outside of Whitechapel. It is used, of course, for a discussion of Anderson's anti-Fenian activities (and his involvement, discreditable or not, in the Parnellism and Crime campaign of 1887 to 1889). But few readers are aware that besides the Ripper material, Anderson's memoirs also discuss two other matters of some controversy, one of which is a mystery thirty years older than Whitechapel dealing with murder and dismemberment.

To get the stories straight actually requires some background on when Sir Robert acquired his knowledge. In the early 1870s Anderson was in London as a political spymaster. Suddenly he was aware of a great opportunity brought about by the collapse of the Second Empire in the Franco – Prussian War: a sudden exodus of secret police talent from France. One of the ex-French spies was a person known to Anderson as 'Maxwell.' Anderson described him as a handsome man who might have been a successful model. Maxwell was a gifted linguist, and had experience as a revolutionary. According to Anderson they had many discussions about many secrets, but only two are discussed to any extent: the death of the famous dandy and artist Count d'Orsay, and the Waterloo Bridge Mystery.

Count Alfred d'Orsay had been a social ornament in France and England from the 1820s to the 1840s. He died in Paris on 4 August 1852. The cause of death given to the public was a carbuncle on the spine, but Maxwell painted a different picture of this. He claimed that d'Orsay died as the result of a bullet in his spine, which he got in the gardens of the Elysée Palace while walking there with Emperor Napoleon III. Apparently the bullet was fired by an assassin at the Emperor but hit d'Orsay instead. So the report of a death by natural causes was a lie. Anderson relates that he got a confirmation of the story from the head of the Sûreté.

The Waterloo Bridge Mystery was one of the great unsolved

London murder cases of the nineteenth century, prior to the Whitechapel murders. On the evening of 8 October 1857 Henry Errington (the toll keeper at the Bridge) helped an elderly woman with a large bag get through the turnstile. Another man, Samuel Ball, followed the woman through the turnstile, but walking faster soon overtook her. Both were walking from the Strand side of the Bridge. Ball saw another man walking from the opposite side. This man never identified himself. It was a foggy night, so activity on the bridge was hidden from sight. The next morning two young men in a boat on the Thames found a bag on the third buttress. They eventually turned the bag over to the police when they saw the contents. The contents were a dismembered human body.

With the assistance of a good police surgeon, Dr R. B. Paynter of F Division, and the noted forensic specialist Dr Alfred Taylor, the police were able to show the deceased was a man wearing clothing of foreign origin who had been stabbed to death. The killer had then cut up the body (after boiling parts of it), to make it easier to transport. It was suggested that the perpetrator (or the woman who was hired to transport the remains) intended to let it sink into the Thames but misjudged the distance between the river and the end of the buttress.

However after the initial stages of discovery and the inquest nothing further was discovered. It was a case that perplexed the public. Charles Dickens even alluded to it in a passage (when describing Waterloo Bridge) in *The Uncommercial Traveller*. Since there were no sequence of further murder victims it never gained the notoriety of the Ripper Case. It became one of many unsolved murders in the nineteenth century.

Anderson said that Maxwell explained who the murderers of the unknown man were and why the murder was committed. It seems that the murdered man was an Italian police agent sent to infiltrate an Italian revolutionary cell. The agent resided at Cranbourne Street in Soho. While the police agent was sleeping the revolutionaries searched his clothing and found his letter of instructions. He was knocked out, dragged to the basement, and 'a quick struggle was quickly ended by the use of the assassins' knives.' After first trying to burn the body the killers decided to get rid of it in the Thames.

Before tackling the truth (or possible truth) of these revelations we should notice the source material a bit. Anderson first reveals these two tales in the serial version of *The Lighter Side of My Official Life* which appeared in *Blackwood's Magazine* for December 1909 on pages 771 to 773. They are both repeated in the fourth chapter of his published book version (1910). There is a little difference between the two versions regarding their conclusions. Maxwell soon came to a point where he had no further information to sell to Anderson. Anderson senses from Maxwell's demeanour and speech that something is up, and confronts him. It turns out that Maxwell felt it would be better for his family if he were out of the way. Anderson said that suicide was no answer and accused Maxwell of being a coward. The man broke down and cried at this point. Here the two accounts differ. In the magazine version Anderson tells Maxwell to come back in a week. We never hear what happens then. In the book version Anderson says Maxwell came back a week later and resolved to abandon his plans for suicide.

Anderson checked into the information about the Waterloo Bridge Mystery. He writes, '[I]nquiries made through the Foreign Office and Scotland Yard brought confirmation of all the main points of the story'. He also mentions (vaguely) checking with the head of the Sûreté but does not mention which head (Monsieur Claude or Gustave Macé). He fails to clarify many points in the story. Who did the murdered police agent spy for: the Austrian interests, Sardinia-Piedmont, the Papal States, the Kingdom of the Two Sicilies? Which revolutionary groups were infiltrated: followers of Mazzini or Cavour or someone else?

At the time of the Waterloo Bridge Mystery there was public comment about foreign agents and spies. The *Illustrated London News* (12 October 1857) said: 'The idea which seems to have gained most acceptance is that the victim was a foreigner, and either a spy or an unfaithful accomplice of some of the refugees who hatched conspiracies here, and that the vengeance of his colleagues has fallen upon him,' In 1857 there was reason for the British to be somewhat less than happy about the policy welcoming foreigners. While some upper class exiles (Louis Phillippe, Guizot) were acceptable, others (Karl Marx, Louis Kossuth) were seen as troublemakers. Others (like the political spy and bully, later murderer, Emmanuel Bartholemy) were definitely undesirables. Therefore, the background was there to support the idea of an assassinated Italian police agent. This makes it a better solution to the mystery than the two other theories that have been presented. Elliot O'Donnell, in *Great Thames Mysteries* (1929) tracked down a possible lead in a *News of the World* story from 1859, but it went nowhere. Percy Fitzgerald, in *Chronicles of Bow Street Police Office* (1888), came up with the rather witless idea that the murder was fake and a practical joke. Anderson's solution seems neat and tidy in comparison to these.

Maybe there is a grain of truth to the Anderson solution of the Waterloo Bridge Mystery. Over the years I have found only one reference to it: George Dilnot quotes a heavily cut version of Anderson's written solution in his book *Great Detectives and Their Methods* (1928). He is the only crime historian of any stature to even mention Sir Robert's information.

Unfortunately the evidence from the inquest does not support Anderson's theory. Two competent physicians studied the actual remains. Granted that in some of the clothing found with the remains knife holes were found, nothing suggested a pack of assassins. In fact, death was due to a single knife thrust penetrating the heart. There was evidence of some of the joints being boiled (probably to make cutting up the body easier), but neither Dr. Paynter nor Dr Taylor suggested the remains showed an attempt to burn the body (there were no scorch marks, nor burned flesh).

When I first examined the Waterloo Bridge Mystery six years ago I tried to put the best view of the Anderson theory to the test. In 1871 or 1909 or even 1997 or 2003 who would Anderson have been hinting at as the head of the Italian Revolutionary group that killed the so-called police agent? My guess remains he was thinking of Felice Orsini and his band of assassins. Orsini and his friends were in the British Isles in 1857 and within a few months of the Waterloo Bridge Mystery would kill over eight people in a bomb attack on the coach of Emperor Napoleon III outside the Paris Opera House. The fact that the bombs were manufactured in

Birmingham and the conspirators had plotted the crime in England strained Anglo-French relations. Lord Palmerston, in a rare lapse of his good sense, prosecuted Orsini's associate (Dr Simon Bernard) to placate France. The acquittal of the doctor led to the fall of Palmerston's government. Certainly Orsini had much to hide in October 1857, and would have not wanted a police spy interfering with his plans.

Another point supporting identifying Orsini's group with the Italian conspirators in Anderson's story is that the juxtaposition of the Waterloo Bridge Mystery anecdote with the d'Orsay anecdote is very telling. Maxwell had been talking about how d'Orsay was killed taking a bullet intended for Emperor Napoleon III in 1852. The Waterloo Bridge Mystery is in 1857. The events Anderson recalls Maxwell talking about are from the early years of the reign of Napoleon III (1851–1871) and appear to deal with assassination plots against that monarch. It would be a subject of interest to Anderson as he spent much of his time watching for similar Fenian plots against the British monarchy (and in 1872, about the time Anderson and Maxwell met, an Irish youth named Arthur O'Connor – a nephew of the Chartist Fergus O'Connor – did confront Queen Victoria with a pistol).

But working against this is Anderson's track record with suspicions concerning minorities. If you recall he did say that the Whitechapel Murderer was a depraved Jew, who was protected by the local population. This is of a piece with rival Italian societies or agents assassinating each other in London – while they may be plotting against foreign regimes. There is a logic that makes us take what Sir Robert says seriously enough to evaluate it – that even makes us think it is possibly true. But there is the suspicion left over that Sir Robert may be a bigot.

Also working against Sir Robert is his confounded reticence about sources. Surely by 1909/10 he could have revealed the real name of Maxwell? Did he really believe that revealing the name of an agent that he last used thirty years before mattered? And why not print or quote from some document to verify his inquiries with the foreign office and the Sûreté or Scotland Yard?

To be fair Sir Robert may have retained his reticence to protect the system of informers and spies he had built up that Scotland Yard (and most police systems to this day) use to fight crime or revolutionaries. It was not a matter of the identity of Maxwell alone, but of all the 'Maxwells' who were part of the system. But there is, even here, another reason that may be less credible for keeping quiet or fuzzy about the story. We have to ask ourselves how Anderson, in 1870–1875, got in touch with Maxwell and his ilk. He would need to contact the officer at Scotland Yard who worked most closely with the French police at the time. In the early 1870s this was Chief Inspector Nathaniel Druscovitch. He was an extremely talented man who handled most of the Yard's continental cases. In 1872 he went to Paris to arrest Marguerite Dixblanc for the murder of her employer, Madame Riel, in Park Lane, London. Druscovitch had first rate contacts with the police on the continent, especially in France. Unfortunately, he took bribes, one in particular from the swindler Harry Benson. Druscovitch and two fellow inspectors were sent to prison in 1877 for this, leaving the Yard with a bad image.

I do not have proof that Druscovitch aided Anderson regarding Maxwell, but it is highly probable. It is even probable they knew each other even earlier. In 1867 Anderson was assisting in the campaign against James Stephens ('the Fenian Chief'), who resided in Paris. An Irish magistrate named De Gernon was sent to spy on Stephens. According to Leon O'Broin's book, *Fenian Fever: An Anglo-American Dilemma* (1971), De Gernon wanted an English detective to travel with him, and wrote, 'I can do nothing . . . without a detective such as Mr Drascovitch [sic].' The talented but corrupt detective would have been known to Anderson. Before the Benson scandal Druscovitch would have been used by Anderson to contact people like Maxwell. But Anderson would not brag of this in 1909 or 1910.

There remains the matter of Count d'Orsay's death. Did the famous dandy die from cancer or from an assassin's bullet? Well, it turns out that there is a degree of confusion regarding his death. It is usually noted that Napoleon III appointed d'Orsay his Director of Fine Arts, but it was a gesture to a man on his deathbed – far too late to be of any use. While in his last days most of d'Orsay's

107

biographers say he met his end with Christian resignation or he enjoyed the spirited piano playing of the nieces of his mistress, Lady Blessington.

In 1997 I wrote to Roger L. Williams, formerly Professor of History at the University of Wyoming and an expert on the Second Empire of France. I asked if he had ever heard of this rumour about d'Orsay's death being the result of an assassination. Professor Williams replied that there was no reference to such a rumour in the numerous literary memoirs of the period. More importantly, the setting for the incident is hard to believe. We are supposed to believe that the Count was shot while with the Emperor at the Elysée Palace in August 1852. The problem is that the friendship between d'Orsay and Louis Napoleon Bonaparte had been strained by the latter's coup d'état of December 1851. The Count had been critical of this act. As a result Napoleon III would have been cool towards his old friend, and they should not have been walking together at all. The deathbed appointment was a typical empty gesture of the Emperor.

Unlike the solution to the Waterloo Bridge Mystery, the story about d'Orsay's demise seems not as plausible. It did get some discussion when it was first expounded by Anderson. In *Notes and Queries*, 11 S.I, 4 June, 1910, p. 447, a Mr. Morgan M'Mahon (while discussing d'Orsay's journals) says, 'A curious statement recently made, on what appears to be good authority – Sir Robert Anderson in Blackwood – concerning d'Orsay's death in Paris in 1852, lends a fresh interest to the story of the man's life.' Even more pointed was a comment by the writer (and criminal historian) W. Teignmouth Shore in his *D'Orsay or the Complete Dandy* (1911), where (while describing the Count's death) he adds this footnote: 'An amazing version of d'Orsay's death has recently been made public, namely that in addition to the disease of the spine, the count suffered from a carbuncle, which "was a euphemism for a bullet aimed at the Emperor while they were walking together in the gardens of the Elysée".' Shore was the last biographer of the Count (that I have found) to mention Anderson's story, or to quote from his book.

So we are left with two more fragments of theories on criminal mysteries (in d'Orsay's case a dubious, suspect mystery) by Sir Robert, to put alongside his 'solution' to the Whitechapel Murders. Do I feel that Sir Robert was striking out totally, zero for three, in the mysteries? Not totally – he was writing of his actual experiences at Scotland Yard, and his reliance on informers. It worked well for him against Fenians and Irish revolutionaries. He grew used to it. With Maxwell he got some information that he felt made sense regarding Waterloo Bridge. In a way it does make sense, but one wishes there was more proof to support it. With d'Orsay he did less well, and I suspect (in the end) he put the story in because it might bring his book to the attention of more readers. The Count was still a colourful, well-known historical figure in the early twentieth century, and please note that the d'Orsay anecdote did cause more contemporary comment (*Notes and Queries* and Teignmouth Shore writing of it contemporaneously to the publication in *Blackwood's*) than the Waterloo Bridge anecdote did (Dilnot did not mention it until nearly twenty years later). In short, for the purpose of stoking public interest in the sale of his memoirs, Count d'Orsay served Sir Robert well.

And the Whitechapel material? Well Jack does have a large audience. But Anderson had been involved (once he returned from his vacation) in the investigation. Unlike Waterloo Bridge and d'Orsay, he was not writing of second-hand stories he had nothing to do with. So we have to give Sir Robert the credit he is due – whatever he writes about Jack he writes from his actual experience and we must respect that. So, do I feel he came to the right conclusion regarding Jack's identity?

Well . . . while I respect Sir Robert's labours, I feel he did far better with Irish revolutionaries than with Jewish East Enders, Italian conspirators, or French assassins.

Acknowledgments

Parts of this essay are reworked from an essay entitled *The Bag Nobody Claimed* that was published in *Medicine, Science and the Law*, Vol. 38, No. 4, (1998), pp. 335–340.

This essay appeared in *Ripperologist* magazine No. 46, May 2003.

4. PEOPLE

Le Grand of the Strand

Gerry Nixon

'GRAND, MR (OR LE GRAND) Private detective of 283 The Strand, employed with his colleague J. H. Batchelor by the Whitechapel Vigilance Committee and certain newspapers (including the *Evening News*) to make enquiries following the night of the double murder.'

Thus runs the slim biographical information available on Le Grand[1] in the *A-Z*, which then accurately proceeds to recount his role, together with Batchelor, of recovering a grape-stalk in Dutfield's Yard as well as interviewing Matthew Packer.

It has always been perceived that the police were less than impressed with the interference of the two private detectives into their investigations. They were even less amused when Le Grand and Batchelor whisked Packer off in a hansom for a personal interview with none other than Sir Charles Warren.

However, the police may also have had other reasons for doubting the integrity of Le Grand in his role as private detective. For this was a man with a shady past and sinister future. In 1877 he had been convicted for a series of thefts and sentenced to eight years penal servitude.[2] This earlier offence, as well as another conviction in 1889, was further added to in 1891 – three years after his work for the Vigilance Committee – following a remarkable affair which the *Newmarket Journal* called 'The Extraordinary Threatening Letters.' Although he was now charged under the name of Charles Grant, it is clear that Grant and Le Grand were one and the same person. On 17 October 1891 it reported that 'James Hall, a clerk employed at the Polytechnic, said he knew the prisoner by the name of Grand, and from 1888 to 1889, was in his services as clerk. The prisoner was then living at 3 York Place, Baker Street, and had formerly lived in Charlotte Street, Portman Square. Prisoner carried on the business of private enquiry agent, and had an office in the Strand.'

The charges against Le Grand in 1891 involved the sending of a series of letters demanding money under threat of death. All the recipients were ladies of some wealth. Three of his intended victims – Mrs Baldock, Baroness Bolsover and Lady Jessel – promptly took the letters to the police. Interestingly, all the letters were written in red ink. To Lady Jessel, Le Grand wrote: 'Take notice, if you do not pay me the sum of £500 within ten days I will dash your brains out by a means that may prove fatal to those surrounding you.' He also threatened that 'Hell itself will not protect you from my hand, far less the English detectives, who could not even find the man who murdered seven or eight women in the open streets of Whitechapel. If you look to protection from them, you might as well look to protection from your lapdog.'

He wrote almost identical lines to Mrs Baldock, adding that: 'Remember, Madam, that desperate men, or rather a man, brought to despair by the villainy of a woman, will do desperate things, and, indeed, a woman shall pay for it.'

The equally unfortunate Baroness Bolsover was threatened with dynamite 'or a thousand other ways by which I may send you into an unknown eternity.' Disarmingly, this letter concluded: 'I hope you will consider my request. It may be that one day I may be able to pay it back to you, only I must have it now. If you knew who I am I am sure you would pity me – to see I am come to act like this, which is highly criminal, and void of all human feeling. I knew you once. But enough.'

It confirmed that the prisoner in the dock at Westminster Police Court was a Dane 'who gave the name of Charles Grant and who is known by the alias of Le Grand.' A week later it informed its readership that his real name was Christian Bnscony, alias Nelson, Le Grand, Grant, 'French Colonel' and Captain Anderson, the last mentioned being the name most recently adopted . . .' It also announced that the prisoner 'is stated to be well connected, his father having held a very respectable position in the Danish diplomatic service.'

The various *Times* accounts of his criminal career, while eventually identifying him as one and the same man, called him Christian Nelson in 1877. By 1889 he was 'Charles Colnette Grandy or Grand.' In 1891 he was initially referred to as 'Charles Grande alias Le Grand.'

Piecing together the court proceedings of the various reports, it seems that Le Grand served only seven of the prescribed eight years for the felony charge and was released in 1884. Under the terms of his sentence he was then supposed to report under police supervision for seven years. But Sergeant Bartells of Scotland Yard told the court in 1891 that on 6 May 1884 the prisoner had merely 'reported himself on his liberation, and had never done so since.' His movements are then unknown until he reinvented himself as Private Detective Le Grand in 1888. In June 1889 he was convicted at the Central Criminal Court of sending letters to a doctor demanding money with threats, in company with a French woman named Amelia Porquoi alias Demay, who seems to have been living with Le Grand as his common-law wife.[3] He was sentenced to two years hard labour. (Curiously, *The Times* originally reported that he was given five years.)

Le Grand was obviously at liberty for only a brief time before sending the threatening letters in 1891. One of the strange features of these letters is that they were signed A. M. M. These were the initials of A. Malcolm Morris, the Harley Street surgeon from whom he had demanded money two years earlier! It was also made clear that Le Grand was never actually short of money when he sent the threatening letters. His landlady Nellie Fisher spoke of a three-day trip he made to Paris during this period. He was also in the habit of leaving large quantities of money ('£40 or £50') on his table.

That Le Grand was suffering from some mental disorder seems beyond doubt. It was reported that in 1887 he had written to the Chief Commissioner of Police, complaining of the conduct of a constable and had threatened to burn down public buildings. This letter was also written 'partly in violet and partly in red ink.'

It is surprising that this enigmatic figure has never before been suggested as a candidate for JTR. There have certainly been less likely suspects nominated. Le Grand appears to have spent much of his life in prison both before and after 1888. Yet during the latter part of that fateful year he was able to wander the streets of Whitechapel as a 'detective' under the auspices of the Mile End Vigilance Committee. It would be interesting to know whether he approached them to offer his services.

It is also clear that he considered women were responsible for his problems and should 'pay for it.' Set against this the fact that his known misdemeanours consisted of threats rather than actual violence. However, Le Grand was not averse to using force. When he was arrested in 1891 at Maldon in Surrey he had in his possession 'an eight-chambered revolver and a life preserver' (a type of cosh). He also endeavoured to push one of the arresting officers 'under a train as it entered the station.' Perhaps further research will throw more light on his criminal career.

The Times described Le Grand in 1891 as a 'tall, well-dressed man of military appearance.' His age in 1888, if was correctly given, would have been thirty-five. The fact that he habitually wrote in red ink certainly conjures up images of 1888 and that other famous letter in red ink. That one concluded 'Don't mind me giving the trade name.' This has always been taken as a reference to the signature 'Jack the Ripper.' Was this just a clever diversion? For there is another well-known line in that same letter which may of course be entirely coincidental: 'Grand work the last job was.'

People

Footnotes

1. Although known as both Grand and Le Grand, I have referred to him throughout by the latter as the more likely name during his detective days. Sergeant Stephen White reported in 1888 that one of the 'private detectives' carried a letter addressed to 'Le Grand & Co., Strand.'
2. The thefts included purses, pocket books and knives(!) – all stolen from shops. Le Grand appears to have been an inveterate shop-lifter and admitted two previous convictions.
3. It was a complicated case which involved a trumped-up claim by Porquoi for breach of promise against Dr Morris. Morris specialized in diseases of the skin. His involvement with Porquoi appears to have begun when he treated Le Grand in 1889 for an unspecified ailment.

Select sources

Newmarket Journal, 17 October 1891; 24 October 1891
Begg, Fido, Skinner, *The Jack the Ripper A-Z* (1996)
The Times: 12 July 1877; 8 June 1889; 27 June 1889; 29 September 1891; 7 October 1891; 13 October 1891

This essay appeared in *Ripperologist* magazine No. 42, August 2002.

Stephen Ryder Nabs 'Squibby'

Ripperologist Editors

F EW WHO HAVE READ the chapter about Jack the Ripper in Walter Dew's *I Caught Crippen* can have failed to be gripped by his account of the arrest of a short but powerful and unsavoury young thug and associate of street gangs nicknamed 'Squibby.'

On this occasion Squibby was wanted by the police because he had accidentally assaulted a young child during a fracas. Dew spotted him at the corner of Dorset Street, but Squibby saw Dew approaching and ran away. A chase ensued and a crowd gathered, somebody thinking the pursued man was Jack the Ripper shouted out and in a short time an ever-growing mob was in pursuit.

If true in its basic details, the story is interesting and important for several reasons. It shows how inflamed public feeling had become – and how quickly. The horrifyingly brutal assault on Emma Smith and the frenzied stabbing of Martha Tabram had hardly generated any press or public interest, yet here, the day after Annie Chapman's murder, we're told that the public's passions were so roused that the police simply giving chase to someone quickly produced a bloodthirsty lynch-mob numbering thousands!

On one point Dew was wrong. He says the crowd yelled out that the man was 'Jack the Ripper.' The correspondence signed 'Jack the Ripper' which bestowed the nickname on the murderer and gave it to posterity had yet to be written, so the crowd could not have yelled out the name. Unless, of course, the nickname existed locally prior to the correspondence and never made it into the newspapers for some reason, but had been picked up and used by the unknown correspondent of the letter and postcard. The probability is that Dew misremembered.

Squibby was also mentioned by Benjamin Leeson in his memoirs *Lost London* (1934). He referred to him rather affectionately when writing about a notorious character named Billy Meers. Squibby is mentioned in passing as a 'well-known character' who was known to use a knife. Interestingly, both Dew and Leeson wrote of Squibby in connection with Dorset Street. Here's Dew's account of Squibby and the exciting chase and terrifying experience:

> I was standing in Commercial Street with a fellow detective named Stacey, when my attention was attracted by a young man standing close to the entrance to Dorset Street. I recognized him at once as a young scoundrel nicknamed 'Squibby,' who had given the police a lot of trouble at one time and another, and was now 'wanted' for assault on a child.
>
> 'Squibby' was an associate of notorious young thieves, and although short of stature he was stockily built, and so powerful that we used to call him the Pocket Hercules.
>
> Whenever this 'charming' young fellow was arrested it took six or eight policemen to get him to the station, and by the time he was brought in he was usually devoid of every stitch of clothing, and the policemen pretty well hors de combat.
>
> This 'mighty atom' of the East End was covered from head to foot with tattoo designs.
>
> Some time previously 'Squibby' had engaged in one of his periodical battles with the police. It was as a result of this that the child was injured. The assault on the girl was not deliberate. 'Squibby' was amusing himself by throwing bricks at a policeman. One of the missiles was badly aimed and hit the child.
>
> Knowing he would be 'wanted' for that, the miniature giant went into hiding, and the morning following the Hanbury Street murder was the first occasion following the offence that he had come under the eyes of a police officer. I have a shrewd suspicion that it was not mere curiosity that caused 'Squibby' to mix among that throng of morbid sightseers. He was not the type of fellow to let an opportunity like that pass.

Unfortunately for me, 'Squibby's' eyes were as sharp as my own. Recognition was mutual. He knew I would be after him, and was determined to give me a hard chase. He made a sudden dash, dived between the legs of a horse, crossed the road, and ran as fast as his short legs could carry him along Commercial Street, in the direction of Aldgate.

Stacey and I gave chase, drawing our truncheons — plain-clothes men carried truncheons during the Ripper murders — as we went.

The sight of a man running away from the scene of a Ripper crime with the police officers in hot pursuit sent the crowd wild with excitement. They jumped to the conclusion that the man on the run was a murder suspect.

'Jack the Ripper! Jack the Ripper! Lynch him!' The cry was started by a few and taken up by hundreds.

Behind us as I ran I could hear the tramp of hundreds of feet.

As I was passing Fashion Street a great, burly brute did his best to trip me by thrusting his legs in front of mine. He possibly thought I was the man the crowd was chasing, but more probably knew me as a police officer. I dealt him a heavy blow with my truncheon and he fell back into a baker's window.

Meantime our quarry had reached Flower-and-Dean Street, and realizing that he was bound to be caught if he continued running, he entered the front door of a house, jumped over a low wall, and entered the adjoining house.

Stacey and I dashed in after him. He led us up the stairs and into a bedroom where we grabbed him just as he was making his way through a back window.

I was done in. So was Stacey. Now for a rough time, I thought. 'Squibby' had never been known to be arrested without the most violent resistance.

But this was a different 'Squibby'. Instead of finding, as we expected, an animal of a man, foaming at the mouth and ready to fight to the last breath, his face was of a ghastly hue and he trembled violently.

In a flash I saw the reason. It was not of Stacey or myself that the wanted man was afraid but of the howling mob outside. They were crying for his blood. Their cries reached us. 'Lynch him. Fetch him out. It's Jack the Ripper,' came from a thousand throats.

The crowd now stretched to Commercial Street. 'Squibby' saw

the danger, and so now did I. His life wouldn't have been worth twopence once that mob got their hands on him.

I told him we would do what we could, but I have often wondered what would have happened had not a number of uniformed police officers followed and, as I discovered afterwards, with great difficulty held the door of the house in which we were marooned.

Precautions had also been taken against a demonstration of mob law. Urgent messages had been sent to the surrounding police stations – Leman Street and Commercial Street – and soon reinforcements of uniformed police arrived on the scene.

The baffled crowd became more bloodthirsty than ever. The very precautions the police were taking confirmed them in their conviction that the man whose life they were demanding could be none other than the East End Terror.

The cries of 'Get him! Lynch him! Murder him!' became more insistent than ever, and I am sure little 'Squibby' was convinced that his last hour had come. No policeman who had previously had the unpleasant task of arresting him would have believed that such a change could come over a man. Abject terror showed in his eyes as again and again he appealed to me for protection.

I myself wouldn't have given much for 'Squibby's' life at that moment, and I was not at all happy as to what might happen to Stacey and myself if the mob reached us.

Presently, however, the yells of the crowd became more subdued, and I ventured down to the front door of the hovel into which our prisoner had led us. The sight I saw filled me with relief. Scores of lusty policemen were clearing a space in front of the house. Never in all my life have I more warmly welcomed the sight of the blue uniform.

Several officers came into the house, and it was only with their assistance that our scared prisoner could be induced to descend the stairs and face the street.

On emerging into Flower-and-Dean Street I realized that our dangers were far from over. At the sight of the little man being shepherded by a posse of police officers the mob seemed to go mad.

They made one mad, concerted rush which threatened for a time to break down the police barrier. Their cries became louder than ever, filthy epithets being intermixed with the demands for 'Squibby's' summary execution.

We gained Commercial Street, but beyond that, despite the strong force of police, we found it impossible to go.

One thoughtful young constable solved our immediate problem by getting a four-wheeled cab from Aldgate into which we bundled our prisoner and proceeded with the police forming a 'guard of honour'.

At last it seemed that our troubles were over. But, oh dear, no! Several ugly rushes were made at the cab, and more than once it came within an ace of being over-turned. A big, burly inspector named Babbington came to our rescue. He suggested that we should be much safer on foot than in our precarious vehicle, and with this I agreed. So out we scrambled, just along Spitalfields Market.

The whole of Commercial Street was now packed by a yelling, hooting mob of frenzied people. Some, I have no doubt, regarded the opportunity as a heaven-sent one to have a go at the police.

A lane was formed all the way to Commercial Street police station, and after what seemed to me an interminable time, and likewise I am sure to 'Squibby,' we fought our way into the grimy-looking building which for once looked really beautiful to me.

This station is, or was, an island. It was immediately surrounded by the mob, now more infuriated than ever because the man they believed to be the 'Ripper' had been delivered safely at the police station.

Even now they did not abandon hope of taking the law into their own hands. The police station was attacked again and again, and it was only the indomitable pluck of the men in blue which prevented an innocent man being crucified. There were many sore heads in Commercial Street that day.

I was told afterwards that from the very first police officers shouted to the crowd to say that the man who had been taken in custody had nothing whatever to do with the Ripper murders. They would have none of it. Their blood was up.

For a long time the shouting crowd surrounded the police station. A few seconds after a space had been cleared it was filled again.

Inspectors went to the upper windows of the police station and tried to explain who the prisoner was, and why he had been arrested. Several other ruses were adopted in order to induce the people to go to their homes. But nothing would convince them they had made a mistake, and it was not until many hours after

'Squibby' had been placed under lock and key that the streets in the vicinity of the police station reverted to their normal peacefulness.

The moment he was put in a cell 'Squibby' began to regain his composure. Much as he hated policemen he had confidence in their ability to protect him in their own police station. Eventually he was sentenced to three months' imprisonment and was quite happy about it.

'I shall be much safer in Pentonville for a bit,' he said with a smile.

After this experience 'Squibby' was a changed man. Whenever he met me he never failed to thank me for 'saving his life,' and as far as I know he never again gave trouble to police officers whose duty it was to arrest him.

I have seen many riotous crowds in my career, but none quite like the one I have described. Every man and woman in that mob was ready to tear a fellow-creature to pieces because some fool, seeing a man pursued by police officers, had shouted 'Jack the Ripper.'

Although this experience may have changed Squibby's attitude to the police, and made him less prone to fiercely resist arrest, he evidently continued his life of violence and crime, as Benjamin Leeson, when writing a book about a man he called Billy Meers, related:

I was passing one day through Dorset Street, Spitalfields, then one of London's worst crime streets – in fact, it was a toss-up whether it, or Ratcliffe Highway, could claim the honour of being the worst. Dorset Street was better known to local people as 'the do as you please' and it quite justified its title, as the dwellers therein certainly did do as they pleased, and it was seeking trouble to go there looking for anything or anybody, unless, of course, you were called there, and even then you could be fairly certain of getting a great deal more than you bargained for.

On this occasion I was nearing the end of the street, when I was startled to see a man nearly fall from a street door, then scramble up again, and dash across the narrow road, just as something flashed behind him and struck the shop shutters on the opposite side. Immediately following this, a man whom I recognised as Billy Meers emerged from the house.

'Blimey, governor,' he said, when he saw me, 'I'm glad it didn't hit yer. It was meant for that "Squibby." He's just been in here, threatening me with a "chiv" (knife), but when he saw me pick up a bigger one, he scooted; I just missed him.'

'Squibby' was another well-known character in those parts, and had been charged more than once for using the knife, and had been at death's door himself as the result of being stabbed.

We crossed the road, and I found a butcher's knife with a foot-long blade sticking perfectly straight in the shutter, the point having passed right through and broken the window on the other side. It had missed 'Squibby' by a few feet, and me by as many inches, but as it was not meant for me, and as the man for whom it was intended was not likely to make any complaint, there the matter ended.

Efforts have been made in the past to identify Squibby and the A–Z suggested that he was either William Squibb, charged at the Thames Police Court in February 1888 with stealing a watch or Charles Squibb, arrested later in 1888 with attempted theft and threatening a policeman. But he was neither. Stephen Ryder, owner of the premier Ripper site on the internet, *Casebook: Jack the Ripper*, has identified Squibby as a man named George Cullen and turned up a contemporary newspaper report mentioning the event written about by Dew:

George Cullen, alias Squibby, 25, was charged, before Mr Bushby, with assaulting Betsy Goldstein. Constable Bates, 166 H, said on the 1st inst. the prisoner accosted him in Commercial Street, and threatened that the next time he was interfered with he would 'do for him.' Cullen was a notorious street gambler, and had been chased the previous Sunday. After his threat he took up a stone and flung it at the officer. It struck the young girl he was now charged with assaulting. On Saturday morning Cullen was seen in Commercial Street and chased by Detective Dew, H division. He dodged under market carts and horses' legs and presently other constables took up the chase, Cullen giving them a smart run though Spitalfields where the cry was raised that it was 'the murderer,' and some thousands of persons gathered in a state of the greatest excitement. Previous convictions for assault on the police having been proved. Mr Bushby sentenced the prisoner to three months' hard labour.

This essay appeared in *Ripperologist* magazine No. 57, January 2005.

Clara Collett and Her Investigations in the East End

Deborah McDonald

IT WAS IN THE AUTUMN OF 1888, just as the news of the Whitechapel murders began to make the headlines, that Clara Collet moved to the East End of London to begin her investigation of women's work for Charles Booth.

The first volume of Booth's investigation into the extent of poverty in the East End of London was almost complete, but he needed someone to collect the statistics and write up the chapter on 'Women's Work.' He had assumed that the important research and writing would be completed by his wife's cousin, Beatrice Potter (later to become Beatrice Webb), who had already completed 'The Tailoring Trade', 'The Docks' and 'The Jewish Community' chapters. Indeed, she was herself considering doing so, though not without worry. She wrote in her diary: 'In dreadful perplexity about my work . . . It would indefinitely postpone "Co-operation" [the next work she had planned to do], on the other, "Female Labour" is a subject of growing importance, one which for practical purposes is more important than "Co-operation" . . . Then the work is needed to complete Charlie's book and I owe him consideration. I have already a mass of material in my head, which could be used for it.'

A few days later Potter's thoughts were elsewhere as the announcement of the forthcoming marriage of Joseph Chamberlain was made. Potter had once harboured ideas of marriage with him and this news unsettled her and caused a period of nervous collapse, thus putting an end to any thoughts Booth may have had of persuading her to complete his work.

Booth had to look elsewhere for a suitable contender to take on this important chapter for his almost completed first series. He needed someone reliable, educated and level-headed who could finish the work by the spring deadline. He chose Clara Collet.

Collet had been born in 1860 in north London. Her family were middle class but far from wealthy, unlike Potter's. Her father, Dobson Collet, was the editor of a small, serious, political journal entitled the *Diplomatic Review* and was a man of radical ideas which were reflected in his journal. Despite being non-revolutionary himself, one of his regular contributors was Karl Marx. As a result of this association, Marx's youngest daughter Eleanor, became a good friend of Collet's, the two of them sharing a common interest in the works of Shakespeare. An informal club was set up for the purpose of having evenings reading the plays together. It was given the light-hearted name of the 'Dogberry Club' and the Marx and Collet families were founder members.

It met once a month and a good time was had by all. Marx and his friend Engels regularly attended the sessions, although Marx refrained from joining in the reading; apparently his German accent was too strong.

The sessions were concluded with games of charades which Marx thoroughly enjoyed and he was often to be seen laughing until the tears ran down his face.

Dobson Collet knew that he would not be able to support his children and therefore sought to secure their future by providing them all, including the girls, with a good education. Clara was lucky enough to be sent to the newly established North London Collegiate School, which gave her a better education than most of her contemporaries, including the much richer Potter who had been forced to rely on governesses for her scant education.

In 1878, Collet began the expected career for an educated middle class woman: she became a schoolmistress. There was little alternative. Collet enjoyed her eight years at the Wyggeston Girls' School in Leicester but she did not feel fulfilled in this profession and her outspoken ideas on life sometimes caused her difficulties.

But she used her time well and completed a BA degree course run by University College, London, one of the few universities to offer degrees to women at this time.

Marriage would have been one way to escape the career into which, as a result of lack of alternatives, she had been forced. Collet had a relationship with a man while working in Leicester, but she refused his offer of marriage. She did not love him and was determined she would not marry merely for the sake of convenience. Instead of accepting this secure route, Collet left teaching and returned to London. She studied for an MA in Political Economy, the first attempted by a woman. She passed easily.

She also joined many societies, including the Royal Statistical Society, the Royal Economic Society, the Charity Organisation Society and the British Association for the Advancement of Science. It was probably at one of these societies that Collet met Booth, for he was a member of all these himself.

Collet was not a 'shrinking violet' who sat quietly while her male colleagues spoke, but participated equally in the debates and wrote fervently for the various journals spawned by the societies. Booth cannot have failed to notice her.

Although Collet kept a diary for much of her early life, it does not document the period she spent working for Booth. Luckily we do have other sources of evidence discussing this period. Booth himself discussed Collet's work in the East End in some detail when he was invited to give evidence for the Royal Commission on Labour. He confirmed that Collet collected her statistical figures during the autumn and winter of 1888–9 and for this purpose took up residency in the area for three months. Unfortunately we do not know where.

The East End with its rubbish-strewn, rat-infested streets, inhabited by poor men and women, sometimes living ten or more to a room, often trying to earn enough during the day to find a bed in a common lodging house for the night, must have been a difficult enough area to live in for those used to nothing else. For Collet it must have seemed like hell.

Potter's own short sojourn into the East End as part of her 'Tailoring Trade' investigation lasted three days, although she had planned to work alongside female 'sweaters' for some weeks in order to be able to understand their work more fully.

Unlike her, Collet did not rush back to the safety and sanity away from the East End. She remained for the full three months – despite the fervour in the area created by the dreadful deeds of the Whitechapel murderer!

Collet interviewed the working girls by first befriending them at their workplace, then inviting them back for tea at her temporary accommodation. She found it difficult to gain the girls' trust, but for the most part she succeeded and they began to candidly discuss their wages, conditions and lifestyles. Collet was thus able to build up a picture of the working women in the East End.

Collet obtained her introduction to the home workers, who made up a large section of the working population, via the local clergy.

Prostitutes were also included in her survey and she may have inadvertently been introduced to the victims of the Whitechapel murderer, or at least many women who were living with the fear that they might be the next victims.

In Collet's opinion women became prostitutes as a result of financial pressures either to fund their bed for the night or pay for food. She also believed that in many cases they were not always from the very poorest class, but were women who wanted to have extra little luxuries in life.

Most Victorians believed that prostitution, alcoholism and the general degeneracy in the East End was a result of the laziness and lack of morality of its inhabitants. They also believed the poor would rather turn to criminal behaviour than do a decent day's work. They thought the poor were beyond help and inherently different from themselves. Collet, conversely, blamed poor wages and lack of availability of regular work as being the causes of such evils.

While Collet may have had an enlightened view of prostitutes, she was certainly wrong if she believed that no prostitutes came from the lowest of the social stratum, as can be evidenced by those victims of Jack the Ripper. These unfortunate women turned to prostitution as their only means of survival. They had all suffered terrible social deprivation earlier in life, bought on by the failure of their relationships and the necessity to find work in order to eat and pay for a bed for the night. They had turned to alcohol as a means of comfort, but by becoming addicted had made it even more difficult to find regular employment. They were surviving by the only means left to them.

Collet was right in her assessment that insufficient wages drove many women to the streets. The better off women she saw were the younger women trying to make an honest living and failing due to the irregularity and lack of employment. They were women on the edge of the slide down into the abyss.

The women the Ripper attacked were out on the street late at night when the more attractive and less desperate younger women had already made enough money for their bed and had returned to their lodgings, relieved that they had survived once again.

Collet completed her chapter on 'Women's Work' on schedule and returned to her home in central London.

Booth's investigation has become one of the most useful tools available to give us a glimpse into Jack the Ripper's world.

Further information

See the Clara Collet website on *www.claracollet.co.uk*

See Marion Comyn (née Skinner), *My Recollections of Karl Marx, The Nineteenth Century and After Vol. 91* (January 1922) pp. 161–169.

For the full report on Collet by Booth see *British Parliamentary Papers – Industrial Relations, Vol. 27, Labour Commission* (Session 1892: Shannon, Ireland: Irish University Press, 1970) p. 489.

See Charles Booth et al, *Women's Work, Life and Labour of the People of London* (London: 1889), Chapter 9, for the full account of Collet's researches and also see the archive library at the London School of Economics for some of her notes for this work.

This essay appeared in *Ripperologist* magazine No. 38, December 2001.

The Search for Jack el Destripador

Eduardo Zinna

O N 27 JULY 1876 the *Standard*, an English-language newspaper founded in Buenos Aires in 1861 by Eduardo T. Mulhall, published a letter to the Editors, which read as follows:

Horrible Murder
Buenos Aires, July 26th
To the Editors of the Standard,

Gentlemen,
   Last night (Tuesday), a horrible murder was committed in Calle Corrientes, a poor girl having her throat cut in her sleep by a man who was occupying the same room. The object of the murder was no doubt plunder, but the other inmates of the house being disturbed, he made off, leaving the greater part of his clothes behind him. On the Comisario being called in, and the clothes examined, it was discovered by a photograph in one of the pockets that the assassin was the same party who had lately complained of being robbed of several gold ounces and a watch and chain whilst staying at the Hotel . . . Having ascertained that his new address was the Hotel . . ., the police immediately proceeded thither, and learned that the man they were in search of had arrived at the Hotel in a state of semi-nudity, told a story of having been robbed and stripped in the street, drank a glass of hot grog, re-dressed himself and disappeared.
   N.

The Search for Jack el Destripador

Argentina's Biblioteca Nacional is housed in a massive, cube-like concrete building perched on the edge of an old riverbank that slopes down gently towards land long reclaimed from the waters. For many years a lovely villa surrounded by a spacious park and a high iron fence stood on that site. Until 1955 it was used as the residence of the Argentine Presidents. Its most famous occupant being Evita Perôn, who died there of cancer in 1952 at the age of thirty-three. In the weeks before her death, thousands of people gathered at the fence to pray for her. At dusk they lit candles. I went to see them one evening: hundred upon hundred of flickering yellow flames encircling the Residencia like a star-belt in the darkness.

Last September I was back in Buenos Aires. At the Biblioteca's old-newspaper department I requested the issues of the Standard for 1876. They brought me the actual newspapers, bound in green leather. As I ran my fingers down the yellowing, brittle pages, I could feel the grain of the paper and the slight raising of the print. It was a direct contact with the past that you don't get when using a microfilm reader!

I read the letter on the Calle Corrientes murder. The Standard had discreetly withheld the name of the murdered girl, that of her suspected killer and the hotels where he had lodged, but thanks to Carl Muusmann, the author of *Who was Jack the Ripper?*, and his translators and editors, Rikki Skipper-Pedersen and Adam Wood, I knew that what I had found was the first report on the murder of Caroline Metz by a suspect called Alois Szemeredy.

I could even supply the missing details: complaining of having been robbed, Szemeredy had moved on 22 July from the Hotel de Provence, located in Calle Cangallo 33, to the Hotel de Roma, in Calle Cangallo 323, a few hundred yards eastwards. In memoirs published in 1881, José Antonio Wilde described the Hotel de Roma as one of the best establishments of its kind in Buenos Aires.[1] As for the Hotel de Provence, an advertisement published regularly in the Standard listed its amenities:

People

HOTELPROVENCE
(Established 1850)
Cangallo, No. 33

Fine Suites of Rooms for Families

Clean Linen; attendance and cuisine of first order

Visitors of short stay in town, Board & Lodging at $50 per day

Families and regular visitors at conventional terms

Orders for Breakfast, Dinners, Suppers, Lunch, Pic-Nics,
Dispatched 'al primer cartelo'

NIGHT PORTER

Charges Moderate

Hotel de Provence
Joseph Perez & Co.,
Proprietor

I continued searching the *Standard* for more news on the Metz murder case. The next day, Thursday 28 July, the following item appeared under Editor's Table:

> The barbarous murder committed in this city on Tuesday night, the particulars of which we published yesterday, has shocked the public mind. The assassin is known, and is being pursued by the police; it is generally thought he will be caught, and let us hope that whilst the particulars of this shocking crime are fresh to the public mind he will be tried. Public opinion is fast centering up on the outrageous impunity for crime which exists in the Plate.[2] For minor offences, punishment is generally certain, whilst for the highest crime which the law has to deal with, the law is impotent. Scarcely a day passes by that there is not some record of murder, either in

town or camp,[3] published in the newspapers. The arrest of the assassin would appear to be almost the vindication of the law, for with regard to the trial we never see a line published in the newspaper; there is not one with a speciality for publishing the trials in the Criminal Court. The murder on Tuesday night was one of the most barbarous in the annals of crime, and perpetrated by a villain who, if we are to believe report, pretended respectability.

The murder was further covered on Friday:

Yesterday we saw a photograph of the unfortunate woman murdered on Tuesday night in Calle Corrientes. Judging from the photograph, she was a young and very handsome woman; her real name is not known, but she went by the name of Metz, probably her native city. The assassin, it was said yesterday evening, is caught, and is a Hungarian. The Chief of Police has been most unceasing in his efforts both night and day to capture the murderer. The Porteòo says that Mr Commissary Wright was very active in his measures from the moment the murder was known.

By Sunday the hard news was scarce and the *Standard* was reduced to discrediting gossip: the rumoured capture of the Calle Corrientes assassin, it said, was incorrect, as evening newspapers had contradicted it. Other news was that Argentine Army troops captured by Indian chieftain Namuncur the previous May south of Buenos Aires were in good health. On 1 August, the international news was that Garnet Wolseley was gathering 27,000 troops in Britain for an undisclosed purpose.[4] Another newspaper, the *Tribuna*, was cited to the effect that two men had been arrested in connection with the Metz murder. But this would turn out to be a false alarm.

Yet another false alarm found its way into the *Standard's* pages on 2 August: the still unnamed Hungarian who had allegedly murdered Caroline Metz had been seen entering a house in Calle Temple on Saturday but eluded capture by making his exit over the wall. On 3 August, Rosario newspapers reported that the Hungarian had committed three previous crimes: one in Milan, one in France and one in Rio de Janeiro. He had later travelled in Argentina, where he had been in prison in Mendoza and San Luis.

People

And then the Metz murder case disappeared completely from the news. As I scanned copies of the *Standard* for the following months, other events caught my eye, but nothing on Szemeredy and his crime.

On 8 August an incident had taken place at the junction of Calles Maipú and Paraguay in central Buenos Aires. Policemen had ordered two soldiers to move so as to allow cattle to be driven up the street. The soldiers refused to budge and in the ensuing mélèe one soldier and one policeman were wounded. In Azul, 150 miles south-west of Buenos Aires, 500 soldiers under Colonel Donovan faced rebellious Indian chieftain Catriel at the head of 4,000 warriors. During the month of August the tramways carried 64,000 passengers in the city of Buenos Aires and 45,000 in the suburban line. The substitution of silk underclothing for cotton attracted comment from the *Standard* on 1 November: 'What next?' asked the newspaper rhetorically, 'or has Folly come to the end of her tether?' On 29 November the news was published of a horrid crime 'which will probably be forgotten in a few days like the murder of Caroline Metz.' And that was it.

Because of a malfunction in the Biblioteca's equipment – a problem that plagues libraries and other public-funded institutions throughout the world – I could not consult other newspapers. I could not look for further information on the elusive Hungarian's flight to Montevideo, his extradition, his trial and his acquittal of the charge of murder – with all of which I was familiar from Muusman's book. Thus ended, for the time being, my search.

However, from my visit to the Biblioteca I had obtained, independent corroboration of the beginnings of Szemeredy's criminal career.

A few months earlier I had found evidence about the end of his career, the last of his crimes and the end of his life.

On a grey July morning in Vienna I climbed the steps of the Österreichische National Bibliothek, the Austrian National Library, which is located in a magnificent palace that was once part of the Hofburg, the home of the Austro-Hungarian Emperors for over six centuries.

The National Bibliothek is famous for its collections of maps, autographs, incunabula, Egyptian papyri and musical instruments. In a vast room in the basement I explained in a combination of English and halting German what I wanted to see. Finally I sat before a microfilm reader, a crank on the side of which allowed me to scroll through page after page of the newspapers *Weiner Tageblatt* and *Neue Freie Presse*. If any mention of Szemeredy existed in that labyrinth of Gothic-scripted German text, I was determined to find it.

In the *Tageblatt's* issue for 1 October 1892 I came across an item entitled 'Der Selbstmôrder von Pressburg' (The Pressburg Suicide). I had found Szemeredy!

Further analysis of contemporary newspapers produced a number of articles on him, which are still awaiting decipherment and study, but a particular tantalizing item found tucked amid advertisements for restaurants and concerts, publicized a Szemeredy exhibition consisting of photographs and documents. One wonders where those photographs and documents are filed now!

I had entertained serious doubts about Szemeredy, not merely about his viability as a Ripper suspect but also about whether he really existed at all. I had a pet theory that Szemeredy was identical with Alonso Maduro, another suspect hailing from Buenos Aires. Adam Wood had reviewed this theory in an article From Brick Lane to Buenos Aires (*Ripperologist*, No. 25) and concluded that the two were different. The news in the *Tageblatt* dispelled any doubts I'd had and proved Adam correct. As soon as I returned home to Geneva, I e-mailed Adam Wood:

'I have some good news which I thought I should share with you. Have you ever suspected that Alois Szemeredy was fictional, that he had been made up by Muusman?'

Adam's sent a reply of remarkable brevity:

'No.'

However, Adam had thought that if either of them was fictional then it was likely to be Maduro. However, in Buenos Aires I was to learn more about Maduro.

Juan-Jacobo Bajarlìa

The grand old man of Argentina's Ripperologìa is without doubt
Juan-Jacobo Bajarlìa, writer, lawyer, criminologist and political
activist. I was taken to meet him by a younger but equally
dedicated Ripperólogo, Juan José Delaney.

We met in his book-lined studio and over vino tinto, home-made
bollitos and Turkish coffee, courtesy of Señora Enriqueta, Bajarlìa
told us about his search for el Destripador.

His interest in the Ripper first awoke during a trip to London in
1963[5] and there he heard about Alonso Maduro.

Supposedly an Argentine financier, in 1888 Maduro had come
to London and befriended Griffith Salway of a City brokerage firm
in Old Broad Street. Salway later came across Maduro in
Whitechapel on the night Emma Smith was murdered and later he
overheard Maduro saying that all prostitutes should be killed. After
the murder of Mary Kelly, Salway had the opportunity to investigate Maduro's trunk and in a secret compartment he found a dark
overcoat, a soft hat and a set of surgical knives. A sticker in the
trunk read 'Paseo de Julio [followed by an illegible number]
Buenos Aires.'

Back home, Bajarlìa looked for confirmation of the story and
after much searching he came across people who had known a
similarly sounding Alfonso Maroni.

Maroni was an enigmatic man who In the early years of the
twentieth century frequented the Bolsa, the Stock Exchange, lived
somewhere in the neighbourhood, and was noted for dressing in a
long dark overcoat and soft felt hat. Maroni died on a rainy
morning in October 1929 at the age of seventy-five years in a hotel
in the Paseo de Julio (named on the sticker in 'Maduro's' trunk),
across from Plaza Mazzini.

Juan José Delaney

My companion that day, Juan José Delaney, is a writer whose
literary output – short story collections, including *Tréboles del
Sur* (*Southern Shamrocks*) and a recent novel, Moira Sullivan
– has almost exclusively concerned the Irish Diaspora in
Argentina.

In the January 1999 issue of the Argentine periodical, *Todo es Historia* he sketched out the first fruits of his Ripper research. The article covered Szemeredy and Maduro, but concentrated on the third and perhaps best-known South American suspect, Dr Stanley. As Ripper scholars round the world know, Dr Stanley is the suspect first revealed by Leonard Matters on 26 December 1926 in the People newspaper and developed by him into a book-length narrative, *The Mystery of Jack the Ripper*.

According to Matters, he had learnt of the Ripper's identity from a Spanish-language article published in a journal in Buenos Aires.[6] The story told how a surgeon named José Riche had written to the author of the article, also a surgeon, summoning him to a major hospital. When the article's author arrived, Riche took him to a patient occupying Bed 58, Ward V, at whose request he had acted. The surgeon recognized the patient as his former professor in London and the man to whom Matters gave name 'Dr Stanley,' but made it clear that this was not his real name. Dr Stanley told his former disciple how he had trodden the streets of the East End in pursuit of Mary Jeannette Kelly, the prostitute who had infected his gifted son with syphilis, thus ending his career and his life and plunging his father into the deepest despair. As soon as he had confessed to the Ripper crimes, the patient fell back on his bed and died. He was buried in the Western Cemetery.

Although Matters did not specify them, the hospital where Dr Stanley died and the cemetery where he was buried are easily identified. The hospital could only be the the Hospital Inglés – later the Británico – the British Hospital, and the Western Cemetery or Cementerio del Oeste is more commonly known as the Chacarita.

Stories and unconfirmed rumours about Dr Stanley abound. Many – maybe most – think that he was merely Matters's invention. Yet Juan José Delaney has obtained independent proof of his existence. In 1989, an aged Irish priest living in Argentina, Father Alfred MacConastair, who died in 1997, told Juan José a story. A former chaplain of the Británico in the 1920s had confided in Father MacConastair that he had been called to the deathbed of a man of 'another faith' – that is to say, not a Catholic – who wanted to clear his conscience. What burdened this man was his responsibility for the Ripper's crimes.

The Hospital Inglés was founded in 1844 to tend to the needs of 8,000 British residents, who constituted the largest foreign community in Buenos Aires (the total population of which was only 65,000) and the numerous British seamen and voyagers. Juan José saw Dr Goodman Mercer, Medical Director of the Británico, and Ms Diana Logan, its external relations head. The possibility of checking staff files at the Británico in search of José Riche and the medical history of all men named Stanley who died in the hospital during the first decades of the nineteenth century was raised, but Dr Goodman Mercer felt that this task would require an enormous effort and he mentioned that Juan José was not the first person to think of it. Some time ago, he said, a British Ripperologist society had written on the same subject.[7]

On another occasion Dr Goodman Mercer underlined that nobody named José Riche had ever worked for the Británico and that no Ward V or Bed 58 had ever existed at the Hospital.

Juan José's next destination was the Western Cemetery, the Chacarita. A section of it is occupied by the British cemetery, which dates back to the mid-nineteenth century, when British nationals came to Argentina in large numbers to work in banking, shipping, insurance companies, the railways, the meat-packing plants, or another of the many economic areas in which Britain had extensive interests at that time. Juan José told me of his many walks among the rows of tombs. Yet Dr Stanley's grave still eludes him.

Not satisfied with these results, Juan José made a stop at the Centro de Estudios Migratorios Latinoamericanos (CEMLA), Centre for Latin American Migration Studies. He learned there that fifty-six people whose surname was Stanley – twenty-four of them women – entered Argentina between 1888 and 1926. CEMLA's files are, unfortunately, incomplete. In some cases they list surnames but not first names and may or may not indicate sex, religion, occupation or nationality. They seem invariably to record the ships in which the voyagers came and the ports of origin, which included Southampton, Liverpool, Durban and Rio de Janeiro.

Sally's Bar

A further link to Buenos Aires is a dive called Sally's Bar. Like many others, Juan José first learnt about Sally's Bar from author Daniel Farson who in his book Jack the Ripper, recalled receiving a letter for a Mr Barca of Streatham in which he wrote about a dive in Buenos Aires that between 1910 and 1920 was allegedly owned by the Ripper.

No confirmation was ever found from another source, except for Professor Enrique Mayochi who assured Juan José that a bar by that name had indeed existed in the financial district during the first years of the century.

For many years, Buenos Aires was one of the great port cities of the world – to the extent that those of us who were born there are known as Porteños – people from the port. A number of disreputable bars and joints catering mostly for foreign seamen could still be found in the late 1950s in Calle 25 de Mayo, not far from both the financial district and the docks.

I can well recall walking with my friends down the street, lit by the harsh pink and blue glare of neon signs and snatches of piano music and the sound of English words wafting from the interior of the bars there. Inside, fair-haired sailors talked to dark-skinned hostesses whose lips always seemed too red. The air was heavy with the smells of strong perfume, cigarette smoke and spilled liquor.

Our favourite was the Texas and on occasion we summoned up our courage and walked in. Hopelessly under-age and utterly devoid of proper ID, we managed once or twice to down a beer quickly before being expelled, firmly but not unkindly by the staff. By the time we were old enough to enter the Texas legitimately we had other interests and I never crossed its threshold. Within a few years I went to sea myself – but that's another story.

Soon the world-wide decline of shipping affected the Buenos

Aires docks. Few merchant ships stop there now and the bars in Calle 25 de Mayo are long gone.

Professor Mayochi established yet another connection between Buenos Aires and the Ripper, though frankly it is a tenuous one.

Many Ripper roads lead to Buenos Aires. No clear evidence has yet been found to confirm or confound the candidacy of Szemeredy or Maduro, Stanley or Maroni to be identified as the Ripper, but the search goes on. There are old newspapers to read and old documents to study, and there is the ever-present hope that some time, somewhere a clue may be unearthed which may bring the mystery a step closer to its solution.

Juan-Jacobo Bajarlìa has been searching – so far in vain – for any records of Szemeredy's trial in a collection of *Procesos Célebres* (*Famous Trials*) published by Argentina's Supreme Court in the nineteenth century. Juan José Delaney is writing his second novel: *Sally's Bar*. We keep trying.

Footnotes

1. Wilde, José Antonio, *Buenos Aires Desde 70 Años Atrás*.
2. The Plate is the generic name for the region adjoining the River Plate. It generally includes Buenos Aires and its environs as well as Montevideo, the capital of Uruguay, on the other shore of the river.
3. 'Camp' is an Anglo-Argentine word, derived from the Spanish word *campo*, which means 'countryside.'
4. Sir Garnet Wolseley (1833–1913) was a celebrated Victorian general who fought the Russians, the Sepoys, the Chinese, the Ashanti, the Basutos and the Zulus, conquered Egypt, gave rise to the expression 'All Sir Garnet', was a tad too late to rescue Gordon from Khartoum and was the very model of a modern major-general in *The Pirates of Penzance*. In 1876, however, he was chief administrator of Natal, and, as far as I have been able to ascertain, he could not have been engaged in raising troops in Britain. Yet another minor mystery.
5. As for me, I read my first book on the Ripper in 1966. It was the Mayflower-Dell paperback edition of Robin Odell's *Jack the Ripper in Fact and Fiction*.
6. Matters apparently was not only fluent in Spanish but an accomplished translator as well. The list of his publications includes *The House of the Ravens* (London: Williams & Norgate, 1924) and his translation of *La Casa de los Cuervos* by Argentine author Hugo Wast (Gustavo Martìnez Zuvirìa).
7. The 'Ripperologist society' was the Cloak and Dagger Club and I was the author of the letter. In April 1998, I wrote to Ms Logan asking for any information available on Dr Stanley, Leonard Matters or the Ripper. I have not yet received a reply.

Select sources

Bajarlìa, Juan-Jacobo, 'Jack el Destripador, Argentino?' *Ellery Queen's Mystery Magazine*, No. 3, February 1976

'El Destripador Era Argentino,' *La Revista-Libro Argentina*, No. 13, October 1979, 'Una Conjetura: Acaso el maniático nació en estas pampas?' *Clarìn*, 3 April 1988

'Jekyll y el Destripador,' *Historias de Monstruos*, 1989

'El Destripador Era Argentino,' *Noticias*, 27 March 1999

Cianciabella, Teresa, 'El Hospital Británico,' *Todo es Historia* No. 378, January 1999

Delaney, Juan José, 'Jack el Destripador: de Londres a Buenos Aires,' *Todo es Historia* No. 378, January 1999

Farson, Daniel, *Jack the Ripper*

Farwell, Byron, *Eminent Victorian Soldiers*

McCormick, Donald, *The Identity of Jack the Ripper*

Matters, Leonard, *The Mystery of Jack the Ripper*

Mayochi, Enrique Mario, *Belgrano: 1855 – Del Pueblo al Barrio – 1993*

Muusmann, Carl, *Who was Jack the Ripper?*

Wilde, José Antonio, *Buenos Aires Desde 70 Años Atrás*

Wood, Adam, 'From Buenos Aires to Brick Lane,' *Ripperologist* No. 25, October 1998

This essay appeared in *Ripperologist* magazine No. 33, February 2001.

5. AUTHORS AND COMMENTATORS

Dickens and the Ripper Legend

Madeleine Murphy

THE HEART OF DICKENSIAN LONDON lies in the eastern half of the city. Most of Dickens' fiction takes place in the area circumscribed by St Giles in the west, Camden to the north, Stepney to the east and the Old Kent Road to the south. It should come as no surprise, then, to find that the East End occupies an important place in his imagination. From Dickensian fiction we derive many of today's clichés about nineteenth-century East End life: the oyster stalls and quaint Cockney antics to be sure, but also the neglected workhouse orphan, the dark streets, the squalor, descriptions of which still shock us a hundred years later. For Dickens' response to the East End did not remain static. The rosy, comic Whitechapel appears in his early writings; his later writings give us a jungle of decaying slums housing a starved, feral people. And although he died in 1870, when the Ripper was most likely a little boy, Dickens is in some measure responsible for the Ripper legend. Again and again, in his fiction, he tried to expose the conditions in which people lived. Again and again he warns us: Beware, from this dark jungle, some unknown beast will spring.

Such forebodings are hard to see in the light-hearted comedy of Pickwick Papers, written when Dickens was only twenty-four. Mr Pickwick's adventures in Ipswich begin at the Bull on Whitechapel Road, then a comfortable coaching inn that Dickens knew well. The mood of the neighborhood is cheerful: proceeding towards the turnpike at Mile End, their coach excites 'the admiration of the whole population of that pretty densely populated quarter.' Its poverty prompts nothing darker than Sam Weller's quaint, if unprophetic observation that 'poverty and oysters always seem to go together.' Another East End episode in Pickwick relates the meeting of the Brick Lane Branch of the United Grand Junction Ebenezer Temperance Association. Dickens had no use for the temperance movement and could be pretty scathing about it. Here, however, he is genial. The ladies of the Association gather in an upstairs warehouse in Brick Lane, to guzzle tea and congratulate themselves on converts like

Betsy Martin, widow, one child and one eye. Goes out charing and washing, by the day; never had more than one eye, but knows her mother drank bottled stout, and shouldn't wonder if that caused it (immense cheering). Thinks it not impossible that if she had always abstained from spirits, she might have had two eyes by this time (tremendous applause).

It's odd to reflect that the warehouse was only a stone's throw from the corner of Thrawl Street, where Mary Ann Nichols – a real-life 'Betsy Martin' – would drink away her doss money, with well-known consequences. But this amiable satire is worlds away from the harsh realities of poverty, homelessness and alcoholism.

The East End also had a kind of Ellis Island romance for the younger Dickens. London was the heart of England and the Empire, a 'world city' to which the adventurous and ambitious flocked to make their fortunes. And for many such, their first glimpse of this world city would be the streets of Whitechapel. Thus its coaching inns and hostels are places of excitement, where dazed newcomers alight from coaches into the rush of the city streets. In *Barnaby Rudge*, Joe Willett runs away 'big with great thoughts of going away for a soldier . . . [and] full of such youthful visions . . . pushed on until the noise of London sounded in his ears, and the Black Lion hove into sight.' Whitechapel also offers David Copperfield his first experience of London, a city already alive in his imagination:

> What an amazing place London was to me when I saw it in the distance, and how I believed all the adventures of all my favourite heroes to be constantly enacting and re-enacting there, and how I vaguely made it out in my own mind to be fuller of wonders and wickedness than all the cities of the earth, I need not stop to relate here. We approached it by degrees, and got, in due time, to the inn in the Whitechapel district for which we were bound. I forget whether it was the Blue Bull or the Blue Boar; but I know it was the Blue Something, and that its likeness was painted up on the back of the coach.

David's destination, incidentally, is a school in Blackheath, 'the most forlorn and miserable place I had ever seen,' where his year is spent in a blur of 'cracked slates, tear-blotted copy books, canings, rulerings, hair-cuttings, rainy Sundays, suet puddings, and a dirty atmosphere of ink surrounding all.' A depressing picture.

Perhaps it's no surprise that at least one Blackheath schoolmaster, the unfortunate M. J. Druitt, ended up in the Thames.

Another positive element to Dickens' view of Whitechapel was its bustle. It was a hive – a bustling, glittering throng of human activity that never ceased to thrill him. An unattributed article in *Household Words* (possibly by Dickens, but certainly written under his influence) takes a breathless tour of this great panorama. The writer explores 'Butcher Row' by the Minories, 'a city of meat! The gas ... lights up a long vista of beef, mutton and veal. Legs, shoulders, loins, ribs, hearts, livers, kidneys, gleam in all the gaudy panoply of scarlet and white on every side.' On the Whitechapel Road, he stops at the pubs 'with queer signs,' including The Grave Maurice and the now legendary Blind Beggar. The article offers hundreds of realistic miniatures – 'a gaunt old man with the bristly beard and the red eyelids' and 'slatternly, frowsy drabs of women, wrangling with wrinkled crones' – but the overall tone is one of enthusiasm for this great stream of diverse humanity: 'But the noise! The yelling, screeching, howling, swearing, laughing, fighting saturnalia; the combination of commerce, fun, frolic, cheating, almsgiving, thieving and devilry; the Geneva-laden tobacco-charged atmosphere.'

It's an image that seems to be indelibly printed in the mind of every BBC set designer. No period production is ever complete without hundreds of howling costermongers, hawking eel pies or taxidermied parrots.

In his earlier writing, then, Dickens saw much that was comic, romantic and exciting in East End life. Yet we already sense darker elements. The bustle had its oppressive side; even the starry-eyed Copperfield finds that it 'confused my weary head beyond description.' And it could be sinister. Mrs Nickleby and her daughter Kate, for instance, are housed near the Minories in 'a large old dingy house in Thames Street . . . An empty dog-kennel, some bones of animals, fragments of iron hoops, and staves of old casks lay strewn about, but no life was stirring there. It was a picture of dark, silent decay.' This darkness comes to dominate his vision of the East End.

Our Mutual Friend, Dickens's last complete novel, is set largely in Limehouse, and it does not present an exciting or romantic picture at all. It is a 'squalid maze of streets and alleys of miserable houses let out into single rooms.' In describing the home of Lizzie Hexam, the novel's working class heroine, Dickens gives us an accurate glimpse of the better class of riverside dwellings:

> The fire was in a rusty brazier, not fitted to the hearth . . . Two or three old sculls and oars stood against the wall, and against another part of the wall was a small dresser, making a spare show of the commonest articles of crockery and cooking-vessels. The roof of the room was not plastered, but was formed of the flooring of the room above.

The people have changed, too. Loyal Sam Weller and his father are long gone. Most of the East Enders here are sharks: the gabbling alcoholic Mr Dolls, the predatory Rogue Riderhood, the cunning Silas Wegg.

Where *Pickwick Papers* focused on the coaching inns of the East End, *Our Mutual Friend* features its graveyards. The aptly-named Bradley Headstone terrifies Lizzie with his ferocious marriage proposal in a churchyard off Leadenhall Street: 'a paved square court, with a raised bank of earth about breast high, in the middle, enclosed by iron rails. Here, conveniently and healthfully elevated above the level of the living, were the dead.' The hero John Rokesmith ponders his doomed love in the yard of Limehouse Church. He 'looked up at the high tower spectrally resisting the wind, and he looked around at the white tombstones, like enough to the dead in their winding-sheets.' Death, it seems, is a permanent presence in these streets.

There is some cheer amid all this bleakness. The Six Jolly Fellowship Porters is thought to be based on The Grapes which backed onto Limehouse Reach, and the detailed description of the interior certainly suggests that it is drawn from life: 'Externally, it was a narrow, lopsided, wooden jumble of corpulent windows heaped one upon the other as you might heap as many toppling oranges, with a crazy wooden verandah impending over the water; indeed the whole house . . . impended over the water, but seemed to have got into the condition of a faint-hearted diver who has paused so long on the brink that he will never go in at all.'

Inside the unprepossessing heap lies 'a bar to soften the human breast,' a tiny firelit haven 'divided from the rough world,' decorated with scarlet curtains, 'cordial-bottles radiant with fictitious grapes in bunches, and lemons in nets, and biscuits in baskets.' But this is no throwback to the Blue Boar or the Bull Inn. It's a refuge from the darkness of the world outside – a world that 'pressed so hard and so close . . . as to leave the hostelry not an inch of ground beyond its door.'

Dickens's vision of the East End is ultimately a dark and menacing one. But is this another kind of romanticism? How well did Dickens know the real East End? The answer is, very well indeed. To most Londoners, working-class Whitechapel was virtually invisible: but Dickens explored it avidly. Such first-hand street knowledge was essential to his fiction. He never wrote about a place or its inhabitants without first becoming familiar with both, and his excursions into the East End are well-documented. During one night-time ramble with Wilkie Collins, Dickens discovered five 'bundles of rags' settled in the mud and rain outside the Whitechapel Workhouse – girls unable to get admittance to the Ward for the night. More horrifying to Dickens than their obvious starvation was their despair. 'They were all dull and languid,' he wrote. 'No one made any sort of profession or complaint; no one cared to look at me; no one thanked me.' Other excursions included an unscheduled visit to a riverside hovel in Stepney, that sounds a lot like the Hexam home.'The woman of the room had picked up some long strips of wood, about some wharf or barge, and they had just now been thrust into the otherwise empty grate . . . The flare of the burning wood enabled me to see a table, and a broken chair or so, and some old cheap crockery ornaments about the chimney piece.' A visit to the Vintners' Almshouses (renamed 'Titbull's') on the Mile End Road prompts his usual vivid description: 'Old iron and fried fish, cough drops and artificial flowers, boiled pigs' feet and household furniture that looks as if it were polished up with lip-salve . . . and saucers full of shell-fish in a green juice which I hope is natural to them when their health is good, garnish the paved sideways as you go to Titbull's.'

Literally as well as figuratively, Dickens knew the streets of the East End.

He also knew about the lives of East Enders. Critics have sometimes accused Dickens of idealizing the poor, and have pointed to sentimental figures like Oliver Twist, the saintly workhouse orphan. But Dickens' fictional characters are just that – fictions. In real life, Dickens was pragmatic and clear-eyed. He was interested in effective reform, and that meant dealing with people as they really were. He reported on literally hundreds of institutions, public and private. He approved of anything neat, organized, useful and cheerful; he loathed bullying and condescension. The 'Self-Supporting Cooking Depot for the Working Classes,' a self-help venture at the corner of Commercial Street and Flower and Dean Street, was just the kind of project that delighted him. He describes how a mere fourpence-halfpenny will buy 'an honest and stout soup,' along with meat, potatoes and pudding, all excellently served. His only objection was to the absence of beer, a precaution that never ceased to irritate him: it told the working man 'in the old wearisome condescending patronising way that he must be goody-poody, and do as he is toldy-poldy.' (One wonders if Catherine Eddowes ever got the chance to eat there; it was still operating in the early 1880s, when she lived with John Kelly a few doors up in Flower and Dean Street.)

Dickens also disliked phony sentimentalism. Teachers in the Ragged Schools, he observed, often made the mistake of pretending that their pupils were innocent young things: 'hulking mudlarks' and 'young women old in the vices of the commonest and worst life were expected to profess themselves enthralled by the good child's book, *The Adventures of Little Margery*, who . . . 'divided her porridge with singing birds.' What those 'vices' were, Dickens knew perfectly well. He and heiress Angela-Burdett Coutts managed Urania Cottage, a home for prostitutes who wanted to leave their street life behind. Coutts provided the funds; Dickens did everything else. The Home itself was not in the East End, but the biographies of its inmates would have been familiar to anyone in Whitechapel: these girls were destitute, mostly homeless, living hand to mouth, prostituting themselves when necessary, drinking when possible. Dickens' advice to Coutts on how to recruit inmates is not the usual Victorian cant about being 'fallen' and failing one's 'duty to society.' It is lucid and sensible. 'Never mind society while she is at that pass,' he urged Miss Coutts, who had a rather evangelical streak. 'Society has used her ill and turned away from her, and she cannot be expected to take much heed of its rights and wrongs.' He was realistic, too, about the psychological damage that many girls would have sustained.

There is no doubt that many of them will go on well for some time, and would then be siezed with a violent fit of the most extraordinary passion, apparently quite motiveless, and insist on going away. There seems to be something inherent in their course of life, which engenders and awakens a sudden restlessness and recklessness which may be long suppressed, but breaks out like a madness.

One thinks of Polly Nichols again. She lasted only three months in service with a family who were, she wrote to her father, 'teetotallers and very religious, so I ought to get on well.' Perhaps she fell prey to a 'violent fit,' or perhaps she had no more use for Methodists than did Dickens. Either way, Dickens would have understood her frailty and restlessness very well.

Dickens' East End, then, is a complex place that changes over time. It contains comedy, nostalgia, the bustle and adventure of life. It is also a real place with real people, whose streets and lives he knew well. But its strongest impression is its last: dark, decaying, fearful, a place of graveyards and mud, of destructive passions fomenting dangerously beneath the surface. Like many of his contemporaries, Dickens came to see urban poverty not just as a tragedy or a social problem, but as a horror, a thickening jungle that threatened to swallow middle-class London. The Victorians were afraid of it; and they were right. The nineteenth century saw cholera epidemics at home and mob violence abroad. Who knew what incurable bitterness was festering in the hearts of those consigned to live like dogs? 'Turn that dog's descendants loose,' Dickens wrote prophetically, 'and in a very few years they will so degenerate that they will lose even their bark—but not their bite.' No wonder, perhaps, that the Ripper's crimes would strike Londoners with such force, and linger in their imaginations. They seemed to embody all the feral savagery of the slums that Dickens had long warned must break loose.

This essay appeared in *Ripperologist* magazine No. 36, August 2001.

Arthur George Morrison:
Was He the Child of the Jago?

Andy and Sue Parlour

IN 1896 ARTHUR GEORGE MORRISON published a book titled *A Child of the Jago*. Morrison's story, a novel, centred around six filthy smelling slum filled streets of London's East End. In fact the novel is a portrait of life of a down and out area of Shoreditch E2, known in the nineteenth century as the Old Nichol. The houses in these wicked few streets were occupied by the lowest of the low.

The London County Council, who were responsible for the Old Nichol did a survey in the Boundary Street area, part of which was the Old Nichol, in 1890. The findings, which are in condensed form, are reprinted here:

The Boundary Street Report
The streets are 20 in number and the average population per room is 2–3 persons, 107 rooms having 5 or more persons in each room. The streets and courts are very narrow, the widest being only 28 ft across.

In many cases there was a great difference between the level of the street and that of the ground floor of the houses, the latter in some cases being 18 inches below the former. A large number of the houses had no back yards and many of the small courts were of a very bad class.

There were 730 houses, of which, 652 were occupied, wholly or partly, by persons of the labouring classes; the remaining 78 houses consisting of 12 public-houses and beer shops, 21 shops and factories, 2 registered lodging-houses (153 beds); and 43 empty houses. The population, exclusive of those in lodging-houses, was 5,566 – viz., 3,370 adults and 2,196 children, who occupied 2,545 rooms.

The LCC report goes: 'That a large proportion of the inhabitants of the area belong to the criminal classes. Living in one street alone there were at one time no less than 64 persons who had served varying times of penal servitude.'

We also learn that the death rate in the Old Nichol area was twice as high as in other parts of Shoreditch and Bethnal Green and four times that of London as a whole; and one child in every four born in the area died before his or her first birthday.

Morrison's *Child of the Jago* was published in 1896, so he had had a full six years to access this devastating LCC report of the living conditions of the Old Nichol. This together with his own research and observations was to be the basis on which he wrote many articles and short stories, as well as three novels.

But what of Arthur Morrison himself? Not much is known of him and his younger days, but our research has opened up a little more of his life. He always stated he was born in Kent. In fact Morrison was born Arthur George Morrison on 1 November 1863 at number 4, John Street, Poplar, to George Richard (engine fitter) and Jane Morrison. His parents had married at the church of St Peter, Stepney on 18 January 1863.

His father George was born in Stepney on 8 December 1839. His mother Jane Cooper was born at Sheerness, Kent in 1840. There were two John Streets in Poplar in 1863 but due to a street renaming programme in 1865 both ceased to exist. The No. 4, John Street where Arthur was born became No. 4, Grundy Street. The other John Street became Rigden Street. At No. 4, Grundy Street Arthur's mother owned a haberdasher's shop (this part of Grundy seemed to have its fair share of shops). In 1881 they are listed in the census at 4, Grundy Street thus: 'Jane Morrison aged 41, widow, Haberdasher, Arthur G. aged 17, Clerk to Architect at East Road, Frederick W. aged 10, and Ada aged 12, both scholars.'

Arthur's father had died some time in 1875, how, when and

where we do not know. By 1886 Arthur was working as a clerk to the Beaumont Trust, a charity, which ran the People's Palace in the Mile End Road. Here he was honing his skills as a writer and journalist. According to one of Morrison's accounts of his early life he was born in Kent, the son of a 'professional man,' and educated at private schools. All three statements contradict what is now positively known, so Morrison's versions of his own life are extremely unreliable. Born, living and working in London's East End, and seeing for himself the hardships that most had to put up with in their miserable day-to-day existence fed Morrison's mind. In October 1891 a story he had written appeared in *Macmillan's Magazine* titled *A Street: a short tale of East London life*. As this extract shows he had a 'feel' for what he wrote:

> The East End is a vast city, as famous in its way as any city men have built. But who knows the East End? It is down through Cornhill and out beyond Leadenhall Street and Aldgate pump and one would say; a shocking place and where he once went with a curate. An evil growth of slums which hide human creeping things; where foul men and women live on a penn'worth of gin, where collars and clean shirts are not yet invented, where every citizen wears a black eye, and no man combs his hair. Our street is not a place like this.

It was articles like this, which drew the attention of publisher W. E. Henly, when learning from Morrison that he intended to publish a series of articles Henly agreed to take the gifted young writer on and offered him a contract. The stories appeared in the National Observer throughout 1893, and in late 1894 they were published collectively and re-titled *Tales of Mean Streets*. In the opening line he sets the scene by telling the reader what the houses were like: 'Of this street there are about one hundred and fifty yards – on the same pattern all. It is not pretty to look at. A dingy little brick house twenty feet high, with three square holes to carry the windows, and an oblong to carry the door, is not a pleasing object; and each side of the street is formed by two or three score of such houses in a row, with one front wall in common.'

Morrison was writing from a personal aspect. He had, and was still living in East London. By 1890 he was a full time journalist. Although trying to hide the fact that he was a child of the East End he wrote with a sense of true 'realism.' When once called upon to answer how he could write with such knowledge he would always defend himself by referring to his time spent at the People's Palace. He once said, 'For a good few years I have lived in the East End of London, and have been, not an occasional visitor, but a familiar and equal friend in the house of the East-Ender'; or, replying angrily to criticisms of his portrayal of East End life, '. . . of which, I do happen to know at first hand, and without the help of a notebook.'

Morrison wanted all to know of his intimate knowledge of the East End and at the same time was trying to hide his and his family's roots within it. But was Morrison being very clever? He is at one time denying his background and on the other hand explaining intimate details of the conditions. The controversy at the time, led to increasing interst in him, and his writing. One person who showed an interest in Morrison's work and approached him in 1894 was the Vicar of Holy Trinity Church the Reverend Arthur Osborne Jay. His parish in Shoreditch included the Old Nichol. He wrote praising Morrison's *The Mean Streets*, saying there were parts in the Old Nichol much coarser and harder than portrayed in the *Tales*. He invited Morrison to visit with him the 'Nichol.' Morrison took up the invitation and after being persuaded of the truth of Jay's assertion began writing *A Child of the Jago*. Over the next twelve months with the Reverend's help he researched more and more on the conditions in which the people of the 'Nichol' were living in which. In 1896 *A Child of the Jago* was published. The story revolves around a young boy Dicky Perrott, growing up among the violent and semi-criminal underclass of the Jago, a fictional area between Shoreditch High Street and Brick Lane, but based entirely on the 'Nichol.' And of his mother desperately struggling to keep the family fed. In the story the Reverend Sturt who throws all his energy into trying to improve the area is of course the Reverend Arthur Osborne Jay. No chirpy Cockneys here. The streetwise and brutal survived the best. Fighting and drunkenness were the best entertainments for men and women. Most sources of income came from the coshing, mugging and the stripping of strangers, lured into the 'Nichol' by the street girls.

Shoplifting and the theft from unguarded carts was rife, and men who did not drink and beat their wives were considered soft. Against all this adversity Dicky Perrott is battling to better himself.

Despite its grim setting the novel fairly rattles along, full of lively turbulent characters, coarse East End dialogue, of the damp, evil, noisy and smelly places, the atmosphere of which leaps out at you from the pages. It is ironic that at the time *A Child of the Jago* was published the Old Nichol was ceasing to exist. It was being demolished to make way for a new, London County Council housing development, of blocks of flats all centred round a circular park. When opening the new estate in 1900 the Prince of Wales (later King Edward VII), made a speech, during which he made a reference to Arthur Morrison and to the Reverend Jay, 'Few, indeed, will forget this site who have read Mr Morrison's pathetic tale *A Child of the Jago*, and all of us are familiar with the labours of that most excellent philanthropist, Mr Jay, in this neighbourhood.' *A Child of the Jago* was published to much critical acclaim and soon became a bestseller. Morrison dedicated his book to the Reverend Jay.

Morrison continued with his writing, publishing various titles and writing on various subjects. He returned to an East End theme with *To London Town* (1899), based on Johnny May who although born in Essex comes to live in London's East End. *The Hole in the Wall* (1902), is a story of Stephen Kemp whose mother has just died when the novel opens, and his father is later murdered (how we do not know) without ever appearing in the book. Was Morrison recalling his own father's demise?

Morrison spent his days buying works of art from the steady influx of immigrants into the East End of London from the Far East. He began to supplement his rudimentary knowledge of Japanese art he had picked up by systematic courses of study under Japanese scholars and painters in London. In 1902 he published a series of articles on the subject in the *Monthly Review*, culminating in a double-volume work in 1911. In 1913 Morrison surprisingly sold his entire art collection for £4,000. Over the years he had amassed a fine collection and was considered by many to be an expert on the subject. In 1892 he married Elizabeth Thatcher and soon after moved to Chingford, Essex, and a little later to Loughton, also in Essex. The

Morrisons had one son, Guy. At the age of fifty Morrison retired and moved to a house at High Beech, Essex, in Epping Forest. His son Guy served in the First World War, dying in 1921 of malaria contracted while in the services. In 1930 Arthur and Elizabeth Morrison moved yet again this time to Chalfont St Peter, adding to his collection of English watercolours and Oriental *objets d'art*. He published his last book *Fiddle o' Dreams* in 1933. In his retirement he worked tirelessly for the Royal Society of Literature (he had been elected a member 1924 and on the board since 1935). He was an honorary member of the Japanese Art Association and also a leading Freemason. When Arthur Morrison died in 1945 aged eighty-two he was wealthy but forgotten. The books that had made his name and fortune were now fifty years old and long out of print. They were not considered then as now of historical interest. Although proud of his working-class fiction he chose to keep his public and private lives apart. After his death, his wife Elizabeth, acting according to his wishes, sold his library, dispersed his art collections and most sadly of all burnt all his personal notebooks, manuscripts and papers. Only the original manuscript of *A Child of the Jago*, which he had presented to Bethnal Green Library in 1936, survives.

More facts about Arthur Morrison
In the 1901 census he his still living at Loughton in Essex, age thirty-seven. His occupation is given as man of letters. He is now giving his place of birth as Blackheath, London.

Also in the 1901 census we find his mother still living at the family home, 4, Grundy Street, Poplar. She is now sixty-one, she is still a widow and carrying on the occupation of haberdasher. Living with her at Grundy Street is her unmarried daughter and Arthur's sister, Ada now aged thirty-two, also a haberdasher. The whereabouts of Morrison's younger brother, Frederick is not known for certain.

Even in 1901 Arthur George Morrison was denying his roots.

This essay appeared in *Ripperologist* magazine No. 47, July 2003.

The Ripper People: William Le Queux

Eduardo Zinna

IN THE CLOSE, SELF-CONTAINED world of Ripperology, no one is more revered – or vilified – than the author, the theorist and the investigator. Their ranks are swollen with policemen, academics, journalists and magistrates, seasoned professionals and gifted amateurs, meticulous researchers and unscrupulous hoaxers. Into their number sauntered, eighty years ago, novelist, traveller, sportsman, gourmet, journalist, marksman, Egyptologist, raconteur, amateur spy, radio enthusiast, inveterate name-dropper and (according to many sources) amiable fibber William Le Queux.

In the fifty-ninth year of his life, in 1923, Le Queux penned a volume of memoirs entitled *Things I Know About Kings, Celebrities and Crooks*. Much of this work was devoted to Le Queux's meetings with the rich and famous. His subjects included the Sultan of Turkey, King Nicholas of Montenegro, 'Carmen Sylva,' Queen of Romania, Princess Luisa of Saxony, Vatt Marashi, Chief of the Skreli Brigands, Petkoff, Prime Minister of Bulgaria, and Dr Crippen. Most of them have been forgotten. And so might be the book and perhaps its author. But, almost as an afterthought, Le Queux purported to reveal to the world, in a couple of pages, the actual facts of the 'Jack the Ripper Mystery,' which, he remarked, still puzzled the whole world. And still does.

William Tufnell Le Queux was born in London to a French father and English mother. His surname, which he pronounced to rhyme with Kew, was an old Norman name meaning simply 'The

Cook' – which didn't prevent him from asserting, years later, that it meant 'The King's Head Cook' and that his family had a distinguished lineage. Le Queux was educated in England, Italy and France, where he studied art. Soon he drifted into journalism, writing first for French newspapers. Back in Britain in the 1880s, he edited *Gossip and Piccadilly*. He later joined the staff of the London *Globe*, for which he claimed to have covered the Jack the Ripper crimes.

After travelling in Russia and writing a series of articles on the revolutionary movement and the condition of exiles in Siberia for *The Times*, he published his first novel, *Guilty Bonds* (1891), which dealt with political conspiracy in Russia. In banning the book, the Russian censors took the first step towards ensuring Le Queux's lasting popularity and fortune. Within two years he had abandoned journalism to devote the rest of his life to the production of nearly 200 fiction and non-fiction books, including a fair share of mysteries, thrillers and spy stories.

The line of military thinking prevailing until the end of the nineteenth century named as the greatest threats to Britain's security her oldest enemy, France, in Africa and on the continent, and France's ally, Russia, in central Asia and the borders of British India. Despite his French ancestry, Le Queux adhered faithfully to this line. His loyalty was rewarded in 1893, when he joined forces for the first time with another staunch nationalist: future press tycoon Alfred Harmsworth – later Lord Northcliffe, founder of the *Daily Mail* and owner of *The Times*. Harmsworth commissioned Le Queux to write a magazine serial entitled *The Poisoned Bullet* relating the fictional invasion of Britain by the combined forces of France and Russia.[1] The fighting started with dreadful carnage, as Britain was treacherously attacked, one evening in 1897, by the enemy, and continued in the same vein for several weeks – until beleaguered Britain repealed the invaders with the assistance of stalwart Germany.[2]

Harmsworth affirmed that the serial was based on the prognostications of the best authorities in modern warfare and was intended to promote public interest in the idea of a larger fleet. Among its admiring readers was Field-Marshal Earl Roberts of Kandahar, hero of India and the Boer War and former Commander-in-Chief. The following year *The Poisoned Bullet* appeared in book form as *The Great War in England in 1897* and sold very well indeed.

Encouraged by his success, Le Queux continued to churn out tales about the exploits of Britain's enemies. The peril of the title in *England's Peril: A Story of the Secret Service* (1899) consisted mainly of spymaster Gaston La Touche, the dashing chief of the French Secret Service. La Touche was possessed of 'an iron nerve and muscles which rendered him practically invulnerable' as well as a robust, down-to-earth sense of humour. He was also an intrepid explorer, the first white man ever to enter Timbuktu, and 'one of the most easy-going, devil-may-care fellows, who seemed to exist at random anywhere and everywhere': 'Today he would be heard of in savage Africa, a week later he would be seen sipping his mazagran in front of the Grand Café in Paris, and a few days afterwards one would read that he had sailed from Havre, Brest or Marseille to another quarter of the globe.'

But La Touche also had a ruthless streak and 'no equal in unscrupulousness.' The woman whom he blackmailed in the pursuit of his dastardly designs upbraided him for his ungentlemanly behaviour: 'You, Gaston la Touche, have no pity for a woman! You know well enough that by your fiendish cunning and your master-stroke of ingenuity you have succeeded in holding me fettered as your slave, so that you can use me as your cat's-paw to attain your despicable ends!'

At the beginning of the novel, Lord Casterton, who had denounced in Parliament the inadequacy of Britain's military preparations, is assassinated. His face has been shattered beyond recognition. We later learn that the crime has been committed with an explosive cigar given to Casterton by his wife, who is in love with La Touche.

But Le Queux's readers could rest assured that La Touche's dire stratagems would always be defeated in the end. He told them that: 'The British Secret Service, although never so prominently before the public as those unscrupulous agents provocateurs of France and Russia, is nevertheless equally active. It works in silence and secrecy, yet many are its successful counterplots against the machinations of England's enemies.'

French spies continued to mount attacks against Britain in a number of Le Queux's semi-fictional works. In *His Majesty's Minister* (1891), a French agent taps the private wire between Windsor Castle and the Foreign Office.

The dauntless hero of *Secrets of the Foreign Service* (1903) was Duckworth Drew, 'secret agent in the employ of the Foreign Office, and, next to his Majesty's Secretary of State for Foreign Affairs, one of the most powerful and important pillars of England's supremacy.' Drew was 'one of the most remarkable of men, possessing tact, shrewdness, cunning and daring that are utterly amazing.' Not only had Le Queux given Drew a name that rhymed with his own but also endowed him with characteristics which resembled him – or, rather, his self-image: Drew had an English mother and a French father and was 'dark, of medium height, about forty, unobtrusive, of perfect manner and a born gentleman.' Scarcely had he arrived in France – where he used his real name, which was, predictably, Dreux – that the French Foreign Minister asked him for one of his excellent Cuban cigars. But – perhaps in retaliation for the cigar that had caused Lord Casterton's death – the cigar given to the Minister had been treated with a solution of *cocculus indicus* which made him unwittingly reveal the secrets Drew had come to collect.

Nor was France's ally, Russia, spared. *A Secret Service: Being Strange Tales of a Nihilist* (1892), which featured a Jewish hero, dealt in some detail with the anti-Semitic pogroms which raged across Russia following the assassination of Tsar Alexander II. Apparently still determined to boost Le Queux's sales, Russia also banned *A Secret Service*.

With the closing of the nineteenth century, a subtle disturbance of the balance of power began to take place. Germany started to throw its weight about, making bellicose noises and building up a fleet to rival Britain's. When Britain and France set aside their old rivalries and signed the Entente Cordiale in 1904, Le Queux was temporarily bereft of dastardly villains. But he soon cast his net about for new enemies. He did not have to search far.

By his own account, Le Queux became aware of the new peril to the nation when a friend disclosed to him the existence of a vast network of German espionage spread over Britain. His sensational revelations, however, failed to awaken the expected interest. 'My voice was, alas, that of someone crying out in the wilderness!' he would complain, years later, in his memoirs. Earl Roberts, a devoted reader of Le Queux's invasion saga, was of a similar frame of mind. He had become convinced that Britain should not rely entirely on the navy for its protection but that universal military conscription and the building of a larger army were indispensable for the defence of the realm. The two men – the Field-Marshal and the thriller-writer – met: 'My dear Le Queux,' said the white-moustached old soldier, holding out his hands in a fatherly manner, 'the world thinks me a lunatic also, because, after my forty years' service in India, I have come home and dared to tell England that she is unprepared for war.'[3]

When the Government of the day failed to be converted to his ideas, Roberts resigned from the Committee of Imperial Defence and founded the National Service League, which would grow in membership from an initial 2,000 to more than 200,000 by the eve of the Great War.

At this point, Harmsworth, now the proprietor of the *Daily Mail*, the first mass-circulation newspaper, stepped in again. Always striving to increase the sales of his newspaper, he had decided that what Britain needed was a new invasion scare substituting the German army for the old enemies. Once more he hired Le Queux to write a serial – this time for the *Daily Mail* – and sent him to work out the most likely route for the German invasion. Le Queux spent four months roaming the east coast of England, scouting invasion beaches and battle sites. Back in London, he plotted together with Roberts the advance of the German army through the English countryside. But Harmsworth's steadfast patriotism did not dull his business acumen. He took exception to a route that – though militarily sound – crossed through far too many small villages and sparsely populated areas. So the route was changed to allow the Germans to cut a wide swathe through big cities and large towns, 'not keep to remote, one-eyed villages where there

158

was no possibility of large *Daily Mail* sales.' In March 1906, Harmsworth launched *The Invasion of 1910* with sandwich men in spike helmets and Prussian blue uniforms marching up and down Oxford Street.

This new invasion of Britain started with the Teutonic hordes massing on the Frisian coast and stealthily crossing the North Sea to attack a nation that slept, short of soldiers, weapons and plans and totally unaware of the foul tide approaching its shores. Worse still, lamented Le Queux, the country was inadequately led, since the Conservatives had been recently replaced by the Liberals at the helm of Britain. 'A strong, aristocratic Government,' he wrote, 'had been replaced by a weak administration swayed by every breath of popular impulse. The peasantry, who were the backbone of the nation, had vanished and been replaced by the weak, excitable population of the towns.'

Not only that, but daring German spies were assisting the invasion by destroying railways and telegraph wires: 'Among the thousands of Germans working in London the hundred or so spies, all trusted soldiers, had passed unnoticed, but, working in unison, each little group of two or three had been allotted its task and previously thoroughly reconnoitred the position and studied the most rapid or effective means.'

Poorly led, unprepared and untrained, the British fight valiantly, but are overwhelmed by the coldly professional German army. Utter savagery prevails on both sides. The invaders kill women and children, force terrified civilians to dig their own graves and slaughter the entire population of a town in retaliation for the ambush of a German supply party. The British, almost as brutal, shoot, stab, hang or throttle any German soldier who falls into their hands.

From his headquarters in Berlin, the Kaiser urges his forces on. 'The pride of these English must be broken,' he thunders. Wave after wave of invading soldiery edge further towards London. They besiege the city, subjecting it to heavy bombardment. When they finally walk in, surrounded by desolation and ruin, they must fight the exhausted survivors in the streets. The Germans capture the city, but their flag will not fly long over it. The whole population rises against the Hun with formidable wrath. Before such an implacable enemy, the Germans lose their will to fight and lay down their arms. The victors exact a terrible price. German prisoners are lynched, torn limb from limb or killed in ways so horrible that Le Queux tactfully declines to describe them. As the fighting ends, Britain's economy, trade and finances are in ruins and, across the sea, Germany is poised for another invasion.

The serial was phenomenally successful. The *Daily Mail* sold out day after day, as special maps were published in the national and provincial press to show which areas the German foe would be invading the following morning. Immediately afterwards *The Invasion of 1910*, with a full account of the siege of London, was issued in book form. In an introductory letter, Earl Roberts stated that 'the catastrophe that may happen if we still remain in the present state of unpreparedness is vividly and forcibly illustrated in Mr Le Queux's new book which I recommend to the perusal of everybody who has the welfare of the British Empire at heart.' Le Queux had already repaid the compliment, as one of his characters declared: 'Had we adopted his [Roberts's] scheme for universal service these dire catastrophes could never had occurred.'

The Invasion of 1910 was translated into twenty-seven languages, including Arabic, Chinese and Japanese, and sold over a million copies. The German translation was issued in 1911 as *Die Invasion von 1910* and in 1914 as *Der Einfall der Deutschen in England*. To the great chagrin of its author, its cover depicted a victorious German army marching into London and its text was revised to allow the soldiers of the Kaiser to remain in possession of Britain's capital.

At the same time as he practised the art of the political, semi-fictional thriller, Le Queux honed his skills as a prolific and prosperous exponent of the novel of glamorous adventure in the posh haunts of the upper classes. The heroine of *The Gamblers* (1901), for instance, leaves Kensington society with her guardian for a tour on the continent. At every turn they run into energetic millionaires, dashing undercover agents, shady croupiers, tow-headed women and villainous Corsicans as they play roulette at the Casino in Monte Carlo and a private gambling den in Paris, cruise the Mediterranean in sumptuous yachts, ride luxury trains across Europe and witness murder at five-star hotels. When the murderer is exposed he obligingly kills himself with his own diabolical invention: a thimble fitted with a hollow spike within which is 'a small chamber filled with a most subtle and deadly poison, extracted from a small lizard peculiar to the Bambara country on the banks of the Upper Niger.'

Le Queux's spy novels were equally set among the powerful and influential: the world of embassies, government offices and diplomatic soirees. His heroes tend to work for the British Government and are likely to pour scorn on the received opinions of the public, politicians and the press, who all underestimate the German danger. Like some latter-day secret agents, they often allow themselves to be captured by enemy agents, be bound and gagged and left alone in a room together with some sort of device set to kill them off in a few minutes, only to contrive some miraculous last-minute escape.

A typical Le Queux hero is the protagonist of *Reveals the Cotton Glove*, a short story included in the collection *Revelations of the Secret Service* (1911). He is a secret agent for the Nameless Bureau – that is to say, the Secret Service Bureau – as well as a member of the upper classes and a distinguished diplomat. His job is to steal other country's secrets, which he generally accomplishes through ingenious schemes, sometimes disguising himself as a working-class man or a hoodlum. But he is first and foremost a member of his class and, as such, all doors are open to him. His life is spent dashing in and out of exclusive clubs, embassy balls and lavish restaurants. A charming Parisienne, a glass of champagne, an expensive cigar – such are the trappings of his trade.

Yet Le Queux's techniques are subtler than they seem. As his upper crust characters frequent the renowned spots of the continent or tramp along the corridors of power, Le Queux flatters his readers by implying their familiarity with the places his characters visit and the circles in which they move. When the protagonists of *The Gamblers* stop at Paris to see the sights of the city, Le Queux remarks: 'Need I describe them? I think not. Those who read these lines probably know them all.' When his protagonists arrive in

Nice, Le Queux addresses his public directly: 'Reader, you probably know the panorama of the Riviera . . .' And when they reach Monte Carlo he recalls that 'White serge is, as you know, always de rigueur at Monte in winter . . .' Most of his readers were probably not acquainted with the sights of Paris or the panorama of the Riviera, and they were undoubtedly unaware of what was de rigueur at Monte – in any season – but they certainly appreciated an author who welcomed them into the world of the ruling classes and the playgrounds of the idle rich.

Following the success of *The Invasion of 1910*, Le Queux became a celebrity at clubs and dinner parties, appreciated as a wit and raconteur and, above all, hailed as 'the man who dared to tell the truth.' Not content with his growing reputation, he decided to enhance it further by embarking on a new career as spy-catcher and international man of mystery by joining a voluntary Secret Service department: 'Half a dozen patriotic men in secret banded themselves together. Each, paying his own expenses, set to work gathering information in Germany and elsewhere that might be useful to our country in case of need.'[4]

From then on Le Queux allegedly carried out secret missions when travelling throughout Europe. By his own account, he went to the Balkans in 1906 and on a special government mission to Macedonia, Montenegro, Serbia and Albania in the following year. On one mission, he said, he disguised himself when visiting a gun factory in Germany and reported later to British intelligence about new German weaponry. He would later hint that he was intimate with the workings of a 'certain nameless department, known only by a code number' (the Secret Service Bureau, the future MI5, created in 1909 under army captain Vernon Kell), and that he knew well 'its splendid staff, its untiring and painstaking efforts, its patriotism and the astuteness of its head director, one of the finest Englishmen of [his] acquaintance.'

By his own account, Le Queux's first major coup came in July 1908, when a German friend asked to meet him in Switzerland. At a hotel in Zurich, Le Queux was given a copy of a speech made by the Kaiser to a council of war a month earlier. Like many statesmen before and after him, Wilhelm II sought to assuage internal discontent by embarking in a foreign war. The chosen target was, of course, Britain. As soon as a vast Zeppelin fleet was assembled, the German forces would descend from the skies upon their unsuspecting foe. In the meantime, Germany's vast army of spies would work to ensure the triumph of its interests throughout the world.

Le Queux's sensational revelations met with mixed reactions. Among those who considered the Kaiser's speech of the first importance were his old allies Earl Roberts and Harmsworth – now Lord Northcliffe – as well as an imposing array of senior military men. But the roster of those who considered Le Queux's disclosures as sheer moonshine was equally impressive. The speech was allegedly stolen from the offices of Le Queux's publishers. 'German secret agents undoubtedly committed the theft,' wrote Le Queux, 'for I have since learnt that my manuscript is in the archives of the Secret Service in Berlin!'

Many doubts were expressed about Le Queux's veracity concerning his adventures and many reservations about the accuracy of his revelations. A number of influential people, however, seem to have believed them implicitly. We have seen that Earl Roberts, Lord Northcliffe and many others gave him strong support. Lieutenant-Colonel James Edmonds, who was charged with counter-intelligence at the War Office from 1907, conferred often with Le Queux, followed up on his reports on German espionage and never doubted his usefulness to Britain's welfare. In the foreword to Le Queux's official biography, Sir Robert Gower, MP, described him as: '. . . a man, a man in thought and deed, whose interest was directed solely to the welfare of his country, who imperturbably risked his life in countless exploits for that country's benefit – exploits far exceeding in their daring the most colourful adventures of his bravest fictional heroes – it is to his credit that in all his Secret Service operations he paid all his expenses out of his own pocket.'[5]

Undeterred by criticism, Le Queux continued his efforts to entrap German spies in Britain. When he was not sussing out secret agents he was compiling reports on German spies or writing up his counter-espionage achievements for the press. In 1909, he decided to place a comprehensive record of his investigations before an appreciative public in the form of a collection of short stories, *Spies of the Kaiser; Plotting the Downfall of England*. He 'refrained from giving actual names and dates' for reasons which seemed obvious to him and presented instead 'the facts in the form of fiction – fiction which, I trust, will point its own patriotic moral.' In the preface, Le Queux stated that Britain was in 'grave danger of invasion by Germany at a date not far distant.' He asserted that 5,000 German agents were active in Britain, being paid between £10 and £30 per month. Most of these agents had been cunningly sent to Scotland, where their guttural accent was much less noticeable.

The book rehashed previous warnings in chapters bearing such titles as *The Back-Door of England*; *The German Plot Against England*; *How the Germans Are Preparing for Invasion*; and *The Peril of London* and celebrated British knowhow in chapters purporting to disclose the secrets of the new gun, the improved 'Dreadnoughts,' the new armour-plates, the new aeroplane and the silent submarine, the plans for all of which the foreign agents were trying desperately to steal.

Spies of the Kaiser was said – mainly by Le Queux himself – to have incensed the German monarch so much that he branded the author a dangerous enemy of Germany. Before the Great War, his agents allegedly trailed Le Queux in London to the point where Scotland Yard provided several guards to protect him against assassination. When the War broke out, Le Queux went about with a revolver in his pocket with which he was prepared to repel an attack which – in the event – never came.

But his books were lapped up by a public ready to believe that the most abominable plots were being secretly hatched against Britain. In *German Spies in England: An Exposure*, published in early 1915, Le Queux denounced a vast network of spies to be found everywhere and in all classes, from hall-porters in the leading hotels and hundreds of 'clever and capable' German prostitutes round Piccadilly at one end of the social scale to 'naturalised' foreign baronets, financiers, merchants, ship-owners and persons of both sexes of high social standing. The book went through six editions in three weeks and received endorsements from the Lord Mayor of London, Sir Arthur Conan Doyle and other prestigious individuals. The *Daily Mail* – owned by Le Queux's old patron, Lord Northcliffe – reviewed *German Spies in England* most favourably and called for action by the Government to stamp out such danger to the realm.

For the rest of the war Le Queux kept up a steady flow of volumes of thrilling adventure and shocking disclosure. Among them were *Britain's Deadly Peril* (1915); *German Atrocities: a Record of Shameless Deeds* (1915); *The Zeppelin Destroyer* (1916); *Hushed Up at German Headquarters* (1917); *Behind the German Lines; Amazing Confessions of Col.-Lieut. Otto von Heynitz, 16th Uhlans, Principal Aide-de-Camp to His Imperial Highness the German Crown Prince in the Field, and Now Detained in Switzerland; Startling Revelations of the Crown Prince's Shameful Actions, disclosed to and edited by William Le Queux* (1917); three volumes of *Secrets of Potsdam*, culminating in *Further Secrets of Potsdam: Startling Exposures of the Inner Life of the Courts of the Kaiser and Crown-Prince, revealed for the first time by Count Ernst von Heltzendorff* (1917); and *Love Intrigues of the Kaiser's Sons* (1918).

Besides semi-fictional accounts of political and military intrigue and espionage novels, Le Queux wrote tales of the occult such as *Stolen Souls* (1895) and low-life London stories such *A Madonna of the Music Halls* (1897). His motorcar tales included *The Count's Chauffeur* (1922) and *Cinders of Harley Street* (1922); his aviation stories, *The Terror of the Air* (1922) and *Beryl of the Bi-Plane* (1922); and his radio romances, *Tracked by Wireless* (1922) and *The Voice from the Void: The Great Wireless Mystery* (1922). Even true crime awoke his interest. In *Landru: His Secret Love Affairs* (1922), Le Queux evoked the career of notorious French lady-killer Henri Désiré Landru and even threw in some previously undisclosed information. He claimed he had been directly involved in the affair, assisting the police in their investigations and being present during some interrogations of the murderer himself.

At the peak of his powers 'The Master of Mystery,' as his publishers had christened him, was a prestigious and best-selling author, allegedly the favourite writer of Queen Alexandra and Prime Minister Lord Balfour. Not everybody, however, held the same opinion of his abilities. While acknowledging his great popularity, G. K. Chesterton compared him unfavourably with Charles Dickens:

> There are no popular authors to-day. We call such authors as Mr Guy Boothby or Mr William Le Queux popular authors. But this is popularity altogether in a weaker sense; not only in quantity, but in quality. The old popularity was positive; the new is negative. There is a great deal of difference between the eager man who wants to read a book, and the tired man who wants a book to read. A man reading a Le Queux mystery wants to get to the end of it. A man reading the Dickens novel wished that it might never end. Men read a Dickens story six times because they knew it so well. If a man can read a Le Queux story six times it is only because he can forget it six times.[6]

But, what did Le Queux know about Jack the Ripper? This is a tale that, though often told, is worth retelling. As we have seen, Le Queux allegedly covered the Whitechapel crimes for the *Globe*. By his own account, Charles Hands of the *Pall Mall Gazette*, Lincoln Springfield of the *Star* and himself 'practically lived as a trio in Whitechapel, and as each murder was committed [they] wrote it up with picturesque and lurid details while standing in the very spot where the tragedy had occurred. One evening Springfield would publish a theory of how the murders had been done; the next night Charlie Hands would have a far better theory and then [he] would weigh in with another theory in the *Globe*.' No independent corroboration of Le Queux's assertion has yet surfaced elsewhere and in no article in the *Globe* has his hand been detected with any certainty. Nor would he appear to have had any theories on the Ripper's identity at that time – or for several decades to come.

But we must backtrack a bit and begin at the beginning. Having exhausted his scandalous revelations about Imperial Germany, Le Queux turned his eyes towards Russia and the most intriguing personage to come out of pre-revolutionary days: Grigori Efimovitch Rasputin. In 1917, Le Queux published *Rasputin, the*

Rascal Monk, Disclosing the Secret Scandal of the Betrayal of Russia by the Mock-Monk Grichka, and the Consequent Ruin of the Romanoffs, allegedly based on documents obtained from the Kerensky government. Despite its lurid title, this was the most accurate of his three books on the subject.

The following year he produced another book, *The Minister of Evil: The Secret History of Rasputin's Betrayal of Russia*. Once again, Le Queux drew for this book upon documents thoughtfully provided by the Kerensky government. In this case, a manuscript by Fedor Rajevski, Rasputin's personal secretary and bodyservant, recounted how the monk's introduction into the Tsar's Palace and his rise to the highest levels of influence over the Royal Family were carefully engineered by Rajevski's supervisor in the secret service, General Kuropatkin. In the summer of 1903, Kuropatkin sent Rasputin to pray for a male heir to the throne in the church consecrated to the recently canonized St Seraphim of Sarov. Upon entering the church, the Tsarina was deeply impressed by the wild-eyed *staretz*'s fervour. Summoned to the Palace, Rasputin insinuated himself into the Tsarina's confidence and conspired together with her – who was German-born – to ensure the defeat of Russia. Rajevski even claimed to have accompanied Rasputin to meet the Kaiser in Berlin during the war. It was in this book that Le Queux first mentioned the existence of a homicidal maniac from Tver who escaped detection for the murder of a young girl.

As though these two volumes were not enough, in 1919 Le Queux published *Rasputin in London*, a semi-fictional account of an erotic religious movement. Rasputin also featured in 'Why the Monk Rasputin Was Murdered,' in *Hushed Up at German Headquarters* (1917) and 'Rasputin's Crucifix,' in *The Elusive Four* (1921).

Yet it was only in 1923, in *Things I Know about Kings, Celebrities and Crooks*, that Le Queux linked the monk with the Ripper. According to him, in 1917 he received from the Kerensky government – no doubt intent on discrediting the Tsarist regime – a large number of documents found in a safe in the cellar of Rasputin's home. Among these documents was a manuscript entitled *Great Russian Criminals*, written in French at Rasputin's dictation.

This manuscript drew upon a report by a Russian agent named Nideroest, who belonged to the Jubilee Street Club, the anarchist centre in the East End of London. One evening another member of the Club, Russian anarchist Nicholas Zverieff, confided to Nideroest that the Ripper was a homicidal maniac, Dr Alexander Pedachenko, formerly with the staff of the Maternity Hospital at Tver. Pedachenko lived with his sister in Westmoreland Road, Walworth and crossed the Thames to commit his murders. He had two accomplices: a London-born man called Levitski – who was Zverieff's source – and a woman, a tailoress, called Winberg. The woman Winberg engaged the victims in conversation and, while Pedachenko carried out the murders and mutilations, Levitski kept an eye out for police patrols. Levitski was also responsible for the letters signed 'Jack the Ripper' sent to the police and the press.

It was in fact the Ochrana, the Russian Secret Police, which had sent Pedachenko to London, because of a certain rivalry with the British Police. On the instructions of the Ministry of the Interior the Ochrana eventually spirited Pedachenko back to Russia. He arrived in Ostend under the name of Count Luiskovo and was escorted to Moscow by a secret agent. Soon afterwards he was caught attempting to murder a woman and was confined to a mental home where he died in 1908. His accomplices had in the meantime entered Russia where it was thought convenient to exile them to Yakutsk. Le Queux explained that he was disclosing these facts at this time – although presumably he had had the relevant papers since 1917 – because he had only now learnt that the homicidal maniac from Tver really existed.

Can one truly believe Le Queux's assertions? Had the confidant of sultans, kings, ministers and generals, the amateur spy who had unmasked so many enemy agents and the well-informed author who had revealed so many secrets truly ascertained the identity of the Ripper? As soon as *Things I Know* was published, the *Star* dismissed his assertions as pure fabrication. It pointed out that Johann Nideroest was in reality German-Swiss, not Russian, and that far from being a cunning spy he was a totally unreliable fraud. Colin Wilson, who met Rasputin's daughter, Maria, has observed that Rasputin had no interest whatsoever in Russian criminals, that he did not know a word of French and that, to boot, he lived in a flat in the fourth floor of a house with no cellar. Le Queux's record, moreover, might lead one to discard his story out of hand, as one would his revelations about the Kaiser's spies or Rasputin's agents. Still, Pedachenko's tale was picked up by Donald McCormick, who elaborated on it in *The Identity of Jack the Ripper*. But that is, as they say, another story.

Footnotes

1. The 'imaginary war' genre had a long tradition in Britain and other countries. For a comprehensive treatment of the subject, see Newman, Kim, *Apocalypse Movies*.
2. It is worth noting that at the same time Commander Driant of the French Army, writing under the pseudonym of Capitaine Danrit, published *La Guerre Fatale*, which dealt with the military defeat of Britain by a Franco-Russian alliance.
3. Le Queux, William, *Things I know About Kings, Celebrities and Crooks*.
4. Le Queux, William, *op. cit.*
5 . In Sladen, N. St Barbe, *The Real Le Queux: The Official Biography of William Le Queux*.
6. See Chesterton, Gilbert Keith, *Charles Dickens*.

Select sources

Andrew, Christopher, *Her Majesty's Secret Service: The Making of the British Intelligence Community*
Bourdier, Jean, *Histoire du Roman Policier*
Massie, Richard K., *Dreadnought: Britain, Germany and the Coming of World War I*
Sladen, N. St Barbe, *The Real Le Queux: The Official Biography of William Le Queux*
  Sutherland, John, *Longman Companion to Victorian Fiction*
Symons, Julian, *Bloody Murder*
Watson, Colin, *Snobbery with Violence*
Wilson, Colin, *Rasputin and the Fall of the Romanovs*

Sources for Le Queux's Ripper tale include works by Paul Begg, Martin Fido, Melvin Harris, Donald McCormick, Donald Rumbelow and Keith Skinner.

This essay appeared in *Ripperologist* magazine No. 46, May 2003.

6. COMMENT

Jack the Redeemer

Robin Odell

DURING ITS MORE THAN TEN YEARS of existence, *Ripperologist* has evolved from a modest magazine dealing with the Jack the Ripper murders into a respected journal embracing East End and Victorian studies. For a decade, its contributors have illumined many dark corners of the East End, lifted the veil from many shadowy figures and added to the knowledge of events occurring over more than a century of social turmoil and change.

Consequently, we have come to know a great deal about a great many people, some involved pivotally, others, peripherally, with the Whitechapel murders. Research over the last thirty years has added immeasurably to our stock of knowledge about Whitechapel and the people who were Jack the Ripper`s contemporaries. But, at the heart of this web of knowledge lies a vacuum – simply not knowing who Jack the Ripper was. In one way, it no longer matters. It is not as if knowing his identity will deliver justice to his victims. Knowing would serve curiosity and solve a mystery. In any case, the likelihood of an identity being found for the murderer that bears the incontrovertible stamp of certainty, is low. Of course, new theories will continue to evolve and add their contribution to the literary barnacles which cling to the essential mystery.

Study of the subject has acquired a life of its own and much of the output is rightly appreciated for what it contributes to our understanding of the social times and culture of London in the 1880s. Following my initial interest in the murders, more than forty years ago, I was impressed by the surge of social reform which followed in the wake of the murders. It seemed as if nature had decided to compensate for the horror of that autumn in 1888 by initiating changes that would lead to improvements in the social conditions of the Ripper's East End killing fields. In a sense, that is the murderer's real legacy.

'Outcast London'

Social reformers were already at work in the East End long before the murders made their searing impact and, by 1887, over a hundred missionary agents were working there. Apart from the distribution of charity to relieve poverty, those concerned about social conditions attempted to give a voice to the poor by writing books and articles describing their plight. These were well-intentioned attempts to stir the consciences of the privileged classes. For the most part, though, these pleas fell on deaf ears. Why should well-heeled, well-fed managers of the successful Victorian economy worry about the welfare of those who provided them with cheap labour?

An anonymous pamphlet published in 1883 with the title *The Bitter Cry of Outcast London* provided a kind of banner under which reformers could group their forces. The author wrote of tens of thousands 'crowded together amidst horrors which call to mind what we have heard of the middle passage of the slave ship.' 'Outcast London' was a theme taken up by George Sale Reaney, subsequently echoed by others, to which he added a note of menace that might create anxiety. He wrote of people living in conditions in which 'a squire would not kennel his dogs' and suggested that 'Tomorrow they may grasp with their terrible might those strong columns upon which we have based and built prosperity and freedom. Who knows what impulse may seize them, these

171

inarticulate thousands and millions when once they feel their power?'

Greater East London extended from the City boundary at Aldgate to Hackney and included the boroughs of Mile End, Poplar and Bethnal Green, stretching down to the London Docks waterfront. At its heart lay the parishes of Whitechapel, Spitalfields and St George's-in-the-East. Running through it, linking the City to the eastern counties, were the arterial routes furnished by Whitechapel and Commercial Roads. Whitechapel Road was a broad highway which inspired the historian and novelist, Sir Walter Besant, to call it 'the noblest thoroughfare in the world.' In the 1880s, the population of this area was over two million, greater than the numbers living at the time in St Petersburg, Berlin or Philadelphia.

Behind this noble thoroughfare lay dark, crumbling streets and alleyways with inter-connecting courts and passages. Row upon row of rotten, shabby houses provided mean shelter for people who lived in poverty, dirt and degradation. This was a human scrap heap in which 40 per cent of the population lived in conditions officially described as a state of poverty. The extent of overcrowding was such that it was possible to make a distinction between the 'poor,' that is 'people living under a struggle to obtain the necessaries of life' and the 'very poor,' who were in 'a state of chronic want.' A weekly census of paupers in London, reported in October 1888, put the total at over 92,000.

With such a high population, overcrowding existed on an epic scale. In parts of Spitalfields, the density was 286 people per acre. Whole streets of tenement properties were run as common lodging houses, often by the most unscrupulous landlords. Single, two-up and two-down houses in Dorset Street housed fifty or sixty people. Defective water supplies, lack of washing facilities and inadequate sanitation added to the misery and made the area prone to disease and epidemics which periodically swept away the weak and infirm.

Dominant features of the East End were the great markets; vegetables at Spitalfields, fish at Billingsgate and meat at Aldgate. And the Empire's trade came and went at the London Docks. Aldgate was popularly known as 'Butchers' Row' or 'Blood Alley' and at peak times animals were slaughtered in the streets.

According to the London Post Office Directory of the time, over five hundred men were employed as slaughterers, butchers or meat vendors in East London, any one of whom might have been Jack the Ripper. Most of the capital city's unsavoury features seemed to be located in the East End and especially abhorrent was the infamous dust-hole in Wentworth Street where, all day long, uncovered carts carrying the fly-blown rubbish produced in the great metropolis was ground down by heavy machinery. This foul work emitted continuous noise and coated everything in the vicinity with a covering of grime and filth.

The people themselves could be divided into two groups – those who made a living out of honest toil and those who did not. Honest men and woman carried the millstone of the sweating system around their necks. The simple fact being that there were far more people than jobs. As a result, honest people seeking employment were prey to a system which forced them to accept the lowest wages and endure slave-like conditions. The alternatives were starvation, begging or crime.

Men, and very often, women and children too, worked twelve or sixteen hours a day, seven days a week. Under the sweating system, the going rate for female labour making match boxes was two pence farthing a gross. Boot makers earned three to five shillings for making six pairs of boots but at least the sweat shop owner provided the leather. As long as work was available, toil continued until the human frame simply broke down under the strain. Men were often burnt out wrecks at the age of forty.

On an average day in the 1880s, some 20,000 men would be out of work in London. The unemployed queued daily outside the gates at London Docks in their hundreds in the hope of being taken on for a day's labour. A prospective docker could earn three shillings and six pence a day if he was fortunate enough to be among the twenty or so able-bodied men taken on each day. The destitute could look to the state to meet their basic needs for food and shelter. Anyone in sufficient want could apply for Poor Law Relief. The reality was that food and accommodation were provided in a manner calculated to discourage the needy from returning. The real penalty was that the wretched relief on offer was not free. Paupers were expected to work for their supper. Women were called on to dismantle the ropes from old ships and men were expected to break half a ton of stone; tasks normally reserved as punishment for the inmates of Her Majesty's prisons.

Despite their daily hardships, the people of the East End were renowned for their good humour and they found ways to relieve the sweat, toil and tears. They let off steam in the public houses and gin palaces when they had money to spend or visited the music halls for laughter, music and entertainment. The Peoples' Palace at Mile End road was a popular venue where Walter Sickert, an *habitué* of such entertainments and a putative Jack the Ripper, probably rubbed shoulders with the locals.

Spiritual privileges
Some Victorians recognized that the East End was a blot on the capital of the Empire. They contributed modestly to their church collections in the fashionable West End, satisfying their moral qualms about doing something to alleviate the distress on the other side of the city. A few made it their personal mission to work among the poor and they helped to co-ordinate the efforts being made to ameliorate some of the worst aspects of social degradation. On the other hand, there were the typically pompous out-of-touch pillars of society, such as Canon Wilberforce, who believed that the state of the poor was 'better than they have deserved at the hands of God.' From the comfort of his drawing room he felt moved to suggest that the existing social order combined 'the greatest measure of temporal comforts and spiritual privileges.'

As the penalty for being honest was the prospect of an early grave, it was small wonder that many East Enders lived on their wits and took to crime as a way of life. In the 1880s, the East End was a refuge for all the criminal elements of London and for many of those who migrated from the great cities of Europe. There were large numbers of Poles, Russians and Germans, many of whom sought asylum from political discrimination in their own countries. This was especially true for Jews fleeing the pogroms of eastern Europe. The laws governing the admission of immigrants to England were lax and, once inside the country, the one-time refugees set up clubs, businesses, brothels and criminal rackets as they pleased without license or proper authority. The East End was a place where an individual could lose his identity, take on another persona and remain beyond the reach of the law. The careers of Severin Klosowski, Michael Ostrog, Alexander Pedachenko and Aaron Kosminski, all Ripper suspects at one time or another, illustrate the point.

Compared with modern standards, most crime was petty in nature. Apart from the street gangs and the activities of the anarchists, there was little organized crime. People took to small-scale crime simply to make a living. Thieving was popular and boys as young as ten or twelve were often committed burglars. Robbery, sneak-thieving, forgery, rent-dodging and begging brought out the full range of human wit and ingenuity. The Bishop of Wakefield, who published a report on prevailing social conditions in 1888, was told by one of his missionaries that of a hundred dock labourers, only about twenty were honest. This kind of thinking fostered the notion of 'The London Savage' and a professional criminal class on whom good works would be wasted.

In the economy of the impoverished, prostitution was an inevitable occupation. The East End was home to both prostitutes and brothels in uncontrollable numbers. As many as 80,000 prostitutes of all types plied their trade in London and, of these, 1,200 worked in Whitechapel alone. Dorset Street, the manor patrolled by Annie Chapman, Mary Kelly and many of their colleagues, was described as 'one vast brothel' and the street had a fearsome reputation. It was known as 'the do as you please' and although policemen always patrolled in pairs, they were often physically as well as verbally abused. The inadequacy of the police at the time of the Ripper murders was a subject that was constantly aired in the correspondence pages of the newspapers of the day. The Metropolitan Police area covered 440,891 acres of London (approximately 688 square miles) and the total distance of the beats patrolled amounted to 7,916 miles. In December 1887, the strength of the Metropolitan Police stood at 14,081 men of all ranks, of which 8,773 were available for street patrols.

Such was the state of deprivation in the East End that many

women were forced onto the streets in order to earn the four pence needed nightly for a bed in a common lodging house. Indeed, so great was their wretchedness that children were turned into the streets at night so that their mothers could use the accommodation to entertain clients. These young outcasts found shelter where they could and in the early 1880s Dr Thomas Barnardo recorded a visit he made with the Earl of Shaftesbury, another of the great reformers, to the London Docks where they counted over seventy boys around the age of fourteen sleeping under tarpaulins in Lower Thames Street.

Barbarians at the gate

The East End was truly a forgotten corner of the Empire. Many who knew of the evils which persisted there and blighted the lives of the people, smugly glossed over them. A correspondent in one of the weekly journals of the time wrote about the joys of living in the East End. 'For four pence a night,' went the narrative, 'one could sleep as soundly as in the grandest hotel. The dreams that visit poor weary people . . . may be as bright and sweet as those of happy youth in a rural home where the morning sunlight when it enters the cottage window is accompanied by the twittering of birds . . .' and so on. The hypocrisy and ignorance that prevailed in Victorian society was breathtaking.

The facts were that the East End was a dark, smelly, over-populated district whose inhabitants were forced to endure the meanest living conditions. Plans to introduce these under-privileged citizens to the benefits of education and religion were favourite topics in the fashionable salons of the West End. One campaigner for universal education wrote, it would 'greatly tend to their happiness and good if . . . it enables them better to appreciate the benefits of thrift and contented industry . . .' Some of the talk was well-intentioned but there were also anxious stirrings at the thought of barbarians at the gate, hinted at earlier in George Reaney's *Outcast London*. The fear was that hordes of deprived citizens in the East End might rise up from their slums and invade the comfort zones of Victorian gentility.

Social reformers had been at work in the East End since the mid-

1870s, preaching goodness and charity. One of these was Reverend Samuel Barnett, whose Bishop when he appointed him to the living at St Jude's Whitechapel, said, 'This is the worst parish in my diocese, inhabited mainly by a criminal population and, I fear, much corrupted by doles.' Only twenty-eight years old at the time, Barnett set about improving the social conditions of his parishioners with great vigour. He started adult education classes, founded a penny bank and a maternity society and, in due course, established Toynbee Hall, the University Settlement, in the heart of Spitalfields, which continues its work today.

The Earl of Shaftesbury, Dr Thomas Barnardo, Beatrice and Sidney Webb, George Bernard Shaw, General William Booth and others began to probe the nation's conscience and its purse regarding the needs of the East End. But the needs were so immense that the social missions were swamped by the demands made on them and the government's response seemed to be limited to Prime Minister Gladstone's personal efforts to reclaim prostitutes from the streets. Picking up the theme of *Outcast London*, W. T. Stead, editor of the *Pall Mall Gazette*, asked 'Where is the leader of men who will preach a new crusade against the crying evil of our times?'

Murderous redeemer

As if in answer to this clarion call, a redeemer appeared on the scene. He did not wear the cloak of the reforming idealist but, rather, the mantle of the murderer. Jack the Ripper succeeded in focusing the eyes of the world on the East End of London in a way that no honest man could. The spectacular butchery which he visited on Whitechapel and Spitalfields lifted the curtain of pretence which Victorian society had draped over this forgotten corner of England.

George Bernard Shaw was quick to seize the moment with a letter entitled 'Blood Money for Whitechapel' published in the *Star* on 24 September 1888. He pulled no punches, famously noting that if the habits of duchesses allowed them to be lured into Whitechapel, 'a single experiment in slaughterhouse anatomy on an aristocratic victim might fetch in a round half million and save the necessity of sacrificing four women of the people.' He railed against a system which first robbed and then pauperized the poor by way of compensation, allowing the rich to 'combine the luxury of the protected thief with the unctious self-satisfaction of the pious philanthropist.' Reverend Samuel Barnett had earlier picked up a similar theme but in more genteel language. Writing in *The Times* on 19 September 1888, he suggested the Whitechapel murders would not be in vain if 'the public conscience awakes to consider the life which these horrors reveal.' And all this happened before the Ripper really got into his stride with his 'double event' and grand finale at Millers Court.

Naturally, Jack the Ripper was no more a social worker for the East End than he was a literary agent for those who came to write about his crimes. But both phenomena were evident after his three-month reign of terror in 1888. At the end of the Lord Mayor's Show on 9 November, while doctors were still examining the brutally dissected remains of Mary Kelly, the citizens of the East End were entertained to a Meat Tea provided by the generosity of the Lord Mayor. Three thousand people crowded into the Great Assembly Hall at Mile End Road and, who knows, Jack the Ripper, his work completed, may have been among them. Each person tucked into half a pound of bread and butter, half a pound of cake, a large pork pie and a quart of tea.

The feast was rounded off with a magic lantern show and a concert performed by the Crusaders Temperance Brass Band. When the feasting was over, the recipients of the Lord Mayor's generosity returned to their lodging houses and sweat shops to work or sleep. Such corporate generosity was symbolic of the attitude to the problems of London's poor. No one bothered to count the cost of a few pork pies if it helped to keep the masses down and glossed over the rottenness of life in the slums.

Rights restored

But the tide was beginning to turn. The Whitechapel murders had seen to that. The spotlight that the Ripper threw on the East End pierced the gloom of this shadowland and laid bare the grim-realities of human existence there. The scales fell from the eyes of decent people who had been unaware of the scale of degradation that lay so close to their own world of privilege. Those in positions of authority who knew only too well were forced to acknowledge that something had to be done.

Possibly the single greatest measurable result was that Dr Barnardo collected close to three million pounds from conscience-stricken Victorians. The cry of 'Outcast London' was being taken up everywhere and the *Daily Telegraph* reported that 'Dark Annie (Annie Chapman) will effect in one way what fifty secretaries of state could never accomplish – focusing attention on East End conditions.'

One of the most urgent needs was that of housing. Samuel Barnett's aim was to rebuild the whole of what he called the 'bad quarter.' For the immediate task of demolishing some of the worst slums in Flower and Dean Street and replacing them with model dwellings, he needed nearly a quarter of a million pounds. In his innocent way, Barnett thought the path would be open for wealthy men of goodwill to come forward and buy up the bad properties in order to banish the festering evils they nurtured. Developers did indeed come forward but they were not so philanthropic as to be content with merely clearing away the slums – they wanted a profit as well.

Prospective financiers argued about the dividends they might expect to gain by buying up slum properties. Their thinking was that such investments would be sounder than English railway securities or Russian bonds. The landlords themselves cashed in demanding absurdly high prices for their crumbling properties. Many were able to retire to comfortable houses in the country on the proceeds of their deals. The Socialist League, in a direct reference to the Ripper murders, spoke out against the exploitation that was rife and referred to 'the opening for profit made literally with the murderer's knife.'

Despite the profiteering, improvements did come about once the extent of neglect in the East End was fully exposed. The indefatigable Barnett set up a building society to help the East Enders acquire accommodation in the new six-storey tenements being built in Flower and Dean, Thrawl and Wentworth Streets to replace houses that had been condemned fifteen years previously.

The authors of *The Survey of London* had no doubt that many of the social improvements which came about at the end of the nineteenth century were largely due to the social backlash created by the Ripper murders. Their assessment was that 'The Whitechapel murders undoubtedly gave a further impetus towards rebuilding . . .' Perhaps encouraged by the turn of the social tide in their favour, many East Enders decided to help their own cause. The Great Dock Strike of 1889 lasted a month and cost the nation an estimated two million pounds and a Women's Trade Union Association was set up when the Match Girls went on strike demanding proper working conditions.

Samuel Barnett continued in the thick of the fight to win social reform and he called for properly-based social research as the best means of assessing needs. He was a great humanitarian who deservedly won the affection of the East Enders who called him the 'Saint of Whitechapel.' He wielded considerable influence and during the scarlet fever and diphtheria epidemics in 1896, the Secretary of the Water Board asked him to use his authority to calm the families distressed by the suffering of their children. Barnett succeeded in calming people's fears and, in return, extracted a promise from the Water Board that piped supplies would be available in the area for six hours a day.

Each battle won added momentum to the campaign for social reform and the government at last began to play its part too. The House of Lords debated the unfairness of sweated labour and the House of Commons reviewed the system of poor law relief and the question of foreign immigration, all matters of great importance to the redevelopment of the East End. Legislation was enacted to register lodging houses and juvenile courts were set up to deal with young offenders. Toynbee Hall established a Poor Man's Lawyer Movement and a Tenants' Protection Committee kept a watchful eye open for unscrupulous landlords.

The right of the people of the East End to live their lives in dignity and to be part of the social structure of their own nation was achieved through their gritty determination and the vision of those who took up their cause. The triumph over the dark oppressive forces of inhumanity owed much to exceptional individuals like the Barnetts, Webbs, Shaftesbury, Shaw and Barnardo and they overcame the smug complacency of Victorian England. No longer would it be possible for a peer of the realm to declare that poverty-stricken East Enders should be despatched to the colonies.

This triumph also owed much to an anonymous benefactor, a creature of the shadows, whose name and actions were synonymous with horror and evil. In a strange way, by shocking the nation with his brutal knife-work, Jack the Ripper rocked the social fabric to its core and inspired a sense of humanity that restored rights and justice to the oppressed people of London's East End.

This essay appeared in *Ripperologist* magazine No. 56, November 2004.

Why We Will Never Forget Jack the Ripper

Anne Perry

LONDON HAS BEEN, in its time, the largest city in the world. It is well over two thousand years old, and has stood at the heart of an empire that spanned the globe. Of all the blood that has been shed, the violence and the secrecy, the rise and fall of dynasties, five murders in the autumn of 1888 have cut more deeply into the memory of horror than any others.

The first was on 31 August, when Mary Ann Nichols was found with her throat cut. The second was Annie Chapman, hideously mutilated on 8 September. On the 30 September, two women were killed: Elizabeth Stride, known as Liz, and Catherine Eddowes. Eddowes was also fearfully slashed, almost beyond recognition. The last, and most terribly torn open and ritually disembowelled, was Mary Jane Kelly, on 9 November.

The perpetrator was never caught, and has passed into history by the name he gave himself – Jack the Ripper.

Why has he not sunk into the grim footnotes of history along with all the myriad other ghastly, unsolved crimes, but remained a century later to bring a unique chill to the blood? He cast such a pall of terror over London then that the Whitechapel murders were the only subject the music hall comedians would not joke about. At mention of him the silence was utter and complete. Joke about any other icon or affliction of mankind you care to name – but not the Whitechapel murderer!

He had assumed the gigantic proportion of myth even in his own time, and the years have not lessened this. Why? Because he struck out of the darkness of narrow streets, gas-lit, wreathed in fog, cobbles echoing with the clip of horses' hooves, hansom cabs looming out of the darkness? The hint of a doomed romance, a royal connection, secrets that might or might not penetrate right to the heart of power, corruption to hide all truth about it, an insane surgeon who put his skills to the devil's service? A man who was sane by daylight, a healer of the sick, and by night a sadist so terrible, covered in human blood, that the very mention of his name paralyzed all thought and sense.

Was it at least in part because he was never caught that he became a symbol of the ultimate horror? He robbed not only life, but the features of the face which make a woman recognizable to others, are part of her identity, and of her womb and entrails which make of her a woman? In the darkness of his anonymity he is everyone, and no one. He has no face. That he walks in some kind of hell, by his own admission in his letters, makes him more terrible, not less.

To give him an ordinary name, a past, a motive, would be to reduce him to humanity, and he has become in our minds something other than that. He is the insane spirit of unquenchable hatred towards not just women, but womanhood. I do not wish to know who he was. He is legend – I say 'is,' because an essence of what we believe of him lives on. Perhaps as we need secrets, we also need devils: people we invest with a mantle beyond humanity, good or evil. Jack is one such person. He has new incarnations in story after story, many of them extraordinarily powerful. His name has so much emotion attached to it that the single word, said rightly, conjures up a world of horror no one else has equalled. He is a black shadow in our folklore, and perhaps art needs darkness as well as light to have the power to move us.

His acts can never, in any light at all, have been good, but perhaps we can use them to learn more of ourselves and our nature, and the understanding of good and evil which are part of us. The fact that we do not forget surely means that it echoes a reality that is woven into our dreams, our nightmares, and so our beliefs of life.

This essay appeared in *Ripperologist* magazine No. 50, November 2003.

7. ANALYSIS

Responses to the Ripper Murders:
Letters to Old Jewry

L. Perry Curtis Jr.

L IKE ANY SENSATIONAL CRIME featured day after day in the mass media the Whitechapel murders provoked a huge response from the public in the form of hundreds of letters addressed to the editors of London's newspapers during 1888–89. In this way Victorians of diverse occupations and disparate education shared their thoughts or fantasies about the perpetrator with their fellow readers. But thousands of others preferred a more private route by writing to the police – both at Scotland Yard and district stations in the City and East End. As William Fishman has observed about the fallout from the murders, 'the weirdos, the eccentrics, the perverts and the inadequates had a field day.'[1] Needless to say, some of these characters identified so strongly with Jack the Ripper that they wrote gloating or taunting letters over that name boasting of more murders to come.

The beautifully produced and carefully compiled book by Stewart P. Evans and Keith Skinner, *Jack the Ripper: Letters From Hell* (2001), provides ample evidence of the macabre fantasies that the mutilation-murders unleashed in obscure misogynists with a penchant for sadism or a compulsion to confess.

All this Ripper mail – whether designed for public or private consumption – constitutes a valuable source of information about the concerns, if not obsessions, of contemporaries at home and abroad. Many letters were addressed to either the Lord Mayor, Sir Polydore de Keyser, or Colonel Sir James Fraser (1814–92), Commissioner of the City of London police, headquartered at 26 Old Jewry. An able commander, Fraser was on the verge of retirement when the Ripper struck. Almost a century later the sterling efforts of Donald Rumbelow resulted in the preservation of more than three hundred of these letters in the Corporation of London Record Office at Guildhall.[2] This mail affords some fascinating, if fleeting, insights into contemporary attitudes towards the sensation-horrors taking place in a part of London notorious for poverty, prostitution, crime, overcrowding, and foreign immigration. This essay constitutes a rough and ready content analysis of the surviving letters sent to Old Jewry during that season of mounting horror.

Compared with the letters to the editor published in the press, the police mail was more spontaneous, candid, eccentric, and at times a good deal cruder. Excluding the cohort of Ripper wannabes, at least half a dozen of the letters sent to Colonel Fraser reveal something about their authors' sexual fantasies. Although the vast majority wanted to see the Whitechapel 'fiend' brought to justice, a handful seemed more concerned with securing the reward money destined for anyone with information leading to the arrest and conviction of the killer.

Although the class and status of these correspondents cannot be accurately gauged by handwriting, style and spelling alone, the latter variables suggest that most belonged to the middle- and lower-middle class. Only a dozen or so writers actually admitted their working-class origins but the style of a dozen other letters smacked of a similar provenance.

Excluding the ten or so decipherable letters in this batch signed by self-styled Jacks, my sample of the Old Jewry mail contains some 320 legible letters written by some 271 people. Only 16 per cent of these writers were anonymous or used such epithets as 'Common Sense,' 'Qui Vive,' 'Nemesis,' or 'Scotus.' By way of contrast,

37 per cent of those in our newspaper sample relied on pseudonyms.[3] No doubt the promise of confidentiality as well as the lure of reward money spurred more of the police correspondents to reveal their identity and address. As for the number of self-proclaimed women writers, the figure of 8.5 per cent came very close to that in the newspaper sample (9 per cent). Concerning residence or point of origin, almost half of the 244 letters bearing an address came from Greater London – defined here as the area within a twelve-mile radius centred on St Paul's. (The comparable figure for the published mail was 68 per cent.) Slightly over a third of this mail originated in the English provinces, mostly the southern counties, while Scotland, Ireland, and Wales yielded eleven, four, and one letters respectively. Eleven came from the United States (several penned by English expatriates), eight from Europe (two being English residents) and three from Australia. No letters emanated from Africa, Asia, India or Latin America.

Just like the newspaper mail the favourite topics of the Old Jewry correspondents were methods of detection and suspects. Thus suspects were mentioned in 143 letters, advice about how to catch the killer in 159, and eighteen dealt with both subjects – making a total of 320 letters. In marked contrast to the newspaper mail, which contained many complaints about the state of lawlessness in London, hardly any of these Old Jewry correspondents had the temerity to accuse the authorities of bungling the investigation. However one might construe all the advice about how to catch the perpetrator as a form of indirect criticism. One or two writers did blame the crimes on metropolitan vice. Thus Susan Fraser, the wife of an Indian civil servant, lamented the rampant immorality of London. She had brought her children home from India to escape all the 'impure' influences there only to find that 'impurity' had triumphed in 'so-called Christian England.' Appalled by these vicious murders, she wondered why 'the women of England do not rise in a body to appeal against such violence being done to any woman however much despised she may be' (2 October).[4]

Suspects and motives

Of the more than 150 suspects nominated in the Old Jewry mail, 101 were English or British subjects, twenty-one were European (including five Jewish immigrants), six were American, three were East Indian, and two were Malay. Among the nationalities or ethnicities receiving at least one mention were a black and a white South African, an Irishman, and an Irish-American. As for occupation, by far the most popular choice – amounting to 46 per cent – was a doctor or surgeon. Other candidates included a religious maniac (thirteen mentions), a butcher (nine), a man disguised as a woman (seven), a night-watchman (six), a woman (six), a policeman (five), a victim of venereal disease (four), a professional man (two), a flasher (two), and a man disguised as a constable (two). One respectable widow from Upper Clapton, reported seeing a 'disgusting' man exposing himself in Devonshire Street and hoped that he would repent 'when in the agony of his own Death' he sought forgiveness from 'Jesus sweet Jesus – Amen' (8 October). Of the twenty-three acknowledged female writers, fourteen chose to deal with suspects and the moral implications of the crimes rather than modes of detection. Not surprisingly, only one of these women thought that the Ripper might be one of her own sex.

Under the heading of human vivisection several correspondents echoed Coroner Wynne E. Baxter's theory by speculating that a fanatic pathologist or surgeon was cutting up women in order to study their genitalia, especially the uterus. Thus an imaginative major in the Royal Fusiliers, Charles Latham, opined that a well-to-do medical student was experimenting with female genitalia in a state of sexual arousal. In loving detail he explained how the killer had grown 'mad enough' – although sane in all other respects – to procure the desired organ 'under a condition of activity and excitement.' With knife in hand along with a bottle of spirits and a damp sponge he would stalk his victim and take her to a dark spot for 'an immoral purpose.' After cutting her throat while 'actually having connection,' he would rip open her stomach, remove the womb, and place it in the bottle so that he could study it in his secret laboratory in Whitechapel (3 October). Although bereft of a motive, Mr I. Tullidge, who owned a London carpet steam-cleaning firm, argued

that the murderer cut the throat of his victim while 'having connection from behind, instead of the natural way.' He urged the police to
question prostitutes about any encounters with men interested in anal
intercourse and recommended the use of East End unfortunates as
'dupes to bring the monster to justice' (2 October).

At least four male writers insisted that the murders were inspired
by revenge against prostitutes for spreading venereal disease.
'Scotus' paraded his medical knowledge by reckoning that the killer
had been 'badly disfigured' by phagedaena, an ulcerative disease,
that might have destroyed his 'privy member.' Here then was the
motive for these crimes. He advised the police to check every
hospital that had recently treated patients for any such disorder (4
October). 'A Thinker' believed that desire for 'morbid revenge and
retaliation for a severe dose of venerial [sic]' lay behind these crimes.
He imagined a scenario wherein the killer would approach his
victim, discuss the price for her services, fondle her from behind, and
pretend to unbutton his trousers. At that point he would pull out a
knife and cut her throat from left to right (3 September). A man from
Thanet College, Margate, Kent, informed Colonel Fraser that the
culprit suffered from softening of the brain caused by consorting
with diseased prostitutes. Acting on 'the vile superstition of the
Chinese and Malays,' he was slaying these women in order to make
a uterine poultice that would 'suck off the virus from his ulcers'
(13 November). Robert Owen, an American from Milldale in
Tuscaloosa county, Alabama, proposed that intimacy with
prostitutes had ruined the mind and body of the murderer, who had
once been a respectable man despite his assumption that the world
was made for his pleasure. 'Reduced to desperation and frenzy by
disease,' he was now running 'a muck [sic]' against the class he held
responsible for his downfall (27 September).

At least one educated writer attributed the Whitechapel horrors to
socialism rather than syphilis. T. J. Nettleship of Oxford Street
speculated that the killer might be one of 'the socialist pedagogues
who hoist the red flag in Hyde Park'. And if this was not the case, then
they knew his identity and were protecting him for political reasons.
After all, he had recently heard one of these demagogues (one
wonders if this could have been G. B. Shaw or H. M. Hyndman)

exclaiming: 'Wait till we get a few murders done up here at the West End, and then you'll see what a howl there'll be' (2 October). Dr P. J. M., a misogynistic American army surgeon, who had run a military hospital in Europe, could not decide if the killer was a man or a woman. But he told the police to be on the lookout for someone dressed as a woman and to keep every 'suspicious' woman under surveillance. And if this 'devilish' criminal did turn out to be a woman, then she had probably lost her lover or husband because he was 'an excessive, lascivious man.' And he did not have to tell the Lord Mayor 'what such a "Fury" is able to do' if only because 'the D_ _ _ _ may know what is often in such a petticoat !!!!'

Relying on his statistical skills, a calculating officer in the London Customs House, E. K. Larkins, compiled a long memorandum filled with data concerning the arrivals and departures of cattle boats along the Thames. Correlating these with the times of each murder, he narrowed the choice down to two vessels and concluded that the killer was a middle-aged Portuguese cattleman who accompanied livestock shipments from Oporto to London (11 January 1889). Along the same lines, the xenophobic Frederick Charles Friend from Peckham suspected a Spanish or Italian sailor on board a vessel plying between the port of London and the continent. This boat arrived at the end of each month and left on the 9th of the next. The 'free use of the knife' as well as the vengeful nature of the attacks clearly pointed to a southern European culprit (3 October and 9 November).

On the other hand several writers preferred Asian or Jewish Jacks. Thus William Gow of Alyth, Perthshire, blamed the murders on a gang of Indian hill tribesmen, who believed in the magical power of the 'generative organs' which they wore as amulets (3 and 9 October). Mary Kidgell, an English teacher living in Turin, Italy, considered the mutilations so precise and neat as to be the handiwork of a 'votary of the Buddhist faith' or maybe a Brahmin 'thug' bent on human sacrifice to 'their deity.' Because such people were 'adept in the bloody rites of an abominable worship' she wanted the police to search every Indian temple in London for evidence of human sacrifice (29 November). John Binny of Tavistock Place, London, cast Jack as a seafaring Malay cook, called 'Alaska', who knew how to butcher animals. Presumably, he had declared war on prostitutes because one of them had robbed him. Since no 'Britisher or American, however depraved, could act so like a fiend of hell,' the killer had to be one of those Malays who were 'well-known to be fiendish in their revenge' (6 October).

As for the small anti-Semitic contingent, by far the fiercest bigot was W. J. Smith of Red Lion Passage, Holborn, who blamed the murders on the influx of 'foreigners' from Eastern Europe. Not only had the Jews taken jobs away from Englishmen but they were also spouting socialist or communist slogans and trampling on the rights of native-born citizens. If this trend continued, there would soon be no English people left and unless the government kicked these undesirables into the sea, 'the City is doomed to destruction.' Smith's tirade did not stop there. He called for ethnic cleansing by arson, in short a holocaust, by setting hundreds of fires in the East End, 'at a given signal – say the sending up of a Balloon that could be seen all over London' (9 October).

The long list of suspects in this mail ran the gamut from a flasher who had exposed himself to several women in the West End to an 'Electro-Biologist,' who mesmerized his victims before killing them. In between these extremes were medical men, butchers or slaughtermen, one or two plebeian Irishmen, and Police Constable Edward Watkins, who had found Eddowes's body in Mitre Square. The prime candidate of one anonymous writer ('M. P.') was Richard Mansfield, the Anglo-American star of the spectacular *Dr Jekyll and Mr Hyde* production at the Lyceum. After all Mansfield was capable of working himself into such a 'dretefull manor' in order to become Hyde and he did not perform on Saturday nights when most of the murders took place (5 October). As for other celebrities, Charles Stewart Parnell received at least one nomination (2 November); and C. J. Denny from Farnborough pointed an accusing finger at L. Forbes Winslow, the vainglorious alienist and asylum operator, because his recent letter to the Globe showed signs of 'incipient insanity' (3 October). Alex de Borra, a doctor from Elsinore, near Riverside, California, thought that Jack was a mad physician who killed female patients in his office and then disposed of them 'at leisure' (12 September).

The most bizarre suspect of all was not a man but an ape that had escaped from a 'wild beast show.' So thought Mrs L. Painter of Ryde, Isle of Wight, who must have owed her inspiration to Poe's razor-wielding Orang-Utan in the *Murders in the Rue Morgue*. She explained how this powerful and agile creature escaped at night, removed a knife hidden in a nearby tree, and then killed his victims silently before returning dutifully to his cage. At this point, however, Mrs Painter shifted her ground. She wondered if the murderer might be a 'mad woman.' But in the end she opted for the ape theory because this beast was so swift, cunning, noiseless, and strong. After denouncing prostitutes, she expressed her hope that the fear provoked by the murders would 'rid our streets of those women who are too often called "unfortunates"' and force them to find an honest living because 'a violent disease requires a violent remedy' (3 October).

Modes of detection

Suggestions by the Old Jewry correspondents for capturing the Ripper ranged from commonsensical to the far side of fanciful. Apart from psychic divination six writers recommended that the police wear noiseless boots or rubber galoshes 'to deaden the sound of their feet'. Ten (including Percy Lindley, the bloodhound breeder and travel writer) advised the use of bloodhounds and two opted for better lighting in Whitechapel. Thirteen writers – mostly men – volunteered to hunt down the killer. And the business manager of the *Financial Times* offered to donate £50 to the reward fund.

By way of contrast with the letters to the editor a higher percentage of the Old Jewry mail (fifty-seven writers in all) urged the police to use human decoys to trap the Ripper. Most thought that these men or women should be disguised as prostitutes and assigned to walk the streets late at night watched over by policemen ready to arrest anyone who threatened them. Of these arm-chair sleuths, thirty-seven recommended that boyish-looking detectives or constables be dressed up to resemble women of the night, while the other twenty preferred to see working-class women from the East End recruited for this dangerous task.

191

Several writers prescribed some kind of body armour in the form of chain mail from chin to thigh concealed beneath lace or velvet collars and dresses in order to ward off a knife attack. Richard Taylor from Long Acre, Clwyd, suggested that the male decoys in drag wear a flexible steel corset and neck-collar. The latter device would be wired to a portable battery powerful enough to administer a severe shock to anyone who grasped their throat (6 October). The even more inventive W. Bryn of Forest Hill, near Lewisham, proposed the construction of mechanical figures resembling prostitutes. Installed in 'dark and lonely' places, these contraptions would contain 'powerful springs' set to release octopus-like arms that would fly out and encircle anyone who raised its chin or squeezed its throat. While grasping its prey in this manner, the robot would emit a loud whistle to alert the police (2 October). A man from Walworth wanted to see police-trained couples strolling around the East End armed with glass syringes filled with a corrosive acid to be sprayed on any suspect, who could then be identified and taken into custody (3 October). William Walton of Kingsley, Cheshire had a simpler idea: the police should give 'unfortunates' pieces of paper smeared with 'Bird Lime.' If attacked, the woman would slap this paper on the back or sleeve of her assailant thereby marking him out for arrest (8 October).

The detective category also included twenty-three letters from self-styled psychics or spiritualists who boasted that they could find the killer by extrasensory means. This mail reflected the fervent belief of so many Victorians in psychical research, the occult, séances, and mesmerism or 'animal magnetism.'[5] Thus several writers claimed that they could track down the Ripper by studying a lock of hair or some other object taken from one of his victims. A respectable woman from Kentish Town with twenty years' experience of 'clairvoyant powers' told Colonel Fraser that she had just visited Old Jewry in the hope of finding something that would connect the Mitre Square victim to herself. In order to 'stop this fearful butchery' she needed to borrow 'one single hair' from Stride or Eddowes or any part of their clothing touched by the killer (3 October).

A devout man from Utica, New York, E. Jay Klinck, shared his vision with the Lord Mayor. After beseeching God to reveal the murderer, he had seen the pale, thin face of a woman standing next to a French or Italian man 'laughing heartily.' This dark-complexioned man had a perfect set of teeth, a full beard and a black moustache with the ends twisted upwards (7 October). A self-proclaimed and importuning psychic from Bedfordshire was responsible for the largest single batch of letters (a dozen in all). Although Jonathan F. Hunt of Biggleswade boasted often about his 'acute mental sensitiveness,' he changed his mind more than once about his prime suspect. However, he never lost sight of the reward money. At the outset he asked for £500 in return for describing the killer as an Italian sculptor or mason. Several letters later he focused on a man suffering from 'recurrent periodical mania . . . much like menstrualation [sic] in females' (3, 6, 8 and 22 October; 13 and 28 November; 7, 8, 24 and 26 December 1888, and 2 January and 4 March 1889). Small wonder that the police dismissed him as a crank. Lastly, a French lady with the patrician name of Cesarine Kestelout de Noyelles of Orbec en Auge, Calvados was convinced that some 'miserable' medical students were stealing and selling female body parts. She urged the police to find the villains by using a hypnotized subject who had communicated with the body of a Ripper victim (26 September). By way of contrast, hardly any of the newspaper correspondents in our sample laid claim to being a psychic or medium capable of identifying the killer.

A courageous young woman from Pentridge told the Lord Mayor shortly after the double event of her plan for capturing the killer. Deeply disturbed by the fate of these 'poor unfortunates,' Lizzie Turncliffe was prepared to 'act the part of a fallen woman' and walk the streets of Whitechapel late at night followed by a detective. If the killer was 'still bent on his fiendish work' and accosted her, she would accompany him to a dark corner whereupon the detective would 'take him red-handed in his crime.' But if the man turned out not to be the culprit, then the detective would save her 'from any other outrage.' Disavowing any interest in reward money, she humbly asked for train fare and living expenses while in London (3 October). Another bold volunteer, John Burke, a working-class youth from New Hartley, Northumberland, wanted to join the CID when he was old enough. He proposed a visit to London to observe how prostitutes plied their trade. He would then dress like a 'street girl' in the hope of luring the killer into his clutches (3 October). George Hammer, a retired London policeman who had emigrated to DeKalb, Indiana and was neither 'precocious youth nor the old crank,' offered to return and join in the hunt for the Ripper (28 November). And a 'stout-hearted' shopkeeper from Hemel Hempstead was willing to pursue 'the clever rouge [sic]' provided the police gave him a new suit of clothes, a pair of rubber-soled shoes, and a thick leather waistcoat for protection.

Five correspondents thought that the police should improve their communications in order to sound the alarm quickly when the murderer struck again. One of these was an expatriate Yorkshireman, J. R. Clark, who had moved to Cleveland, Ohio, where he worked for an electric bell company. His plan involved the laying down of wires in the gutters of Whitechapel equipped with numbered buttons placed at thirty-foot intervals and connected to a large bell-box at police headquarters. When anything suspicious occurred, a detective disguised as a woman would push the nearest button to summon help. Clark's Hibernophobia came to the fore when he declared: 'on no account must you let an irish (sic) Detective peep at it. He must be an Englishman' (19 November). On a more strategic note Harry Green from Canonbury was so worried about the inadequacy of police patrols in the East End that he wanted the German Emperor to lend 'his beloved Royal Grandmother' one thousand 'skilled detectives' from Berlin. And if he complied, then perhaps the Emperor of Russia and the President of France would follow suit and send an equal number of sleuths into the East End (1 October).

Five writers shared the popular belief that the victims's eyes retained an image of their killer's features and pressed the police to photograph their retinas.[6] A German from Bremerhaven, who hankered after the £500 reward, offered some technical advice. To obtain a clear image of the killer the victim's optic nerve should be stimulated electrically and an incandescent lamp placed behind the eye (12 September, 1889). Several graphologists tendered their services to the police. James Gibbins, the resident handwriting expert of the comic weekly, *Ally Sloper's Half Holiday*, was willing to analyze the letter and card sent by Jack to the Central News agency (3 and 12 October). Almost absent from this police mail was the bloodhound lobby that had accounted for almost 20 per cent of the letters to the editor dealing with modes of detection.

If more of the Old Jewry correspondents showed interest in the reward money than did those who wrote to the press, not all of the former were mercenary. For example, one suppliant from the East End craved social, not financial, gain. Rather brazenly – or pathetically – N. A. Benelins revealed his burning desire for an introduction to the rich and famous, including the Lord Mayor and his 'family circle' because this would enable him to 'come in my right sphere' (18 October). For sheer gall or chutzpah, however, no one topped Francis Zysler of Cambridge Heath, London who solicited the Lord Mayor in March 1890 for the reward money because no more Ripper murders had taken place since he had last written to the police almost two years before (15 March, 1890).

The meticulous work of Evans and Skinner makes it unnecessary to delve into the over two hundred letters, cards, and telegrams sent by wannabe Jacks to Scotland Yard (available in the Public Record Office at Kew) and the ten or so letters, cards, and telegrams from 'hoaxers' that survived the winnowing process at Old Jewry. Suffice to say that these demented outpourings antici-pated the response of 'weirdos' or 'kooks' in Germany in 1929 to the arrest and trial of Peter Kurten, 'the monster of Düsseldorf.' In that year the police and the press received some 160 letters from people claiming to be the murderer and mutilator of at least thirty women and children. Most of the 'letters from Hell' written in 1888–9 were filled with crude and barely literate boasts about the murders. Often addressed to 'Dear Boss,' they contained promises of more attacks to come, punctuated by exclamations like 'Ha ! Ha! Ha!' Needless to say, this fantasy-driven mail would make fine grist for the mill of any psychiatrist interested in the psyches of people who relish the vicarious role of serial killer.

In sum, all this Ripper mail – whether reasonable and coherent or the exact opposite – represented the outpourings of people who were profoundly moved in some way or another by the murders. The utterly baffling nature of these crimes and the porosities of the Ripper reportage created a vacuum into which all these correspondents were drawn. Unfortunately, the other side of this mail is missing so we do not know if the authorities ever followed up any of the suggestions made. In any event much the same vacuum persists to this day, exerting a powerful pull on all of us post-Victorians – whether amateur or professional Ripperologists – who are still pursuing the ever-elusive Jack.

Footnotes

1. Fishman, W. J. *East End 1888: Life in a London Borough Among the Labouring Poor*, (London: Duckworth, 1988), p. 216.
2. According to Evans and Skinner, the surviving Old Jewry mail contains 'about 363 communications sent by some 301 correspondents.' *Jack the Ripper – Letters From Hell*, (Stroud, Gloucestershire: Sutton) p. 149. However, the letters that I found there in the early 1990s amounted to 320 – including some ten legible letters and cards signed 'Jack the Ripper' or its equivalent.
3. See Curtis, L. Perry Jr, *Jack the Ripper and the London Press*, (New Haven: Yale University Press, 2001) p. 240.
4. To save space I have omitted the archival references to all the letters cited here, which are deposited in the CLRO, Guildhall, under the heading of Police Box 3.13 to P. B. 3.22. The author will supply individual call numbers upon request. Unless otherwise indicated, all the dates in parentheses refer to 1888.
5. For this largely middle-class fascination with spirits or ghosts, seances, and psychic research, see Oppenheim, Janet, *The Other World – Spiritualism and Psychical Research in England, 1850–1914* (Cambridge: Cambridge University Press, 1985) and Alison Winter, *Mesmerized – Powers of Mind in Victorian Britain* (Chicago: University of Chicago Press, 1998).
6. Two of these writers mentioned that this technique had been used to solve several murders recently in both England and France. But the editor of the *Photographic News* dismissed the notion of retinal imaging as useless. See *Photographic News*, 21 September 1888, p. 608. T. H. Rundle of Camborne, Cornwall, also urged the police to 'treat the eyes of Ripper victims scientifically' (16 October). See also Philip Sugden, *The Complete History of Jack the Ripper* (New York: Carroll & Graf, 1994) pp. 137–8.

This essay appeared in *Ripperologist* magazine No. 40, April 2002.

The Irish Dimension of the Ripper Saga

L. Perry Curtis Jr.

RIPPERPHILES MAY WELL scratch their heads in wonderment at the title of this essay and exclaim with a mixture of scepticism and dismay: 'Well, I always knew there was a Jewish dimension but I have never heard of an Irish one.' Such doubts might seem justified on several counts. After all, no Irishman loomed large in the long list of suspects at the time and hardly any of the leading police and detectives in the case – as distinct from some London journalists – had strong Hibernian connections. Not until the late twentieth century did two Irish suspects surface and in both cases the so-called evidence of their guilt falls into the category of wishful thinking. As an Irish historian, however, I could not resist the temptation to search for the elusive green thread that runs through the East End murders and their aftermath. As we all know, ethnicity and its concomitant customs and loyalties counted heavily at the time and continue to do so no matter how assimilated the non-indigenous inhabitants of the British Isles may have become over the years. In the realm of literary criticism, if not always history, moreover, there are times when the pursuit of silences in the text pays some dividends.

The two most obvious points of Irish interest involve victims and suspects. First and foremost, the last of the five presumed victims, Mary Jane or Jeanette Kelly, seems to have been the only one with overtly Irish antecedents, even though a few Welsh newspapers tried to claim her for one of their own. Despite the

197

dearth of hard evidence there is a consensus that she was born in Limerick around 1863.[1] But was this Limerick town or county? And what circumstances drove her father to leave with his young family and head for Wales? Alas, there are no firm answers. We are told that her father found a job in an ironworks in either Carmarthenshire or Carnarvonshire, where Mary married a coal-miner while still in her teens. After her husband died in a coal-mine explosion, she moved to Cardiff and apparently embarked on a career in the sex industry. Because virtually every book about the murders foregrounds Kelly's spiralling descent from an affluent clientele in the West End to plebeian customers in Whitechapel, there is no need to repeat the few known facts and fictions about her life before that fateful encounter on the night of 8/9 November. According to Ripper lore, Kelly was the youngest and most attractive of the five victims. As she told one of her female friends, she missed Ireland and hoped to earn enough money in London to return to 'her people' there.

Historians of prostitution in Victorian England have suggested that relatively few Irish women entered the oldest female profession – whether out of religious scruples or fear of shame and parental punishment. Because the census did not provide an ethnic breakdown of known street-women, we cannot estimate the percentage of Irish-born women who pursued this livelihood. But Frances Finnegan has stressed the 'disproportionately low number' of Irish women in mid-Victorian York, even though there is no way of knowing how many women engaged in part-time or casual prostitution depending on personal exigencies.[2] Whatever the percentage of Irish-born street walkers in London at the time, there is no doubt that the Ripper singled Kelly out for his most maniacal mutilation.

A much fainter Irish connection in the context of Kelly's murder involves John M'Carthy, the landlord of Kelly's abode with a 'gentlemanly' appearance. Although he was supposedly born in France, we may assume that his origins were Irish. The notorious lodgings in Miller's Court were known as 'M'Carthy's Rents.' This small businessman also owned a chandler's shop or grocery in Dorset Street. Needless to say, his discovery of Kelly's ravaged body inside that charnel-house room earned him a mite of enduring fame.

What is somewhat surprising about the fall-out from the serial murders is the absence of any serious Irish suspects during that autumn. Given the ubiquity of Irish-born families in Whitechapel and the extent of Hibernophobia in England during a decade of intense political agitation by Irish nationalists this silence is hard to explain. Throughout the 1880s the leading newspapers were filled with reports of the Parnellite agitation for Irish Home Rule, the land war, the assassination of the Irish Chief Secretary and his Permanent Under-Secretary in Phoenix Park on 6 May 1882, sensationalized accounts of agrarian outrage, bombs detonated in central London by Fenian dynamiters in 1884–85, and the renewed attack on Irish landlordism by agents of the Plan of Campaign after 1886. In the light of all the negative publicity flowing out of Ireland it is strange that hardly any of the leading Ripper suspects who were denounced or roughly handled by small crowds had Irish surnames. Certainly, to our knowledge, no Ripper-related anti-Irish graffiti appeared on the walls of Goulston Street or elsewhere; and only one or two of the suspects reported in the press had reddish hair and fair complexions, let alone freckles and a snub nose. No more than four out of 272 correspondents who sent letters to the City of London police about the murders lived in Ireland. Moreover, only four of all these writers singled out Irish suspects despite the fact that the popular image of the wild Irishman addicted to drink and violence had not disappeared since the ending of the Fenian offensive around 1868. As for weapons of choice, no doubt most Londoners associated the ape-like figure of rebel Paddy found in caricatures with fists, a shillelagh, a blunder-buss, or a bomb but not a knife. And yet the Invincibles had used long knives to kill their elite victims in Phoenix Park.

Most Irish-born East Enders, especially those who arrived in the wake of the famine, had first-hand knowledge of anti-Catholic and Anglo-Saxonist prejudices, and no doubt they were delighted to be spared the additional burden of serving as a collective scapegoat for the mutilation murders. What saved them from the kind of suspicion that fell on other out-groups was the dramatic surge in the number of Jewish refugees pouring into Whitechapel and environs after 1870. The ferocious pogroms in Eastern Europe drove hordes of these victims into the East End, where their numbers reached almost 45,000 by 1887.[3] If this influx was dwarfed by the (minimal) figure of 178,000 Londoners who were either Irish-born or could claim Irish ancestry during the 1860s, the profoundly 'alien' nature of the Jewish community made itself felt all the way from their core settlement area in Spitalfields to the peripheral enclaves in other parts of Tower Hamlets. Perhaps as many as one-quarter of these new immigrants had attained some middle-class comforts by this time, but most of them were trapped in varying degrees of poverty.[4]

For better or worse, the London Irish lacked a comparable ghetto. Most of them were scattered all over four parishes: St Giles in the Fields, St Mary, Whitechapel, St George-in-the-East, and St Olave, Southwark. To quote Lynn Lees, 'They lived close to the English, but they remained apart . . . The result was a chain of Irish buildings and enclaves located within English working-class territory.'[5] Charles Booth's team of researchers (including Beatrice Potter) stressed the concentration of foreigners in Whitechapel but seemed at times to exclude the Irish from that category, emphasizing instead the dark complexions, high cheek-bones, and prominent noses of the Eastern European contingents.[6] Booth's famous survey of London's inhabitants and streets thus singled out such foreigners as the Chinese, Malays, Swedes, Danes, Germans, Poles, Spaniards, and Italians but treated the Scots, Welsh, and Irish as almost assimilated into the indigenous populace.

The more skilled workers of Irish origins were dispersed around town and the most upwardly mobile among them could almost pass as British – until, that is, they started to speak or went to Mass. On the other hand, Beatrice Potter (Webb) had little time for the poorest London Irish, endorsing the verdict of a London school board visitor: 'The worst scoundrel is the Cockney-born Irishman. The woman is the Chinaman of the place: drudges as the women of savage races; she slaves all day and night . . . They never read. Except Catholics, they never go to church.'[7]

The persistent racializing or 'othering' of the Irish in Britain proved mild by comparison with the fate of the refugees from the sacked shtetls of Eastern Europe. Pronounced differences in speech, attire, patterns of worship, diet, work habits, and physiognomy all enhanced their foreignness and made immigrants from Ireland as well as western Europe seem almost British. In short, the latent xenophobia of Tower Hamlet's indigenous population became much more overt in the face of all these Orientalized Jews. In addition, mounting resentment at the business acumen and usurious activities of these new arrivals fueled the long-burning fires of anti-Semitism. By 1888 ardent English nativists like Arnold White and the Rev. R. C. Billing were calling for a halt to Jewish – but not Irish – immigration, and they had many supporters in the East End.[8] For these compelling reasons the plebeian Irish were spared the intense hostility that rained down on the heads of adult male Jews once the mutilation murders began. Hardly any of the men detained by the police for questioning had Irish surnames or so-called Irish features.

One exception to this rule surfaced in mid-October. A man from Belfast named John Foster was arrested in Glasgow while carrying a bag filled with knives and razors. But this suspect disappeared from the newspaper as rapidly as he had surfaced.[9] By contrast, the first and most famous suspect after the death of Polly Nichols, named John Pizer or 'Leather Apron,' could not have been more Jewish. And most of the police circulars describing men seen with or near the Ripper's victims focused on black hair, beards, and clothing along with dark complexions and heavy accents.[10] Given all the attention lavished on Jewish suspects, one cannot help wondering how Whitechapel's Irish residents would have fared had no Jews settled there.

One of the most interesting aspects of the Irish dimension concerns the letters sent by private citizens to the police accusing Irishmen of being the villain. Amidst all the speculation about 'whodunem' a few Irish candidates did emerge even though they were outnumbered by Jews, Lascars, Malays and southern Europeans – not to mention Englishmen. Reflecting some of the Hibernophobia also prevalent in America, an electrician wrote from Cleveland, Ohio, to the Lord Mayor of London urging the police to install a series of electric bells attached to wires laid down in the gutters of Whitechapel. By pressing the nearest bell-button, any potential victim or policeman could alert Scotland Yard to an attack. At the same time this Yorkshire-born writer insisted that 'on no account must you let an Irish Detective peep' at this contraption.[11]

My sample of some 272 authors who sent 320 legible letters to the City of London police or the Lord Mayor contains 244 writers who gave an address. Only four of the latter lived in Ireland, compared with eleven in Scotland, and one in Wales. Four other correspondents asserted that the Ripper came from Ireland. Three of the Irish writers were absorbed by methods of detection, advocating the use of female decoys or detectives disguised as women to catch the killer. For example, William Bridge of Parsonstown, King's County, suggested that several detectives dress like 'unfortunates' and walk through the East End at night armed with revolvers. John Macready of 3 Dawson Street, Dublin urged Colonel Sir James Fraser, the City's Police Commissioner, to hire a few prostitutes for the same purpose. To protect their necks from the killer's knife, he recommended that they wear 'chain armor collars or steel plates' hidden beneath a lace or silk scarf. They should also be equipped with a whistle to summon assistance. Macready did show some sympathy for these 'poor things' who were 'desperate and reckless enough' to volunteer for this dangerous task, and he thought that they should be rewarded for their efforts.[12] Henry Carr, whose name also had a distinctly Protestant ring, wrote from Maryborough, Queen's County two days after Kelly's death declaring that these 'outrages against poor unfortunates' could be stopped if only the police would arrest every woman found on the streets after dark and lock them up in a building until 'the scoundrel' had been caught. He also suggested dressing a few policemen in women's attire and sending them forth to walk the streets at night.[13]

The strangest communication from Ireland took the form of a telegram sent to the Rotherhithe police in December 1889 by a man named J. Fogarty, who reported the arrest of a man in Dublin named 'Palermo Nagro alias Wilmo' for the Whitechapel murders.

This message turned out to be a complete hoax. As the super-intendent of the Dublin Metropolitan Police informed his opposite number in the City Police, Fogarty was a salesman from Antrim who had gone on a drinking binge in Cork and wound up in Dublin 'suffering from Delirium Tremens.' The Dublin authorities dismissed Fogarty's telegram as the handiwork of a madman and did not bother to prosecute him.[14]

Irish males, in fact, composed a tiny minority of the various ethnic and national suspects proposed by members of the public. One anonymous Londoner promoted the candidacy of Charles Stewart Parnell, whose features, he insisted, strongly resembled those of the man seen leaving Mitre Square after Eddowes's murder carrying a black bag. This writer urged the police to keep Parnell under surveillance and to search his house for blood-stained clothes.[15] Not to be outdone, a clergyman from Newmarket had a dream that he shared with Colonel Fraser. In his vision, he saw two slender and well-dressed young men who would appear two days hence at precisely 4.10 p.m. walking past 22 Gresham Street in the City. Answering to the names Pat Murphy and Tom Slaney, they had to be 'the perpetrators of these horrible crimes.' For good measure, the writer assured the commissioner that he was 'not mad.'[16]

One of Colonel Fraser's most persistent and eccentric corre-spondents was an elderly man from Penzance, Cornwall, named Henry Armitage, who claimed to have served as an officer or police inspector on the West Cornwall railway. Worried about 'the welfare' of England, he averred that the killer was an Irish-American dynamiter. As evidence he cited the word 'Boss' used in the first letter sent by 'Jack the Ripper' to the Central News Agency shortly before the double event of 30 September. Only Americans, he contended, including those working in Cornish mines, used this form of address. In his view, the killer was seeking to avenge the capture and conviction of a Scottish-born American member of the Clan na Gael – presumably Thomas Gallagher – who had been arrested along with five other would-be dynamiters in April 1883. In the course of six letters Armitage argued that this unnamed Fenian was cast in the same mold as the Phoenix Park assassins. Far from being a madman, as the medical doctors thought, Jack was a political fanatic bent on intimidating the nation.[17]

This brand of anti-Fenian paranoia was not all that rare after the 1860s on either side of the Atlantic. An admittedly extreme case may be found in Simon Winchester's fascinating account of lunacy and etymology in Victorian England. A demented surgeon, William Chester Minor, who had graduated from Yale, suffered from a morbid or lethal fear of Irishmen after a traumatic incident during the US Civil War. Obsessed by delusions that they were pursuing and abusing him both physically and sexually, he ventured to London, where on a moonlit night in February 1872 he pulled out his .38 Colt revolver and killed an innocent Lambeth man whom he mistook for a Fenian. At his trial, Dr Minor was declared insane and committed to Broadmoor, the 'special hospital' for the criminally insane, where he spent most of his life collecting old books, compiling lists of words, defining them, and noting the contexts in which they were used. He sent all of his findings to the eminent editor of the forthcoming Oxford English Dictionary, James Murray.[18]

Although not named in the London press during 1888–89, two distinctly Irish suspects eventually emerged from the relentless pursuit of the Whitechapel murderer by latter-day Ripperologists. The first and least plausible of these candidates is James Kelly – a man with no fixed place of birth, address, or occupation, who apparently died in 1929. A victim of chronic mental instability, he murdered his wife in 1883, for which he received the death sentence. Somehow he won a reprieve and ended up in Broadmoor, where he may well have run into Dr Minor. After escaping from the asylum in January 1888, he then proceeded – according to John Morrison – to commit those ghastly crimes in Whitechapel. Later he fled to America and after many years returned to England in 1927 and committed himself to Broadmoor. According to the authors of *The Jack the Ripper A–Z*, the case built by John Morrison is 'unique in the annals of the Ripper, inasmuch as it is presented with no supporting evidence.'[19] Well, maybe not quite unique – but this one certainly lies beyond the pale of serious historical inquiry.

Last but by no means least, there is the Canadian born quack doctor and adventurer, Francis J. Tumblety, who became the 'very likely' choice of John George Littlechild, the head of Scotland Yard's Special Branch from 1883 to 1893. Because this Chief Inspector had spent five months in Dublin investigating the Phoenix Park murders he knew a great deal about political extremists – whether Irish republicans, Russian anarchists or German-Jewish socialists. One may assume that he had no great affection for Irish nationalists. Tumblety was a professional charlatan, an amateur misogynist, a sexual deviant, and a supporter of Irish independence, who rose from rags to riches on the strength of a bogus cure for pimples. Devoid of any formal medical training, he boasted about his service as a brigade surgeon in the Union army and strutted about town in a fancy uniform of his own design, wearing diamond rings and accompanied by several large hounds. He also owned a collection of human organs, including a number of uteri, stored in glass jars.

On 7 November 1888 Tumblety was arrested in London for 'unnatural offenses' or 'gross indecency' – a euphemism for homoerotic activities. Exactly when he was released from custody remains moot. Evidently some Scotland Yard officers suspected him of involvement in the Whitechapel murders, and they would not have done so had he been incarcerated on the night of 8/9 November. He was arrested again on 12 November – this time as a suspect in the murders. Four days later he made bail. Scheduled for trial at the Old Bailey on 10 December, he went into hiding, fled to France, and then sailed to New York, where the police kept him under surveillance. Not the least curious aspect of the Tumblety case is why the London press remained silent about his suspect status when a number of American papers ran feature stories about his possible guilt. Moreover, Littlechild did not promote Tumblety's candidacy until the early 1900s, when he wrote a letter in response to queries from George R. Sims. This letter did not come to light until 1993, when Stewart Evans and Paul Gainey pounced on it and constructed their case for Tumblety's guilt in their 1995 book.[20] One thing remains certain about this elusive Canadian-American-Irishman. When it came to the category of weirdo, he ranked right next to such colourful suspects as Robert D'Onston Stephenson, Michael Ostrog and Alexander Pedachenko.

One more Irish connection deserves mention. Several weeks after the double event a young woman named Milligan was walking with two friends near Kilkeel, county Down, when a man suddenly jumped out of a hedge brandishing a knife and shouting: 'I'm Jack the Ripper.' Poor Miss Milligan never recovered from this shock. Hysteria gave way to a coma and she ran a high fever. Confined to bed, she died several days later.[21] Whatever the autopsy may have revealed it would seem that the power of the Ripper mythos to incite thrills as well as alarms extended well into Ireland not to mention other parts of the world.

Footnotes

1. Begg, Paul, Fido, Martin and Skinner, Keith (eds.), *The Jack the Ripper A–Z* (London: 1991), pp. 219–20.
2. Finnegan, Frances, *Poverty and Prostitution: a Study of Victorian Prostitutes in York* (Cambridge, 1979), pp. 32, 53–4, 173.
3. Quoted in Fishman, William J., *East End 1888* (London: 1988), p. 131. Booth counted some 29,000 Jews in Whitechapel alone in 1887.
4. Ibid.
5. Of course the density of Irish residents varied widely from one street and one parish to another. While Irish residents comprised between 2% and 4% of Goodman's Fields in St Mary's, Whitechapel, they came close to 75% of those living in such alleys or wynds as Glass House Yard and Crown Court. Lees, Lynn H., *Exiles of Erin – Irish Migrants in Victorian London* (Ithaca, 1979), pp. 64–8.
6. See Booth, Charles, *Life and Labour of the People in London, First Series:Poverty, Vol. 3* (London: 1902), p. 100.
7. Webb, Beatrice, *My Apprenticeship* (London: 1926), p. 256.
8. Fishman, *East End 1888*, pp. 144–68.
9. *Lloyd's and Reynolds's*, 14 October 1888.
10. See, for example, *Star*, 5 September 1888.
11. J. R. Clark to the Lord Mayor, 19 November 1888, Police Box 3.13, ff. 38–9, Corporation of London Records Office (hereafter, CLRO).
12. Macready to Col. Fraser, 1 October 1888, Police Box 3.16, f. 134, Ibid.
13. Henry Carr to the Lord Mayor, 19 November 1888, Police Box 3.19, f. 251, Ibid. Carr's uncle, Nassau Smith O'Brien, had served as Superintendent of Scotland Yard from 1853 to 1863. See Smith, Philip T., *Policing Victorian London* (Westport, Conn.: 1985), pp. 127–36.
14. See Fogarty's telegram of 5 December, 1889, and Superintendent William Reddy, DMP to Superintendent of Detectives, James McWilliam, City of London Police, 6 December, 1889, Police Box 3.14, ff. 68-9, CLRO.

15. Anonymous to Col. Fraser, 24 November 1888, Police Box 3.22, f. 379a, CLRO.
16. Rev. William Harrison of Moulton, Newmarket to Col. Fraser, 26 November 1888, Police Box 3.15, f. 87, ibid.
17. Henry Armitage to Col. Fraser, 2, 3 and 8 October and 28 November 1888 and 19 July 1889, Police Box 3.18, f. 231 and 3.19, ff. 232–6, ibid. When Gallagher and his co-conspirators were arrested, they had some 500 pounds of nitroglycerine in their possession. Short, K. R. M., 'The Gallagher Team' in *The Dynamite War*, (Atlantic Highlands, N.J.: 1979), pp. 125–50.
18. Winchester, Simon, *The Professor and the Madman: A Tale of Murder, Insanity and the Making of the Oxford English Dictionary* (New York: 1998), esp. pp. 2–21, 59–73.
19. Begg et al, *The Jack the Ripper A–Z*, p. 218. Kelly's complicity is dismissed for want of any evidence in the Ripper website *www.casebook.org*
20. The case for Tumblety's guilt is set forth in Stewart P. Evans and Paul Gainey, *Jack the Ripper: First American Serial Killer* (New York: 1995), esp. pp. 177–235. The surname Tumblety is presumably a corruption of the Gaelic name, Tomaltaigh or Tumulty. Significantly, his name was spelled Tumuelty on his gravestone in Rochester. See also *www.casebook.org*
21. *Lloyd's and Weekly Times*, 28 October 1888.

This essay appeared in *Ripperologist* magazine No. 50, November 2003.

Cut-throat: A Detailed Examination of the Neck Wounds Sustained by the Whitechapel Murder Victims

Karyo Magellan

EVEN AFTER WELL OVER a century of discussion and analysis, there is still no consensus as to exactly how many of the Whitechapel murder victims were killed by the same assailant. This fundamental prerequisite to establishing the identity of the serial killer remains elusive, and in consideration of opportunities and alibis it is always important to accurately determine how many victims were the work of the same killer. Many researchers and authors continue to rely upon the canonical list of Ripper victims as defined by then Chief Constable Sir Melville Macnaghten in 1894, but this list of victims has an arbitrary basis and is largely unsubstantiated. Through a particularisation and objective analysis of crime scene and pathology data, it is possible to establish links between individual murders or to exclude others as being the work of a serial killer. Such investigations require a detailed examination of each murder to identify the relevant components, followed by a standardized comparison between the murders. This is quite a challenge, given the nature of the raw information surrounding the Whitechapel murders, much of which cannot be relied upon because it is either not first-hand or is otherwise not from a reliable professional source. I have already documented at length the crime scene details of the Whitechapel murders as part of a much more extensive investigation. The present contribution is an additional and more detailed assessment of the neck wounds inflicted on those Whitechapel murder victims killed by such means.[1] For the purposes of this examination, I have used exclusively the descriptions provided by contemporaneous professional medical examiners. No other information is relevant to this work and the victims compared are the canonical Ripper victims identified by Macnaghten, namely Mary Ann Nichols, Annie Chapman, Elisabeth Stride, Catharine Eddowes and Mary Jane Kelly, together with Alice McKenzie and Frances Coles. The descriptions provided by the medical examiners are taken from inquest testimony, as reported in official transcripts or in *The Times* or the *Daily Telegraph*, or from other formal documentation. Although the medical testimony is first hand, with one or two exceptions the reporting is not, and newspaper reports do not always accurately represent what was said at the inquests. However, we must be thankful that the newspapers of the period did such a thorough job of reporting the inquest details since, in the absence of archived original inquest reports for many of the victims, there would otherwise be huge gaps in the accumulated information. Unfortunately, the descriptions given by medical professionals were not always consistent in detail and there are inevitably shortfalls. Nonetheless, in most cases there is sufficient detail to reliably represent, in general terms, the direction and path of the major or fatal cut, or where two cuts coincide, the path of the composite wound. In witness descriptions and in later discussions all references to left and right relate to the victim's body and not as viewed. The detailed descriptions of wounds from all sources for each victim are as follows:

Mary Ann Nichols
Inquest testimony of Dr Rees Llewellyn.[2] 'On the left side of the neck, about an inch below the jaw, there was an incision about four inches long and running from a point immediately below the ear. An inch below on the same side, and commencing about an inch in front of it, was a circular incision terminating at a point about three inches below the right jaw. This incision completely severs all the tissues down to the vertebrae. The large vessels of the neck on both sides were severed. The incision is about eight inches long. These

cuts must have been caused with a long-bladed knife, moderately sharp, and used with great violence. No blood at all was found on the breast either of the body or clothes.'

Annie Chapman

Inquest testimony of Dr George Phillips:[3] 'The throat was dissevered deeply. I noticed that the incision of the skin was jagged, and reached right around the neck. The incisions of the skin indicated that they had been made from the left side of the neck on a line with the angle of the jaw, carried entirely round and again in front of the neck, and ending at a point about midway between the jaw and the sternum or breast bone on the right hand. There were two distinct clean cuts on the body of the vertebrae on the left side of the spine. They were parallel to each other, and separated by about half an inch. The muscular structures between the side processes of bone of the vertebrae had an appearance as if an attempt had been made to separate the bones of the neck.'

Elisabeth Stride

Inquest testimony of Dr William Blackwell:[4] 'There was a check silk scarf around the neck, the bow of which was turned to the left side and pulled very tightly. There was a long incision in the neck, which exactly corresponded with the lower border of the scarf. The lower edge of the scarf was slightly frayed, as if by a sharp knife. The incision in the neck commenced on the left side, two and one half inches below the angle of the jaw, and almost in a direct line with it, nearly severing the vessels on that side, cutting the windpipe completely in two, and terminating on the opposite side one and one half inches below the angle of the right jaw, but without severing the vessels on that side. Deceased would have bled to death comparatively slowly, on account of the vessels on one side only being severed, and the artery not being completely severed. The deceased could not have cried out after the injuries were inflicted as the windpipe was severed. I formed the opinion that the murderer probably took hold of the silk scarf, at the back of it, and then pulled the deceased backwards, but I cannot say whether the throat was cut while the woman was standing or after she was pulled backwards. Deceased would have taken a minute or a minute and a half to bleed to death.'

Inquest testimony of Dr Phillips:[5] 'There was a clean-cut incision on the neck. It was six inches in length and commenced two and a half inches in a straight line below the angle of the jaw, three quarters of an inch over an undivided muscle, and then, becoming deeper, dividing the sheath. The cut was very clean and deviated a little downwards. The artery and other vessels contained in the sheath were all cut through. The cut through the tissues on the right side was more superficial, and tailed off to about two inches below the right angle of the jaw. The deep vessels on that side were uninjured. From this it was evident that the haemorrhage was caused through the partial severance of the left carotid artery. [The cause of death was] undoubtedly from the loss of blood from the left carotid artery and the division of the windpipe.'

Catharine Eddowes

Inquest testimony of Dr Frederick Brown:[6] 'The throat was cut across to the extent of about six or seven inches. A superficial cut commenced about an inch and a half below the lobe and about two and a half inches behind the left ear and extended across the throat to about three inches below the lobe of the right ear. The big muscle across the throat was divided through on the left side – the large vessels on the left side of the neck were severed – the larynx was severed below the vocal chords. All the deep structures were severed to the bone the knife marking intervertebral cartilages – the sheath of the vessels on the right side was just opened, the carotid artery had a fine hole opening. The internal jugular vein was opened an inch and a half not divided. The blood vessels contained clot. All these injuries were performed by a sharp instrument like a knife and pointed. The cause of death was haemorrhage from the left common carotid artery. The death was immediate and the mutilations were inflicted after death.'

Mary Jane Kelly

Inquest testimony of Dr Phillips:[7] 'The mutilated remains of a woman were lying two-thirds over, towards the edge of the bedstead, nearest the door. Deceased had only an under linen garment upon her, and by subsequent examination I am sure the body had been removed, after the injury which caused death, from that side of the bedstead which was nearest to the wooden partition previously mentioned. The large quantity of blood under the bedstead, the saturated condition of the palliasse, pillow, and sheet at the top corner of the bedstead nearest to the partition leads me to the conclusion that the severance of the right carotid artery, which was the immediate cause of death, was inflicted while the deceased was lying at the right side of the bedstead and her head and neck in the top right-hand corner.'

Post mortem report (notes) by Dr Thomas Bond:[8] 'The bed clothing at the right corner was saturated with blood, and on the floor beneath was a pool of blood covering about two feet square. The wall by the right side of the bed and in a line with the neck was marked by blood which had struck it in a number of separate splashes. The neck was cut through the skin and other tissues right down to the vertebrae, the fifth and sixth being deeply notched. The skin cuts in the front of the neck showed distinct ecchymosis. The air passage was cut at the lower part of the larynx through the cricoid cartilage.'

Alice McKenzie

Inquest testimony of Dr Phillips:[9] 'The wound in the neck was 4 in. long, reaching from the back part of the muscles, which were almost entirely divided. It reached to the fore part of the neck to a point 4 in. below the chin. There was a second incision, which must have commenced from behind and immediately below the first. The cause of death was syncope, arising from the loss of blood through the divided carotid vessels, and such death probably was almost instantaneous. I should think the [knife] had a shortish blade and was pointed. I cannot tell whether it was the first or second cut that terminated the woman's life. The first cut, whether it was the important one or not, would probably prevent the woman from crying out on account of the shock. The whole of the air passages were uninjured, so that if she was first forced on to the ground she might have called out.'

Post-mortem report (notes) of Dr Phillips [amended for clarity by this author]:[10] 'Death was caused through syncope arising from the division of the vessels of the left side of the neck. The wounds were caused by a sharp cutting instrument with at least two strokes and were not suicidal. The wounds were made from left to right while the body was on the ground and effected by someone who knew the position of the vessels or at any rate knew where to cut with reference to causing speedy death. There was no physiological reason why the woman should not have uttered a cry because her larynx/trachea was not severed. The wound to the throat tending to confirm the conclusion submitted as to the wounds of the abdominal wall in that death almost immediately followed from incision of the neck, the woman did not move after the incision, and all other wounds were made after death. The wound in the neck was deeper and cleaner than appeared at first sight. More superficial wounds – two jagged wounds commencing from behind the left sterno mastoid muscle leaving a triangular piece of skin attached by its base to the outside (remaining) skin about an inch long and four inches forward and upwards. Deeper wounds – the deepest incision divides the sterno mastoid muscle except for a few posterior fibres, the vessels of the neck and sheath, the division of the common carotid artery being above the omo hyoid muscle, down to the transverse process of the cervical vertebra. There were four jagged cuts over the angle of the jaw where instrument had been arrested over the cut under jaw.'

Letter from Dr Bond to Assistant Commissioner Robert Anderson:[11] 'I was able to form an opinion that there could be no doubt that the cuts were made from left to right & as far as I was able to make out, the knife appears to have been plunged into the neck on the left side of the victim below the sterno mastoid muscle & brought out by a tailed incision just above the larynx on the same side. There appeared to have been two stabs, & the knife then carried forward in the same skin wound, except that a small tongue of skin remained between the two stabs. The incisions appeared to me to be in a direction from above downwards and forwards with several small superficial cuts extending upwards & tailing off into mere scratches. The two main cuts appeared to be about 3 inches long but Dr Phillips stated that before the parts were disturbed the cuts which I saw extending downwards, really were in a direction upwards. The cuts appeared to have been inflicted with a sharp strong knife. I could form no opinion as to the width of the blade or the length of the knife, but undoubtedly the cuts might have been done with a short knife; it must in my opinion have had a sharp point. I believe the cuts were made from the front while the woman's head was thrown back on the ground. There were two bruises high up on the chest which looked as if the murderer had made the cuts with his right hand while he held the woman down with his left. There were no bruises on the woman's face or lips.'

Frances Coles

Inquest testimony of Dr Phillips:[12] 'I made a minute examination of the incision in the throat. There was an external wound, the edges of the skin being not exactly cut through, there being a portion of about an inch long undivided. In my opinion, there were three distinct passings of the knife across the throat – one from left to right, one from right to left, and the third from left to right. Below the wound there was an abrasion, as if caused by a fingernail. Above the wound there were four abrasions, possibly caused by fingernails. From the position of these marks I opine that the left hand was used. There were some contused wounds on the back of the head, which I am of opinion were caused by the head coming into violent contact with paving stones. I came to the conclusion that death had been almost instantaneous, occasioned by the severance of the carotid arteries and other vessels on the left side. In my opinion, the deceased was on the ground when her throat was cut. I think that her assailant used his right hand in making the incisions in the throat, and that he had used his left hand to hold her head back by the chin; that he was on the right side of the body when he made the cuts. The tilting of the body to the left was to prevent the perpetrator from being stained with blood.' In additional inquest reporting, Dr Frederick Oxley[13] suggested that Coles's throat had been cut while she was on the ground but he told the inquest that although there was but one incision of the skin there must have been two wounds because the larynx had been opened in two places and he thought that the wounds had been made by someone standing in front of the victim and not to the right of the victim as Phillips had suggested. The cuts were thus partially across the front of the throat with emphasis on the left side which is where the vessels were severed. There is no mention of vessels on the right side of the neck being divided but clearly the windpipe was at least partially severed. An interpretation of these descriptions provides paths and directions of cut for each victim. It must be stressed that it is impossible to accurately interpret the descriptions and such cuts are rarely as clean and constant as one might imagine. Uniform sweeping arcs are unlikely as expediency necessitates some degree of hacking. It is evident that six of the seven victims received fatal wounds to predominantly the left side of the neck (Nichols, Chapman, Stride, Eddowes, McKenzie and Coles), that being the location of the point of entry, with the laceration being inflicted from left to right across the front of the neck. In each of these six cases death was a consequence of exsanguination via the blood vessels on the left side of the neck, significantly the left carotid artery, which was severed, partially or completely, in all six instances. In two instances (Nichols and Chapman) the vessels on both sides were completely severed. Only a right-handed assailant could have inflicted such wounds and on the balance of probability it seems that the attack must have been from behind with the victims standing. The absence of any significant distribution of blood at the crime scene in any instance does not contradict this assertion – the killer's technique alone could prevent this as the victim was lowered to the ground, instantly silenced by shock or by a severed windpipe. In addition, the absence of any signs of a struggle for any of these six victims, except Chapman, reinforces the instantaneous and surprise nature of the attack that could only be prosecuted from behind with the victim upright. The knife has clearly been drawn across the front of the throat in some instances, a manoeuvre that would be difficult from the front of the victim and the passage of the knife around the throat would be impeded with the victim lying on the ground. Mary Jane Kelly received fatal wounds to the right side of the neck and she bled to death from the vessels on that side. This is further reinforced by inquest testimony suggesting that the wall to the right of Kelly and the bed was spattered with blood as it spurted from the carotid artery.

215

This is also the only instance in which there is any evidence of blood spurting from a neck wound regardless as to the supposed position of the victim when the wounds were inflicted. Because Kelly was probably to the right of the bed when her throat was cut her killer must have been on the bed to her left. In this position the balance of likelihood is that her killer was left-handed, since it would be far more likely that a left-handed assailant would steady the victim's head or stifle her response with his right hand and cut with a knife held in his left hand. There is sufficient evidence from the Whitechapel murder series to suggest that the same individual was responsible for several of the murders, but controversy prevails as to the number of victims murdered by the same killer and, more significantly, was Mary Jane Kelly one of the series? Macnaghten, in his memorandum of 1894, has been regarded as authoritative in ascribing victims to the same serial killer, but his selection is unsubstantiated. On pathology evidence alone it is certainly possible to include Nichols, Chapman, Stride and Eddowes in the same series. Logically one cannot exclude victims from a series because of what did not happen to them, because this may have been a function of opportunity rather than intention; thus, if Elisabeth Stride is included in the series, then there is no good reason to exclude either Alice McKenzie or Frances Coles, although the neck wounds in both of these cases were more lateral than for other victims. Mary Jane Kelly continues to be an anomaly and it is likely that she was murdered by a left-handed assailant. Could the killer have been ambidextrous? This argument is often used by those desperate to reconcile the irreconcilable. Two murderers are more likely than one able to cut instinctively and accurately with a knife in either hand. This is another contribution to the growing evidence suggesting that the man who murdered Mary Jane Kelly was not the same killer who attacked Nichols, Chapman, Stride, Eddowes and, probably, also McKenzie and Coles. This evaluation reinforces the doubts surrounding Mary Jane Kelly and also reveals that Alice McKenzie and Frances Coles cannot be ruled out of the series.

Cut-throat

Footnotes

1. Magellan, K. *By Ear and Eyes: The Whitechapel Murders, Jack the Ripper and the Murder of Mary Jane Kelly* (Derby: Longshot Publishing, 2005).
2 The *Daily Telegraph*, 3 September 1888.
3. The *Daily Telegraph*, 14 September 1888.
4. *The Times*, 3 October 1888.
5. *The Times*, 4 October 1888.
6. Coroner's inquest (L), 1888, No. 135, Catherine Eddowes inquest, 1888 (Corporation of London Record Office).
7. The *Daily Telegraph*, 13 November 1888.
8. MEPO 3/3153, ff.10–18.
9. *The Times*, 18 July 1889 and 15 August 1889.
10. MEPO 3/140, ff.263–27111 MEPO 3/140, ff. 259–262.
12. *The Times*, 24 February 1891.
13. The *Daily Telegraph*, 24 February 1891.

This essay appeared in *Ripperologist* magazine No. 61, September 2005.

The Art of Profiling an Historical Case:
The Whitechapel Murders

James A. Bailey

WHEN THE WHITECHAPEL MURDERS occurred in 1888, profiling was an undeveloped scientific investigative method. As we will see, a type of profiling did take place in the case even then, even if the term 'profiling' was not used. Today, criminal profiling has evolved into an investigative technique used by a number of law enforcement agencies. The purpose of criminal profiling is to provide investigators with additional leads to pursue in an investigation which may lead to an arrest.[1] Crime genre enthusiasts are familiar with the process because the entertainment industry has popularized profiling, which is a central theme in numerous television programs and motion pictures today. One of the most popular novels about profiling, *The Silence of the Lambs* by Thomas Harris, was made into the hit motion picture of the same name with Jodie Foster and Sir Anthony Hopkins. That movie and its sequels probably have had more influence on popular opinion about criminal profiling than any other single source. As depicted in *The Silence of the Lambs* and other fictional settings, profiling is often portrayed as an exact science. However, in actual investigations, compared to fictional portrayals, profiling does not show the same success. Despite the portrayal by the entertainment industry that criminal profiling provides quick leads in solving cases, investigators are painfully aware of its limitations in solving criminal cases.

Dr George Bagster Phillips and early profiling

Throughout police history, investigators have made observations pertaining to unsolved cases. This was a form of criminal profiling even if it was not termed by that name at the time. For example, Dr George Bagster Phillips, the police surgeon for the Metropolitan Police during the Whitechapel murders, used a profiling model to evaluate the offender's behaviour based on the interpretation of wound pattern analysis. Because of the precision of the incisions in the removal of Annie Chapman's organs, Dr Phillips believed the perpetrator to be knowledgeable and with anatomic knowledge, and in fact in his testimony he all but said that the killer was quite possibly a man skilled in medical dissection.[2] Dr Phillips testified in the Chapman inquest at the Working Lads' Institute, Whitechapel Road, on Monday, 10 September 1888. The next day's *Daily Telegraph* reported on the exchanges between him and the Coroner, Wynne Baxter, as follows:

Coroner: Was there any anatomical knowledge displayed?

Dr Phillips: I think there was. There were indications of it. *My own impression is that that anatomical knowledge was only less displayed or indicated in consequence of haste. The person evidently was hindered from making a more complete dissection in consequence of the haste* [emphasis mine].

Coroner: Was the whole of the body there?

Dr Phillips: No; the absent portions being from the abdomen.

Coroner: Are those portions such as would require anatomical knowledge to extract?

Dr Phillips: I think the mode in which they were extracted did show some anatomical knowledge.[3]

Although Dr Phillips's assessment of the case is not referred to in the literature at the time as a profile, by today's criminal investigative techniques it was a criminal profile, giving some idea of the killer's level of anatomical skill.

The beginnings of modern profiling

The modern concept of profiling dates to the early half of the twentieth century. One of the early profilers in the United States

219

was William Langer, a psychiatrist employed by the Office of Strategic Services (OSS) to develop a psychological profile of Adolph Hitler. Langer compiled a description of Hitler's personality, his mental condition and some predictions of his behaviour under certain conditions.[4] Although others have profiled various individuals, Dr James A. Burssel, a New York psychiatrist, may have been one of the first to engage in criminal profiling. Dr Burssel used crime scene behaviour to diagnose the offender's disorder. He associated body physique with certain types of mental illness and consequently was able to give investigators a profile of the offender's physical characteristics. Dr Burssel assisted the police in the 1940s and 1950s during the investigation of the 'Mad Bomber' cases. During this period, the man eventually apprehended, George Metesky, detonated bombs in train stations and theatres in the city. When Metesky was arrested, Dr Burssel's profile was determined to be an accurate profile of the bomber.[5]

Following upon Dr Burssel's profiling efforts came Howard Teten, a former California police officer who became a special agent with the Federal Bureau of Investigation (FBI). In 1970, at the FBI National Academy, Teten began to teach criminal profiling as an investigative aid. Later, he teamed up with Pat Mullany and incorporated the study of abnormal behaviour into lectures on how evidence found at the crime scene could be used to determine aspects of the offender's behaviour.[6] In 1972, the FBI formed the Behavioral Sciences Unit (BSU) to manage the efforts of the profiling agents. These agents were assigned to examine and develop profiles for unsolved cases. Other well-known agents who worked in the unit and profiled important cases were Roy Hazelwood, John Douglas and Robert Ressler. By the 1990s, the unit responsible for profiling cases had changed its name to the National Center for the Analysis of Violent Crime (NCAVC).[7] Today, this unit continues to profile cases. Robert Ressler defines psychological profiling as a process of identifying individual psychological characteristics based on an analysis of their crimes to provide a general description of the offender. The five steps in the process include studying the criminal act and the types of previous offenders, analysis of the crime scene evidence, the background and activities of the victim and known suspects, any motivating factors for all parties, and development of a description of the offender.[8] Richard Ault and James Resse, Special Agents with the FBI Behavioral Science Unit, suggest that the profile varies depending on the type of information the profilers have to assess. The information in a profile generally includes: the offender's race, sex, age group, marital status, general employment, attitude toward police, sexual maturity, the probability of additional crimes, possible past offences and the possibility of a criminal record.[9] Other researchers have developed different profiling strategies and profiling procedures; however, the overall goal of assisting the investigative process is the same.[10] American state and local police agencies began to take advantage of profiling techniques developed by the FBI and others as they began profiling their own cases. Agencies formed special task forces to adapt profiling approaches to solve crimes. Routinely, local agencies investigate a serious crime until it is solved or until another crime occurs. When additional crimes take place, investigators' resources are diluted and the amount of time allotted to a case decreases as new cases are assigned to the investigator. Developing profiles provided investigators with additional investigative leads that sometimes aided in the solution of unsolved cases. The strategy for profiling modern criminal cases and its application to the investigation of the Whitechapel murders could provide some insight into the 117-year-old case. It will not likely offer a solution to the case, but it might point well us in the right direction towards a likely type of individual who was the killer.

Use of a modern criminal case as a means to work up a profile of 'Jack'

The same profiling techniques employed in a modern criminal case in Wilmington, North Carolina, will be used to develop a profile of Jack the Ripper. Like other police agencies around the United States, in 1986 the Wilmington Police Department created a special task force to profile unsolved homicides. The task force consisted of the captain of detectives, a psychologist, the investigating detective and a criminal justice instructor. The purpose of the task force was to profile cases and develop new leads in unsolved homicide cases. In each case, the investigating detective was assigned to the task force as a profiling member. Including the detective as a member on the task force provided the detective with an additional stake in the investigation. Without the detective's involvement and input into the profiling process, the detective operating independently of the task force is less likely to be as co-operative and enthusiastic in executing the investigation.After the task force members were appointed, a police administrator selected and assigned the case to the task force. The case selection is gener-ally an administrative decision by the agency. The criteria used for selecting cases may be whether or not the crime is a high profile case. A high profile status could result from the type of crime, the victim, or the media coverage of the case. Case selection can range from the most recently unsolved case to the oldest case. At any rate, a police administrator usually selects the case to profile. This releases the task force from sifting through the cases trying to decide which one to examine first.The case selected for the Wilmington Police Department task force was a recent robbery homicide investigation of a full-service gas station. Once the case was selected the original investigators presented a detailed chronology of the investigation. During the next several meetings, the task force reviewed the files. The items of physical evidence were exhibited in the meetings and photographs were examined. In order to develop new leads, the task force discussed case details. The leads that developed were prioritized before the detective began the investigative process. During the profiling process, the team focused on the same five-step process as that developed by the FBI. This included: examining the criminal act, analysis of the crime scene, study of the background and activities of the victim, motivating factors for all parties, and then developing a profile for the suspect. A summary of the case revealed that the owner, a Caucasian male, arrived early to open the store one morning. The first customer arrived, entered the station and called to the station attendant for assistance. When he received no response, he proceeded into the station and found the victim lying behind the counter. The customer telephoned emergency services and when they arrived the attendant was found to be deceased. Later, the autopsy revealed that the victim's death was caused by a small gunshot wound to the chest. The investigation yielded numerous unidentified latent fingerprints. There was no money in the cash register and a large ring of keys was found in the keyway of the interior station door. Without any information about the case, the team could have developed a profile based on statistical information from similar crimes. However, in this case the team decided to analyze the available crime information and only consider a statistical profile if one could not be developed from this information. As the team re-enacted what had happened during the commission of the crime based on the information and evidence, one aspect of the crime scene that was puzzling was the key in the front door lock on the inside of the store. The final question contemplated was what type of person would commit a crime like this. It was the team's consensus that the offender probably knew the owner and may have had some type of relationship with him, either business or personal. The offender came to the station while it was still closed and the owner opened the door and voluntarily permitted the perpetrator to enter. The lock was of a dead-bolt type and the team believed that the owner would not have allowed a stranger in the business before it was time to open. Besides, had it been time to open, he would not have left the keyring in the lock. The initial profile of the offender was thus that the offender was someone known to the victim. Based on this profile, the investigative strategy was to re-interview close associates and employees of the victim. The detective accordingly began locating individuals who had a close association with the victim. By this time, several months had passed and one of the employees, the victim's son-in-law, had moved away from the area. When the investigator examined his background, several people who knew him described him as deviant and impulsive. He lived in the county. It was not unusual for him to drink a few beers on Saturday night and periodically go outside and fire his rifle in the air. Through family member interviews, the investigator located the son-in-law's estranged wife, the victim's step-daughter, who was living in another state. By this time her husband had left her. During the

223

interview, she described their relationship as abusive. The investigator had already visited the location where the husband fired his rifle into the air hoping to retrieve some spent cartridges but found none. Information obtained from the step-daughter, however, led to the arrest and conviction of her estranged husband. When the step-daughter's husband was first questioned by investigators, he told them he only worked at the station part time and had been off for three days. The offender could just as well have been someone else and the investigators did not pursue him as a suspect. In this investigation, the profile did not solve the case but offered new leads in the investigation which ultimately led to an arrest. The profiling team did not develop a statistical profile of the offender because the investigative leads from the study of the crime led to an arrest. Human behaviour is not always predictable. The victim could have opened the door to a stranger asking for assistance. If this had been the case, the profiling outcome would have been different. Profiles are rarely 100 per cent accurate. The FBI reported that, out of 192 cases profiled, only eighty-eight cases were solved, and of those, only in fifteen cases were profiles useful in the identification of the suspect. That is 17 per cent of the solved cases or 8 per cent of the total cases.[11] As a general rule, as offender specificity increases, the accuracy of the profile decreases.

Applying profiling to an historical case
The same principles apply to profiling a case whether it is a modern or historical case. The objective of a profile is to provide additional information that can be used in an investigation. The only disadvantage in profiling an historical case is that an investigator cannot follow newly developed leads, re-examine the witnesses, or view the physical evidence. In some historic cases, physical evidence exists but, as with the Jack the Ripper case, it is usually not as abundant as in modern cases. Applying the same five-step process to the Whitechapel murders as applied to the Wilmington robbery homicide investigation can yield a profile of the offender as well. However, in the Whitechapel murders, a statistical profile of Jack the Ripper will be developed prior to considering the five-step process. A statistical profile of a case is

developed by comparing modern statistical data to the case. The comparison is not the same as if data from the 1880s were used, but even with the lack of data pertaining to serial murderers during that period, current data could be used to profile possible characteristics of the nineteenth-century serial killer. Even though the statistical profile provides some useful information, it does not provide enough specific information about the suspect to direct the investigation. By combining statistical data with specific information from cases, a more comprehensive profile may be developed.

Statistical profile of modern serial killers

For serial killers, one source of statistical data for the age distribution suggests that 12 per cent of killers are aged 32–36 years, 17 per cent are aged 18–25, 18 per cent are over age 42, 25 per cent are aged 37–42 and 28 per cent are aged 26–31 years; 95 per cent of the offenders are male and 5 per cent are female; and at least in the United States, 82 per cent are Caucasian, 16 per cent African-American and 2 per cent Hispanic. Around half, 51 per cent, of the killers are employed; 56 per cent do not complete high school and 80 per cent are not married. Around 90 per cent of the victims are strangers to the offender, and 69 per cent of the offenders have some type of psychiatric assessment or confinement history. Sometimes there is an assumption that serial killers have no criminal record; however, 61 per cent have a prior conviction of theft, burglary, or robbery.[12] Other research suggests that a significant number of serial killers are psychopathic sexual sadists who derive pleasure from torturing victims.[13] An analysis of these statistics will be included in the profile developed for Jack the Ripper following the victims' case summaries. Furthermore, to develop a comprehensive profile of Jack the Ripper, a review of his victims and their injuries will be examined in the order in which their deaths occurred. The information about the victims and their injuries is summarized from Donald Rumbelow's *Jack the Ripper: The Complete Casebook*.[14] Students of the case will be aware that there is disagreement about the number of victims who fell prey to Jack the Ripper. For purposes of discussion, five victims, Mary Ann Nichols, Annie Chapman, Elisabeth Stride, Catherine Eddowes and Mary Jane Kelly (usually termed the 'canonical five') will be considered for profiling. Each case will be reviewed individually and then collectively to complete the profile.

Mary Ann Nichols

The first victim was found about 3.40 a.m. on Friday, 31 August 1888, in Buck's Row, near London Hospital, by two carmen on their way to work. Her name was Mary Ann 'Polly' Nichols, an estranged wife and alleged prostitute, with a history of alcohol abuse. Polly was a forty-two-year-old Caucasian female, 5 feet 2 inches in height, with brownish-grey hair and missing five front teeth. She had last been seen intoxicated about 2.00 a.m. that morning in Whitechapel Road. Her body was found in the doorway to a stable-yard just off the dimly lit street. She was lying on her back with one hand near her bonnet and the other reaching towards the stable gate. Her dress was up around her waist and her body was cold to the touch. The first policeman arriving in the scene, however, reported the body to be still warm to the touch above the elbows. Because of the lack of light, the carmen who found the body did not observe any blood. At first, they believed the woman was intoxicated and proceeded to find a policeman to give her assistance. When the policeman arrived with a light, they noticed two cuts to her throat. One cut located just below her left ear, about one inch below her jaw, was about four inches long. The second cut, about one inch below the first cut, was about 8 inches long. The cut was also so deep that it had severed the windpipe and gone to the spinal column. The main arteries had been severed. When the victim was moved to a stretcher, it was noted that blood had collected on her back and had been absorbed by her clothes down to her waist. After the body was removed, there was a blood stain about 6 inches in diameter on the pavement where it had been found. Her post mortem interval was estimated to be 30 minutes. Polly was wearing an overcoat, dress, wool stockings, one flannel slip and one wool slip. During the removal of the clothing, a deep, jagged incision on the left side of the lower abdomen was observed. The abdomen was cut from the centre of the bottom ribs on the right side to the left side of the stomach. There was also bruising on the lower left jaw and a circular bruise on the right side of the face. There were two minor stab wounds to the genital area. In reviewing the injuries sustained by Mary Ann Nichols, the cuts to her throat and abdomen suggest that the attacker was armed with a knife and that he was of considerable strength. Even with a sharp knife, substantial force is required to cut the throat to the vertebral column. The bruising on the face around the jaw could have resulted from an attempt to muffle any sounds from the victim. Considering the victim's history of alleged prostitution, the encounter could have been for sexual exploitation.

Annie Chapman

The second canonical victim, Annie Chapman, estranged wife and alleged prostitute, with a history of alcohol abuse, was found on 8 September 1888 in the back yard of a lodging house on Hanbury Street by one of the lodgers. She was a Caucasian female, about forty-five-years-old, 5 feet tall, with a large, wide nose and dark-brown wavy hair, blue eyes and two teeth missing from her bottom jaw. She was last seen at 5.30 a.m. in the company of a man by a woman on her way to the market. Annie was found lying on her back next to a fence. Her knees were bent with feet on the ground and legs spread open. Her left arm was over her left breast. Her face and hands were bloody. Her throat had been cut twice; the cuts were parallel and about a quarter of an inch apart. One wound was deep and jagged and almost decapitated the victim. Her long overcoat and skirt were pushed up over her stockings. She had been eviscerated and the mesentery of the intestines had been cut in order to stretch the intestines, which had been draped on the victim's shoulder. The uterus, including part of the vagina and two-thirds of the bladder, had been removed. Two pieces of skin from the abdomen were located above the victim's left shoulder in a puddle of blood. Her face and tongue were swollen and there were bruises on her face. She also had abrasions on her ring finger. A brass ring had been removed and was located at the bottom of her feet. Blood stains were found about 14 inches high on the fence from the ground. Blood stains ranging in size from a pinhead to half an inch in diameter were also found on the back of the house.The body mutilations to Chapman provide more insight into the offender's psychological state, even though little is still understood about the offender's behaviour concerning evisceration. In this case, the victim had some organs removed and the mesentery along the length of the intestines was cut, permitting them to be stretched out; however, this does not suggest medical or surgical training. Sexual deviance in this case does provide the investigator with an offender's signature: a cut throat and evisceration. In other words, future cases involving this type of behaviour would suggest the same offender. There is little evidence to suggest robbery, since lodging was paid for on a daily basis. Furthermore, the victim was known as a prostitute in the vicinity.

Elisabeth stride

The third victim was found at 1.00 a.m., 30 September 1888, lying on the ground in Dutfield's Yard, Berner Street, by Louis Diemschutz, arriving with his horse and cart. She was a Swedish woman called Elisabeth Stride, a widow and alleged prostitute, with a history of alcohol abuse. Her common-law husband was Michael Kidney. Elisabeth was about forty-five years old, had blue eyes, brown hair, a straight nose, and was recently treated for venereal disease. When she was found, her dark clothing was wet from the rain, but her body was still warm. She was on her back with a bag of cachous in her left hand and her right hand was bloodstained and on her chest. Her throat had been cut on the left side 2.5 inches below the jaw. The cut continued to the right side 1.5 inches below the jaw. The cut coincided with the lower edge of a scarf around her neck. The bow of the scarf appeared to be pulled tightly to the left side. The cut was deep, severing the windpipe and carotid on the left side but not as deep on the right side. Coagulated blood was observed beneath the body and bruising on both shoulders and the collarbone but no bruising to the face. The left side of the body was soiled with more mud than the right side. Approximately 2 quarts of blood had spilt on to the pavement. There were no mutilations similar to those of the other victims. It's difficult to say whether this victim was killed by the same offender as the other victims because of the lack of mutilations. However, her murder occurred in the same area as the other crimes and her cause of death was her throat being cut. The traditional view is that the attacker fled the scene to avoid detection before he had an opportunity to perform post-mortem mutilation.

Catherine Eddowes

The fourth victim was found at 1.45 a.m. on 30 September 1888, the same day as Elisabeth Stride, in Mitre Square. She was Catherine Eddowes, a 45-year-old Caucasian female with a history of alcohol abuse. Her common-law husband was called John Kelly. The beat policeman had checked the place where Catherine would be murdered 15 minutes before the body was discovered. Catherine was lying on her back with arms beside her body. She wore an ankle-length skirt and three slips. Her left leg was extended and her right leg was bent. The body was warm when discovered. Her throat and the left carotid artery were cut to the spinal column. The incision was about 6 inches in length. Marks from the knife blade were on the vertebral cartilage. The carotid artery on the right had a small opening in it and the jugular vein was cut open as well. The cartilage below the vocal chords was severed. She had a cut on her right cheek and the tip of her nose and lobe of her right ear had been severed. The wall of the abdomen was cut and laid below the breast. The liver had two incisions. She had been cut open from the rectum to the sternum and disembowelled. The intestines were placed on her right side with the exception of one piece that was placed between the body and the left arm. There was no bruising on her face. Prior to her death she had been in police custody and released about midnight. Her body was located about a half-mile from the police station.This is the same signature killing as Nichols and Chapman. All four victims had similar socio-economic circumstances and lifestyles. The geographic proximity of the crime scenes is consistent with a single killer.

Mary Jane Kelly

The fifth victim was discovered murdered in her room at 13 Miller's Court. She was an Irishwoman called Mary Jane Kelly, who was estranged from her common-law husband, Joe Barnett, and believed (at least by some sources) to be pregnant. The twenty-four-year-old Caucasian female and alleged prostitute had a history of alcohol abuse. She was last seen alive at about 11.45 p.m. on 8 November and found deceased at 10.45 a.m. on 9 November by Thomas Bowyer, the rent collector for her landlord, Mr McCarthy. Bowyer knocked at the door. When there was no answer, he looked in through the window and saw her corpse on the bed. She was lying in bed dressed in her undergarments. Her face was cut and disfigured beyond recognition and her throat was cut almost severing the head from the body. The abdomen was cut open and the viscera removed. The intestines were on the right side of the body. Her breasts were cut off. The left arm was cut and attached to the body by a small piece of skin. The nose had been cut off and the thighs stripped of skin down to the feet. The breast, nose and flesh from the thighs were on a table next to the bed. Time of death was estimated between 3.30 and 4.00 a.m. This is the same signature as used in the murders of Nichols, Chapman and Eddowes. The victim's background is similar. The degree of mutilation, however, was more extensive in this case. This might be attributable to the attacker having felt more secure in a room out of public view, where he was able to act out his fantasy without fear of discovery by witnesses.

Conclusions as to a profile of Jack the Ripper
Based on my interpretation of the statistical data collected on the 1888 case together with the information analyzed in modern cases, a profile of the Ripper would characterize him as a Caucasian male aged 26–31 years. He apparently had little education but was employed in some type of vocation. He also most likely had some type of psychological problem that may have been brought to the attention of the mental health medical community. Indeed, the Ripper's identity may have been known to the police because of past convictions for petty crimes such as theft, burglary or robbery. A further analysis of the crimes would indicate that it's likely that the killer was able to gain the trust of the victims. He probably knew or developed a brief relationship with the victims, but because of their past involvement with

prostitution, it is likely that they were approachable by strangers. In one study of eighty-three modern cases, 28 per cent of the victims offered no resistance to the attacker, 31 per cent attempted verbal negations, 7 per cent refused verbally, 10 per cent screamed, 5 per cent attempted escape and 19 per cent resisted the attacker. In two-thirds of the cases, the attacker countered the victim's resistance and the victim was subjected to greater force and aggression.[15] The attacker was most likely a male of considerable strength, proportional to the amount of force required to cut a victim's throat through to the vertebral column. Even if the knife used was sharp, it would have required substantial force to cut through skin, muscle, and vessels to the vertebrae. Large quantities of blood would be present at the scene as a result of the type and location of injuries inflicted on the victims. Some of the victims had bruises on their faces; however, that does not necessarily indicate that a struggle occurred, because alcohol abusers bruise and bleed freely if cut or handled roughly.[16] Even though there was no reported evidence of an initial struggle, a victim's natural instinct in a life-threatening assault is to resist an attacker. Victims generally will resist up to sustaining severe injuries to the hands, arms, or other non-vital parts of the body when attacked.[17] However, there appear to be no defence wounds on any of the victims with the exception of the last one, Mary Jane Kelly. It seems therefore likely that in the majority of the murders the offender manipulated the victim after a brief encounter so that he was able to grab her from behind. Jack the Ripper had a distinctive signature of cutting the throat and post-mortem mutilation by evisceration. The signature of a criminal is different from the modus operandi. The signature has been defined as 'behavior that goes beyond the action needed to commit the crime; it is a fantasy-based ritual or combinations of rituals that represent a unique and personal expression of the offender.'[18] It is estimated that in 1888, the East End of London, a few square miles of area, was populated with about 900,000 inhabitants. Most lived in impoverished conditions and about 50 per cent of the children died before the age of five. About 80,000 people lived in Whitechapel, 8,500 of them in boarding houses with five to seven people occupying each room. The Metropolitan Police estimated that there were about 1,200 prostitutes walking the streets. Even though some of the crime scenes were a considerable distance apart, all the victims lived within a few hundred yards of each other.[19] Due to the proximity in which the victims lived, their killer probably lived and worked in the same geographical setting and thus could well have frequented the same public houses as his victims. Another noteworthy distinction about the Whitechapel murders is that, unlike many modern serial killers, the murderer did not mutilate the body for purposes of torture. The psychopathic sexual sadist tortures the victim for pleasure; however, in the Whitechapel murders the reported medical evidence suggests that the victims were dead when the body mutilations occurred. This post mortem finding is based on the lack of blood from the mutilated areas on the body. Therefore, the killer's sexual fantasy was unlikely to have been sadistic but some other psychopathological condition that caused morbid desires. The assailant travelled the streets late at night or in the early hours of the morning without attracting attention from patrolling policeman. Even if the attacker had been wearing bloodstained clothes, the dim gas lights and dark clothing possibly would have prevented persons on the street from detecting a wet substance like blood at night. Blood would not show on dark clothes in dim lights. After the death of Mary Jane Kelly, the signature killing of Jack the Ripper ended.

Trace evidence in modern cases

A major difference between the 1888 crime scene analysis and modern forensic investigations is the concept of searching for trace evidence that might be useful in identifying the offender. The investigative process that includes identifying witnesses, interviewing citizens in the vicinity, determining when the victim was last seen and who saw the victim, was similar to an investigative process today. Unfortunately, twenty-first century techniques and technology were unavailable to the investigators at the time. Since the 1888 murders, modern crime-scene investigations include the analysis of crime-scene bloodstains and the search for evidence such as hairs, fibres, fingerprints, the assailant's DNA or impression evidence. Each of these types of evidence would be a source for additional information about the killer had the investigators collected such evidence in 1888. A thorough post-mortem examination of the victims by a forensic pathologist using radiography, detailed photographs and the ever-evolving tests of a modern forensic laboratory would have exposed even more evidence for analysis and consideration.

Conclusion

Disagreement will always exist among investigators and Ripperologists about the profile and identity of Jack the Ripper. That's what makes this case – or any unsolved historical case – an interesting challenge worthy of investigative debate. As researchers continue to learn more about serial killers and to refine profiling techniques, more investigators will be able to adapt profiling techniques to profile historical cases such as the 'Ripper' crimes. The mystery and intrigue of Jack the Ripper's identity will keep many searching for innovative methods to answer questions about the 117-year-old case.

Footnotes

1. Cook, Patrick and Hinman, Dayle, L., 'Criminal Profiling', *Journal of Contemporary Criminal Justice 15* (1999), pp. 230–41.
2. Turvey, Brent, *Criminal Profiling: An Introduction to Behavioral Evidence Analysis* (San Diego, California: Academic Press, 1999) pp. 5–6.
3. *Daily Telegraph*, Tuesday 11 September 1888.
4. Turco, Ronald N., 'Psychological Profiling,' *International Journal of Offender Therapy and Comparative Criminology* 43.2 (1990) pp. 147–152.
5. Pinizzotto, Anthony J. 'Forensic Psychology: Criminal Personality Profiling,' *Journal of Police Science and Administration 12* (1984) pp. 32–40.
6. Egger, Steven A., 'Psychological Profiling: Past, Present and Future,' *Journal of Contemporary Criminal Justice 15.3* (1999), pp. 242–61.
7. Osterburg, James W. and Ward, Richard H., *Criminal Investigation: A Method for Reconstructing the Past* (Cincinnati, Ohio: Anderson Publishing Co., 1992) pp. 647–649.
8. Egger, Steven A., *The Killers Among Us: An Examination of Serial Murder and Its Investigation* (Upper Saddle River, New Jersey: Prentice Hall, Inc., 1998) p. 214.
9. Ault, Richard, Jr, and Reese, James T., 'A Psychological Assessment of Crime Profiling,' *FBI Law Enforcement Bulletin 49* (March 1980) pp. 22–5.

10. 'Psychological Profiling: Past, Present and Future' in Egger, *The Killers Among Us*, pp. 242–61.

11. Thornton, William E. 'Investigative (Psychological) Profiling' in Wright, Richard A., and Miller, J. Michael (eds.), *Encyclopedia of Criminology* (New York: Routledge, 2004).

12. Godwin, Maurice, *Hunting Serial Predators: A Multivariate Classification Approach to Profiling Violent Behavior* (Boca Raton, Florida: CRC Press, 2000) pp. 69–76.

13. Geberth, Vernon J., *Sex-Related Homicide and Death Investigation: Practical and Clinical Perspectives* (Boca Raton, Florida: CRC Press, 2003) pp. 24–25.

14. Rumbelow, Donald, *Jack the Ripper: The Complete Casebook* (Chicago: Contemporary Books Inc., 1988).

15. Ressler, Robert K., Burgess, Ann W. and Douglas, John E., *Sexual Homicide:Patterns and Motives* (New York: Lexington Books, 1988) p. 201.

16. Knight, Bernard, *Forensic Pathology* 2nd ed. (London: Edward Arnold, 1996) pp. 141–2.

17. Knight, Bernard, *Simpson's Forensic Medicine* 10th ed. (London: Edward Arnold, 1992), pp. 85–6.

18. Rossmo, D. Kim, *Geographic Profiling* (Boca Raton, Florida: CRC Press, 2000), p. 58.

19. Honeycombe, Gordon, *The Murders of the Black Museum 1870–1970* (London: W. H. Allen & Company Ltd, 1983) pp. 5–14.

This essay appeared in *Ripperologist* magazine No. 59, May 2005.

Jack by Gaslight: The Problem of Illumination in Mitre Square

Neil Bell

QUESTION: What do John Clayton, Stephen Hales, Carlisle Spedding, George Dixon, Archibald Cochrane, the 9th Earl of Dundonald, William Murdoch, and Phillippe Lebon all have in common? Nope, not it's not the forward line of that great Leicester Tigers Rugby Football team of 1898. No, these chaps had a hand, whether by scientific experimentation, invention, or innovation, in creating a piece of equipment which, along with the top hat and Gladstone bag, remains one of the iconic images in the world of Jack the Ripper: the gas lamp. To me, the image conjures up the idea of 'unfortunates' huddled under such lamps hunting for trade and keeping warm while the glow of the lamps shine like beacons through the fog. However, while image is one thing, as I am sure you know, reality is something completely different.

The advent of gas lighting

Frederick Windsor erected London's first street gas lamps in Pall Mall in 1807 and by 1812 he had succeeded in creating The Gas, Light and Coke Company in Horseferry Road, London. It was this firm that was granted a Royal Charter to light the City of London, Westminster, and the Borough of Southwark. Within a couple of years, other private gas companies had been set up and vied to supply the rest of the capital with light. London was soon aglow, well, in truth, more, shall we say, shimmering dimly. The gas burners fitted to the lamps gave out all sorts of differently shaped flames. These flames were given wonderful names such as 'rat tail,' 'fish tail,' 'cockspur' and 'cockscomb.' I could go on, but I'm here to talk about Jack. What has all this to do with the Whitechapel murders of 1888, I hear you ask. Well, to be honest, quite a bit. Among Ripperologists, there has been a debate with regard to the lighting situation at the murder sites and at one site in particular – Mitre Square, Aldgate, the murder site of the fourth canonical victim, Catherine Eddowes, early on the morning of 30 September 1888.

The gas lighting in Mitre Square

Ripperologists have for some time wrestled with the problem of the available illumination in Mitre Square and how the street lighting or the lack thereof affected the killer's ability to carry out the mutilations committed on Eddowes' body. How well could the murderer see to commit such mutilations? If visibility was poor, does this indicate a person skilled in knife-work or anatomy or both? What about the timing? How could the killer have committed these cuts in the estimated time between police beats and in such poor lighting too? I hope to shed a little light on this subject . . . and, yes, that was an intentional pun. You have my permission to groan now. Before I start going into the specifics of the problem at hand, I would like to give you an idea of the layout of the Mitre Square on that bloody night.

The layout of Mitre Square

Mitre Square is located off Aldgate High Street, and is found between Mitre Street to the south-west, Duke Street to the north-east, and St James Place to the north-west. Two passages led into the square. One ran from Duke Street – it was 85 feet long and was known as Church Passage. This passage had a lamp situated on the wall at the Mitre Square end. The passage opened out from only 5 feet wide to an 18-foot span at the Mitre Square end, all within 12 feet. The other passage ran from Mitre Square to St James Place and was called, not surprisingly, St James Passage. This passage was shorter at 55 feet long and at the Mitre Square end had two bollards. Both passages were paved. One final, larger entrance into the square leads from Mitre Street. At 25 feet wide, it was the only access wide enough to allow carriages and carts to enter. There were no other exits from the square. Buildings in Mitre Square consisted of a mixture of huge, looming warehouses and the rears of a shop and dwellings, most empty. Two Kearley & Tonge tea and grocery warehouses (with offices) dominated. One Kearley & Tonge warehouse was situated in the square's north-eastern corner. This building ran approximately 54 feet south-west from St James Passage to an old empty house. The entrance to this warehouse was via some railings and was to be found 31 feet from St James Passage. Next to the empty house was the home of off-duty Police Constable Richard Pearce. Railings began from the Kearley and Tonge warehouse and started 10 feet from the corner of St James Passage, came out towards the square for 12 feet and ran south-westwards for 54 feet, curved back towards PC Pearce's home for 6 feet, south-west again for a further 7 feet before turning back the final remaining 6 feet to the constable's residence. This completed the north-west side of Mitre Square. The next building on from Pearce's house (on the left as viewed) was another warehouse, belonging to Williams & Co. This building jutted out from Pearce's residence for around 21 feet and formed a corner of the square along with Pearce's house. Moving south-east from the Williams & Co. warehouse was the entrance to the square from Mitre Street. Across from this was the rear of Mr Taylor's picture framing shop. Next to Taylor's premises was the back of an empty cottage, one of three that stood together on Mitre Street but the only one whose rear backed onto the square. At the rear of these premises, located in the square, were two coalholes, one for Mr Taylor's shop and one for the empty cottage.Turning north-east, at a 90-degree angle, was a yard wall which ran from the empty cottage. The wall only stood a few feet high, was topped by high railings, and ran from the empty cottage for 22 feet. This formed the south-western corner. The entrance to this yard was found only 3 feet away from the empty dwelling. Still moving north-east was yet another warehouse belonging to Horner & Co. Located north-west across the entrance of Church Passage was the second warehouse belonging to Kearley & Tonge. This building was by far the largest (possibly due to the offices) and it went from Church Passage all along the north-eastern side of Mitre Square back to St James Passage. The nightwatchman working in this building on the night of the Eddowes murder was ex-Metropolitan police officer George Morris. The square itself was cobbled. A pavement ran into the square from Mitre Street, along the outside and back into Mitre Street, The only breaks in this pavement occur at the entrance of Kearley & Tonge (north-west warehouse) and directly opposite Church Passage for 10 feet before continuing along Horner & Co. and back out into the street.

The gas lighting in Mitre Square

Three gas lamps provided light in Mitre Square:

1. A fixed wall gas lamp was situated on Williams & Co.'s corner wall located in Mitre Street. This lamp gave little light into Mitre Square but did illuminate the street entrance to the square.
2. A freestanding lamp was located 18 feet outside Kearley & Tonge's north-west warehouse and 26 feet from their north-east warehouse.
3. The third lamp was another fixed lamp attached to Kearley & Tonge's north-east warehouse at the corner of Church Passage, just at the point where the passage widened from 5 feet to 18 feet.

The City of London Police

Mitre Square, EC1, came under the jurisdiction of The City of London police. The City police force was formally established in 1839, ten years after the Metropolitan police. Their duty was to provide police protection for the City of London. The City police area stetched from the Barbican in the north to the River Thames in the south and from the Holborn-Fleet Street area in the west to Aldgate-Liverpool Street in the east, basically the original area of the ancient City of London. When it came to organizing beats the two forces used similar methods (as did most forces). That is, each beat was numbered and entered onto a register. This register could be referred to at any time to know where an individual police officer on the beat should be at any particular moment. Recorded in this register was the name of every street, alley, square, etc., on the beat. The timing expected to complete a beat was also noted. This was estimated by ascertaining the distance of the beat, including various jobs to be done, such as to check that doors and gates were locked, and multiplying this by the speed it was expected to be completed, which was 2 miles per hour. A group of beats were gathered into 'sections' and a sergeant was allocated a section of which he was in charge. His job was to ensure that each man under his responsibility conducted himself correctly. The sergeant patrolled his section constantly to make sure that things were correct and in order. Two-thirds of the whole force was employed at night. The night beats were expected to be up and running by 10 p.m. and continued till the day beats relieved their brother constables at 6 a.m. Each police officer takes his turn of eight months night duty and four months day duty throughout the whole year. Each officer knew the duties expected from him during his patrol. These were laid down in a book of *General Regulations, Instructions and Orders*. Ultimately then, as today, the primary object of a police officer is the detection and prevention of crime. Beat officers were then and are still expected to know thoroughly each route on their beats, each street, alley, cul de sac, court, house etc. Not only that but in 1888 he would have been expected to know each person in the houses in his area as well as shopkeepers, lodging deputies, publicans, street vendors and warehouse night-watchmen. He had to check that doors, window and yard gates were securely fastened. He had to check that coalholes and trapdoors were safe and secure and make a report if they were not. He also had to keep an eye out for any suspicious characters while keeping a particularly close eye on public houses. A PC's duties were endless and it's a wonder any copper ever completed a beat.

PC Edward Watkins

In 1871, seventeen years prior to the murders, Edward Watkins joined the City police as City police constable 881. Watkins was regarded as a fine officer by his superiors. He was on duty to patrol his beat at 9.45 p.m., the change-over time, and by 10 p.m. he was walking his beat continuously. In his own words, Watkins's route would have taken him from Duke Street, Aldgate, through Heneage Lane, a portion of Bury Street, through Cree Lane, into Leadenhall Street, along eastward into Mitre Street, then into Mitre Square, round the square again into Mitre Street, then into King Street to St James's Place, round the place, then into Duke Street, where I started from. Watkins indicated that his beat took him around twelve to fourteen minutes to complete. Before venturing out, Watkins equipped himself with his bull's eye lantern, a standard issue portable lamp comprising an oil container with an adjustable wick contained within the lamp. Made of tin, these lamps had a single, round magnified lens. The crinkled cowl at the top was multi-levelled, a design that enabled heat and fumes to escape yet let out no chink of light. To adjust the amount of light given off, the cowl was turned. In order to enable aa constable to move with stealth the lamps had a spring-loaded shutter that stopped the light shining forth. This also reduced the need to extinguish and relight the lamp. To carry the lantern, two moveable handles were fitted at the rear. The constable could also carry the lantern on his belt thanks to the belt hook and lip which also doubled up as a heat shield, not that that it helped much. Users complained of burnt fingers, staining of uniform and even blackened faces. Obviously, though, as time progressed the lamps improved. It wasn't uncommon for constables to heat up cups of tea inside them and during the winter they became a valuable heat source. These lamps would also have been used as a signalling device and if needs be, a weapon. During some stage on his beat, Watkins would have noted that the freestanding lamp (outside Kearley & Tonge Warehouse) in Mitre Square was deficient. That is to state that the quality of gas was poor and therefore the lamp was not working to its full capacity. It would have been part of Watkins's duty to report any such events involving gas lamps and no doubt it would have been recorded in his notebook. The constable commenced his beat by 'working left-handed.' Sometimes the beat officers altered the way they made their beats so as not to be predictable. Beats were basically worked in loops. You started at point A and walked around the streets until you returned to point A again. Therefore you made either more left-handed or right-handed turns. When Watkins stated that he worked his beat 'left-handed' it means that the majority of the turns he made during that beat were left-handed turns. He entered Mitre Square from Mitre Street at 1.30 a.m. on the morning of 30 September 1888, checking each corner. No doubt Watkins checked the yard gates were locked and correct, the coalholes were safe, that the empty houses were secured. He would also have looked up Church and St James passages as he passed. On previous nights, he would have exchanged words with Morris but this being a Saturday night/Sunday morning, Morris had other duties to perform, as every weekend. Nothing out of the ordinary grabbed Watkins's attention. Proceeding, he continued back out via Mitre Street and onto King Street.

PC James Harvey

City police constable 964 James Harvey joined the force in 1876. On the night of 29–30 September, Harvey came on duty at the same time as Watkins and, like Watkins, he patrolled his beat left-handed (one suspects that all City beat constables were ordered to operate left-handed that night). He testified that his beat route was from Bevis Marks to Duke Street, into Little Duke Street, to Houndsditch, from Houndsditch back to Duke Street, along Duke Street to Church Passage, back again into Duke Street, to Aldgate, from there to Mitre Street, back again to Houndsditch, up Houndsditch, to Little Duke Street, again back to Houndsditch, to Goring Street, up Goring Street to Bevis Marks. At around 1.40 a.m. Harvey ventured up Church Passage from Duke Street as far as Mitre Square. He stated he saw no one and heard no cry or noise. Then he departed back towards Duke Street and on to Aldgate. Apart from the two constables, only one other figure had a known active presence in Mitre Square that night. As mentioned earlier, George Morris was an ex-police officer, and was now a night-watchman for Kearley & Tonge. He was in the north-eastern warehouse as Watkins patrolled the square at 1.30 a.m. His duties for Saturday night into Sunday morning prevented him from his usual habit of standing at the open door of the warehouse looking out from 1 till 2 a.m. Any other night of the week, Morris stated, he would have been smoking his pipe and speaking to the police officer as he patrolled by. Around 1.40–1.45 a.m., Morris had walked through the warehouse to the door, opened it, apparently taking a quick look out onto the square, and returned to work with the door ajar.

Discovery of the body
At approximately 1.44 a.m., PC Watkins entered the square again. Approaching northwards along Mitre Street, he turned right into the square. Pausing at the square entrance, he checked up and down Mitre Street before walking past the picture frame makers on his right. His lamp was on as he turned right again and proceeded towards the coalhole in the southeast corner of Mitre Square. It was this coalhole that Watkins would have had to check was securely and safely shut. And it was at this coalhole that he discovered the body of a woman. On her back, with her throat severely cut. Stomach ripped and pulled open. Her insides had been lifted out onto the pavement and her face had been awfully mutilated. This was the sight that greeted the constable. He then turned to run and find Morris who was working away in the warehouse. Pushing the slightly open door, he called for Morris with the words, 'For God's sake, mate, come to my assistance.' Well, those were the official words recorded but I cannot help feeling that the actual vocabulary was a little more direct and coarser. Morris located a lamp and accompanied Watkins back to the victim. Once he viewed the body for himself Morris immediately departed the square blowing his whistle. City police, unlike their Met brothers, had not been issued with whistles. Morris ventured out of the square via the Mitre Street entrance and turned left (south) and hurried toward Aldgate. It was there he met up with PC Harvey and PC Holland. While Watkins was alone with the body, he noted that he could see no sign of a struggle. No footmarks were apparent and the only finger markings were upon the victim's chemise that Watkins determined had been moved out of the way by the killer. According to his testimony 'her clothing was filthy.' There occurred a flurry of activity once Morris had returned with Harvey and Holland.

Holland went straight for the nearest doctor, Dr George William Sequeira of 34 Jewry St, Aldgate, and other officers arrived along with City Detectives Halse, Outram and Marriott. Also to arrive was another doctor, Dr Frederick Gordon Brown, the City of London police surgeon.

Just how dark was Mitre Square?

I wanted to find out for myself how light or dark Mitre Square was early on the morning of 30 September 1888. Some who argue that Jack had some sort of medical background or knowledge imply that he could have committed these terrible mutilations with his eyes shut never mind in the dark. So clarification of the situation is an important issue. In Leicester, where I live, we are fortunate to have a museum dedicated to the history of British gas, the National Gas Museum. Good place to start, I thought. I contacted the curator, Mr Maurice Martin. He explained he was unable to assist me due to the lack of information regarding the actual lamps in Mitre Square and their location. However, he put me in touch with a gas lamp enthusiast by the name of Alex Marrack.

Conditions in Mitre Square

The first thing Mr Marrack and I discussed was natural light. The moon was in the second day of its last quarter and 39 per cent of a waning disk was visible. Not the brightest of moons, then. The weather conditions early that morning were more favourable than late Saturday night. Heavy rain had fallen in Whitechapel earlier that night and cloud cover for London was recorded at 100 per cent. Later on Sunday, 30 September, that day would be recorded as a 'brilliant autumnal day' with 30 per cent cloud cover, although unofficial records show 50 per cent. Also to be considered were the high-sided buildings in the square such as the four warehouses, which must have affected how much natural light entered Mitre Square. That said, I think it reasonable to conclude that although rain had stopped around midnight, cloud cover was still fairly dominant and therefore it is probable that very limited moonlight, if any, could have lit the square. The next factor was eyesight. Comparing evenings in 1888 London with the London of today is like comparing Las Vegas and the inside of my wallet which, true to legend, is indeed a very dark and empty place. However, compared to nothing, gas lamps were an improvement but they were merely markers at best. Something to focus on as you made your way and not a source of great illumination. It would stand to reason that to make up for this lack of light your average everyday (or night) Victorian had very acute eyesight. I'm not saying that their 'night sight' was better than ours today but they would have been more used to seeing and working in the dark.

The gas lamps around Mitre Square

As noted, ascertaining the exact lighting situation within the square on the night of the murder was impossible. Each lamp shone differently and all such lamps were dependent on various factors such as gas supply, mantle etc. So the best we could achieve was an approximation. On average, the light given out by the lamps would have been the equivalent of a fridge light – and those were the good lamps. The fixed lamp on Williams & Co.'s warehouse was situated in Mitre Street. This lamp, at the entrance to the square, would have shone little if any light into the actual square. As for the corner where the body was found, the location of Mr Taylor's shop blocked any light from that lamp reaching that spot. This leaves the two lamps in the square itself. Another fixed lamp was located at the Church Passage entrance of the square. Fixed to the Kearley & Tonge warehouse and at 74 feet away from the spot where Watkins found Eddowes' body, this lamp was too far away to light that corner. Yet this lamp could still have had a bearing on the events of that morning. PC Harvey stated that he patrolled Church Passage. If his and Drs Brown and Philips's times are correct, then he should have been at the end of the passage at the entrance to Mitre Square while Jack was in the corner mutilating Eddowes's. Yet Harvey said he saw nothing. This statement has been dismissed by some Ripperologists. I myself have doubted Harvey's recollection of events. I feel it is worth analyzing his testimony. It should be remembered that Harvey's beat did not include Mitre Square. That was Watkins' responsibility and, being from the same force, Harvey would have known this. Harvey's job was to patrol and secure all premises on his beat including Church Passage. He had no reason to look into the square and therefore should not be criticized or questioned for stating he saw nothing. The Church Passage lamp already mentioned overhung the wall and extended out 2 feet making it hang almost overhead, slap bang in the middle of the passageway. The lamp also 'protruded' towards the square due to the fixed angle of the lamp's mounting. So in fact the lamp was ahead of Harvey as he reached and turned at the end of the passage. The light source would have been stronger closer to the lamp, making it more difficult to see past it. Although the strength of the light was weak, I feel that Harvey wouldn't have seen much if anything due to the glare and the simple fact he wasn't looking, and nor should he have been. The final lamp in the square was the freestanding lamp outside Kearley & Tonge's north-western warehouse. This lamp was the closest in the square to Eddowes' body (64 feet). If working correctly, the light from this lamp would have failed to light the corner in which the body was found. However, this lamp was deficient. That is to say, either the quality of the gas supplied to the lamp was poor, gas pressure was low, or the mantle had corroded. Whatever the reason, this lamp was not working to its maximum capacity. Therefore the square was darker than usual. Thus, we concluded that on that night Mitre Square was a dark place. An ideal place for a prostitute to take her client. That said, a little light was available from the lamps situated in the square. I think the fact that Watkins used his lamp in the square indicates that there were dark spots. Morris's action in obtaining a lamp before following Watkins to the body also supports this idea. These two men had enough local knowledge to realize a lamp was needed.

How did the murderer perform the mutilations?
Portable lamps were fairly common in this age, especially within the criminal fraternity. Such easy-to-carry lamps ranged from the sophisticated police bull's eye to the cheaper candle lamp. Candle lamps were easily obtainable, maintainable and very affordable. They were also easy to hide in the pocket of an overcoat. The drawbacks were that these lamps got fairly hot and easily

extinguished themselves. I felt that this idea was not workable. To have to stop and light a lamp is an obstacle to efficiency and if Jack was anything he was efficient. Also the fact that this murder was committed in the darkest corner of the square indicates that any light source emanating from there would shine out like the Eddystone Lighthouse. Though it does make one remember the inventory entry of Eddowes's possessions that stated, 'One tin match box empty'. Could he have borrowed a match? I doubt it as no used matches were reported at the scene. That doesn't mean, however, that they weren't taken away. Dr Brown's initial examination at the scene and his later post-mortem report led him to say at the inquest that the killer would have been 'somebody who knew what he was about.' A person who at the very least possessed some knowledge with regards to 'cutting up animals.' Dr Sequeira seems to have disagreed, stating that he believed the murderer 'was not possessed of any great anatomical skill' – yet you could interpret him as saying that the killer possessed some skill even if he was no brain surgeon. The killer of Catherine Eddowes was obviously a dangerous man. According to Drs Brown and Sequeria, he had some anatomical knowledge. In my opinion, there would have been enough light to see what he was doing. I theorise that Eddowes was killed with her murderer standing behind her, possibly with Eddowes against the wall, and that he pulled her back while drawing a knife across her throat as she was on her way down. This act would have been very swift, because of the lack of blood spilled. The post mortem findings indicated that Eddowes was placed on her back after death or during the act of dying, because there was a lack of bruising to the scalp, back, and elbows. The signature act of mutilation was the next stage. The removal of part of the uterus and the kidney would indicate to me that this was killer's objective. Because removal of these organs was a hallmark shared with the murders of Nichols, Chapman and Kelly, the removal of the uterus and kidney evidently was very important to him. Would he have needed light to conduct this mutilation or did he have enough skill to operate in the dark? The final proof for me that the murderer was able to see to some extent is in the mutilation to Eddowes' face, which was 'carved' for the want of a better

246

word. The forming of the two cuts to produce a 'V', which would need one cut to connect with the other, is an indicator. This cannot be done unless you can see where the other cut began or ended. There is no overlap recorded by Dr Brown nor shown on the drawing provided for the inquest. Precise cuts over the eyelids and also the possibility that Eddowes' belongings were searched by the killer all indicate that this man could see what he was doing.

Conclusion

After speaking to both gas lighting experts Marrack and Martin, assessing the natural light (moonlight) that night and weather conditions, looking into the artificial light situation (gas lamps) and also taking into consideration Dr Brown's post-mortem report, my views agree with those of Dr George William Sequeira who stated at the inquest into the death of Catharine Eddowes, 'I am well acquainted with the locality and the position of the lamps in the square.' Where this murder was committed was probably the darkest part of the square, but there was sufficient light at least to enable the miscreant to perpetrate the deed. While we cannot at this point finally put to bed the debate with regard to the lighting in Mitre Square, I do hope this investigation has helped to shed some light on the situation.

Select sources

Begg, Paul, Fido, Martin and Skinner, Keith, *The Jack the Ripper A–Z*, (London: Headline Books, 1992)

Evans, Stewart P., and Skinner, Keith, *The Ultimate Jack the Ripper Companion* (New York: Carroll & Graf, 2000)

Yost, Dave, 'Elisabeth Stride: Her Killer and Time of Death' at casebook.org/dissertations/dst-yost.html

Yost, Dave, 'Matthew Packer – Final Thoughts' at casebook.org/dissertations/dstyost-packer.html (contains weather records for the night of 29–30 September 1888)

Acknowledgments

The author would like to thank Maurice Martin of the National Gas Museum, Alex Marrack, Chris George, Paul Begg, and Dave Yost.

This essay appeared in *Ripperologist* magazine No. 58, March 2005.